Cultural Memory

in

the

Present

Mieke Bal and Hent de Vries, Editors

REFLECTIONS OF EQUALITY

Christoph Menke

Translated by Howard Rouse and
Andrei Denejkine

STANFORD UNIVERSITY PRESS

STANFORD, CALIFORNIA

2006

Stanford University Press
Stanford, California

The publication of this work was supported by a grant from the Goethe-Institut.

The Annex to Chapter 2 was originally published in 27 *Cardozo Law Review* 595
(2005). © *Cardozo Law Review.*

Reflections of Equality was originally published in German in 2000 under the title
Spiegelungen der Gleichheit © 2000, Akademie Verlag.

Assistance for the translation was provided by Inter Nationes.

Library of Congress Cataloging-in-Publication Data

Menke, Christoph, 1958–
    [Spiegelungen der Gleichheit. English]
    Reflections of equality / Christoph Menke ; translated by Howard Rouse and
Andrei Denejkine.
        p. cm. — (Cultural memory in the present)
    Translation of: Spiegelungen der Gleichheit.
    Includes bibliographical references and index.
    ISBN-10: 0-8047-4473-4 (cloth : alk. paper)
    ISBN-10: 0-8047-4474-2 (pbk. : alk. paper)
    ISBN-13: 978-0-8047-4473-7 (cloth : alk. paper)
    ISBN-13: 978-0-8047-4474-4 (pbk. : alk. paper)
    1. Equality.   I. Title.   II. Series.

JC575.M4613 2006
323.42   dc22

2006011774

Contents

Preface: Equality—Political, Not Metaphysical

These metaphysic rights entering into common life, like rays of light which pierce into dense medium, are by the laws of nature refracted from their straight line. Indeed, in the gross and complicated mass of human passions and concerns the primitive rights of men undergo such a variety of *refractions and reflections* that it becomes absurd to talk of them as if they continued in the simplicity of their original direction.[1]

The "metaphysic rights" which Burke speaks about here are the rights of equality which the French Revolution had set up, with the declaration of human rights, as the basis of the new political order. Burke calls the equality established by the revolution, equality before the law and in legislation, a "metaphysical" idea. The antithesis of "metaphysical," for Burke, is "political." In the revolutionary constitution that spells out the idea of equality there is, according to Burke, "much, but bad, metaphysics; much, but bad, geometry; much, but false, proportionate arithmetic."[2] The problem is not, however, that the metaphysics, geometry, and arithmetic of equality is bad or wrong: "but if it were all as exact as metaphysics, geometry and arithmetic ought to be, and if their schemes were perfectly consistent in all their parts, it would make only a more fair and sightly vision."[3] The problem with the revolutionary establishment of equality is that "not one reference whatsoever is to be found [in it] to anything moral or anything politic, nothing that relates to the concerns, the actions, the passions, the interests of men. *Hominem non sapiunt.*"[4] What is metaphysical is the conception of equality that is given expression in the revolutionary act and its philosophical articulations: a conception that only considers its own validity and does not relate to the concerns, actions, passions, and interests of human beings. This relation takes place, however, in a *political* consideration of equality. The political reflection of equality that Burke undertakes in his *Reflections on the Revolution in France* is one of the "variety of refractions and reflections" of and upon what human beings are and want.

In the title of a famous essay, John Rawls has again taken up Burke's programmatic formula for a political replacement of the metaphysical consideration of equality; Rawls too wants to treat justice "politically and not metaphysically."[5] In this respect, Rawls calls an understanding of justice (as fairness or equality) "political" when it presupposes "no particular metaphysical doctrine about the nature of persons."[6] That is, when it relies upon an understanding of equality which does not depend, in its grounding, upon any assumptions concerning the "essence" of human beings. In the liberal state, such assumptions have to be "avoided" because of their contentiousness. With this concept of a "political liberalism," Rawls has put his finger on a process of the self-reflection of liberal societies which has been practically effective—especially since the 1960s. His aim is to free the basic liberal principles from the rationalistic, bourgeois, chauvinistic, and racist convictions with which their implementation and maintenance have been historically bound up. Rawls's political liberalism is clearly opposed, in this aim, to the political reflection of equality carried out by Burke. For Burke was concerned to show how liberal equality is opposed to the concerns, actions, passions, and interests of human beings. Rawls, by contrast, is concerned with a new understanding of liberal equality— one that no longer makes any "metaphysical" assumptions about the true concerns, actions, passions, and interests of human beings.

This is, however, only one side. The other side is constituted by the fact that political liberalism presupposes and, what is more, remains at the mercy of the political reflection of equality proposed by Burke. From Burke's critique of the traditional, that is, "metaphysical," understanding of liberal equality, it follows that political liberalism has to be preceded by a reflection of equality similar to the political consideration practiced by him. For the traditional understanding of liberal equality is certainly not wrong *because* it makes metaphysical presuppositions. (And the metaphysical is certainly not wrong only because it is metaphysical.) We recognize and criticize these presuppositions as metaphysical, rather, because, in a political consideration, we realize that liberal equality in its traditional understanding has repressive consequences for the concerns, actions, passions, and interests of some human beings. At the origin of the political understanding of liberal equality in Rawls's sense—as an understanding which is no longer metaphysical—there lies a political consideration of liberal equality in Burke's sense: a particular understanding of liberal equality in its refractions and reflections, in its consequences and meanings for the concerns, actions, passions, and interests of human beings.

A great number of poststructuralist, communitarian, and feminist arguments in the philosophical debates of the last few decades can be understood as wanting to bring to consciousness this political reflection of equality in political liberalism—a reflection which is presupposed just as much as it is concealed. It is to these arguments that I refer here while trying, partly in direct confrontation with them, to more precisely grasp the concept of a reflection of equality. Over and above this, I want to draw attention to a critical distinction in these arguments and conceptions. The political reflection of equality is frequently understood as the criticism of an existing, exclusive, and oppressive understanding of liberal equality from the perspective of an anticipated, extended, and power-free understanding. This is, however, a misinterpretation. The reflection of equality that Burke calls "political" is a consideration of equality from outside: a consideration from the point of view of the concerns, actions, passions, and interests of *individual* human beings. The reflection of equality allows this consideration to reflect and refract the fundamentally nonequal, which can be called the individual. The reflection of liberal equality does not only serve to improve equality; it also puts it in question by pointing to its irrevocable limits with regard to the individual. This is the element of truth in Burke's *critique* of equality, something that has been seen not only by Nietzsche and Schmitt but also, with entirely different political consequences, by Adorno and Derrida.

The program that the essays in this volume carry out can thus be described as an attempt to reformulate, with respect to the present form of liberalism, the political reflection of equality drawn up by Burke (and others). At the same time, it is a further attempt to find an adequate articulation for this program. In a first approach, I have undertaken this program by means of a reading of Hegel's interpretation of modernity as a "tragedy in ethical life."[7] In the essays collected in this volume, this program will be further worked out by means of a confrontation with contemporary, or more recent, conceptions that are important to it, including those of Nietzsche, Schmitt, Adorno, Luhmann, Taylor, Rawls, and Derrida. The two essays in the second part are thus intended to clarify the opposition to individuality which the reflection of equality leads to. The two essays in the third part consider two forms of the "sovereign" treatment of this opposition: revolution and mercy. The texts of these two parts stand in a close argumentative interrelation, even if they were conceived and worked out for different occasions. They are preceded by a first part which presents, in an interrelated form, some central structural determinations of the undertaking of a "questioning of equality" (Chapter 1), and which offers a comparative profile of three varieties of this questioning (Chapter 2). This first part was written later as a programmatic introduction to the following chapters. It brings into a general schema that which is later considered in its details and consequences.

REFLECTIONS OF EQUALITY

PART I

A QUESTIONING OF EQUALITY

1

The Self-Reflection of Equality

Modern ethics and politics, no less in theory than in practice, are determined by a struggle concerning equality.[1] One side of this struggle is characterized by a desire to justify the idea of equality and expand its scope. The other side is characterized by a desire to question the idea of equality and restrict its scope. The first side argues from the perspective of everyone, the second from the perspective of the particular individual. The first side believes that the modern idea of equality refers to everyone *as* an individual; the second wants to show that there is an unbridgeable gap between every individual and everyone else—insofar as individuals are understood as particular individuals. The first party therefore suspects the second of wanting to substitute the equality of everyone with the privileges of a few. And the second party suspects the first of wanting to reduce or level out the difference and particularity of individuals. Both suspicions are false, but have a good basis in the position they are directed against. For both sides in the modern struggle concerning equality—the position of its justification and expansion and the position of its questioning and restriction—do not understand themselves correctly in their confrontation with the other.

In both chapters of this programmatic first part, I want to show this from the perspective of the second of these two conflicting positions—from the perspective of the questioning and restriction of equality. I want to show, that is, how this position must be understood in order to be defended. This can only be shown, however, when the position of the justification and expansion of equality is understood in a different way. We are thus concerned, in the end, with a different understanding of *both* positions in the modern struggle concerning equality. I thereby proceed in this first chapter by first describing the modern struggle about equality (A); I go on to put into question its central presupposition (B); and, finally, rather than attempting to smooth out or dissolve this struggle, I seek to undermine it (C).

A. Dialectic of Equality

The Modern Idea of Equality

If we ask about the duties and rights that we possess with respect to one another, the first answer of modernity is that they are the duties and rights of equality: equality is the principal normative idea of modernity. The modern struggle over equality takes this observation as its point of departure. What is called for first of all, then, is an elucidation of the three elements of this observation: the concept of equality (1); the field of the normative (2); and the claim to primacy (3).

(1) *The concept of equality.* In the preliminary formulation mentioned above, the expression "equality" means the equal consideration of everyone. The meaning of the modern idea of equality does not consist in the state of being equal or, even less, the attempt to make equal, nor does it consist in an equal distribution. Equality as *being* equal refers to qualities and their ascertainment (and equality as *equalizing* to qualities and their production). The modern idea of equality is not concerned, however, with the qualities that everyone already has or will eventually have, but with how they ought to be treated. Equality does not have a theoretical meaning here, according to which no distinction can be ascertained between the observed elements; it has, instead, a practical meaning: no distinction ought to be *made* between these elements. In the version of the concept of equal *distribution* this means that everyone should receive the same share of all social goods as everyone else. This, for the most part, is how egalitarian positions have understood the modern idea of equality, and the critics of these positions have rejected this idea for good reasons.[2] The basic thought of the modern idea of equality, formulated by Kantianism and

utilitarianism at the end of the eighteenth century, is, however, another one: the modern idea of equality does not mean equal distribution to everyone, and certainly not the equal distribution of everything to everyone. It means instead the equal consideration of everyone. Equality does not mean that everyone ought to receive the same amount, but that everyone ought to count equally. As the equal consideration of everyone, equality relates neither to qualities nor to shares, but to weightings. In deciding upon modes of action, to treat equally means to accord the same weight to everyone—including oneself.

From the practical standpoint of equality, we are concerned with the equal consideration of persons. Even this, however, is ambiguous: the requirement of the equal consideration of persons can be understood in two different ways. In the weak sense, the equal consideration of persons consists in the fact that they are subjected to the same rule. The paradigm of such equal consideration in the weak sense is the impartial judge, who treats equal cases equally and unequal cases unequally. To treat everyone equally means, for him, to give preference to no one, and this means to apply a rule regardless of person, that is, in a manner that is always equal. The rule can also be a rule of inequality: a rule that establishes privileges, for instance, for particular groups of people. To treat persons equally in the weak sense thus means, for instance, to accord them the appropriate privileges when they are a member of this group and to deny them these privileges when they are not. The equal consideration of everyone in the weak sense, practiced by the impartial judge, is rule-relative; it implies nothing about the content of the rule.

In contrast to this, the equal consideration of everyone in the strong sense describes the content of the rule itself, and not only the impartial mode of its application. The paradigm of this strong idea of equal treatment that has become decisive in modernity is not that of the judge who impartially decides upon individual cases, but that of the legislator who only establishes those rules that consider everyone in an equal measure. Equal treatment is here an idea full of content, and not only a formal idea: it determines the content of normative rules, not only the mode of their application. Everyone counts as much as everyone else; nobody possesses a privilege by reason of which the claim to the equal treatment of others can be disputed.

(2) *The field of the normative.* Equality—and this is the observation with which I began—is the principal normative idea of modernity. This should imply that the idea of equal consideration, in its strong, contentful sense, stands at the center of the two spheres distinguished in the modern conception of the normative: the legal and the moral. The idea of equality is the encompassing idea of modern law and modern morality. It is the basic idea of modern law because the latter is concerned with the realization of the equal rights of everyone. This is the new determination of law according to natural right, which moors the law in subjective rights. In modern constitutions, this reordering of the system of law according to the idea of equality is given expression by the role of basic rights. In the same move, equality becomes the central idea in the modern understanding of morality. For in the modern understanding, those obligations that everyone has with regard to everyone else move into the center of morality. On the one hand, this means that in modern morality nonsocial obligations, with respect to God and oneself, for instance, become inapplicable or acquire a derivative status. On the other hand, it means that the ground of moral obligations does not find its source in a transcendent authority (as the imperative of which these obligations are understood), but only in the recognition of the fact that everyone else has a status fundamentally equal to one's own.

Both modern law and modern morality take as a starting point their own specific question: law begins with the question concerning the laws that everyone is subjected to; morality begins with the question concerning the duties that everyone has with regard to everyone else. Law embodies a vertical perspective, the perspective on everyone from above, and morality a horizontal perspective, the perspective of one among all people. At the same time, however, modern law and modern morality draw attention, in different ways, to the same "strong" idea of equality. Modern law does this by formulating and making obligatory universal rules by means of which everyone is considered equally; modern morality by demanding of every individual that he treat himself as equal to everybody else. The laws of modern law and the standpoint of modern morality are two different mediums for the realization of the same egalitarian understanding of normative rightness: a practical decision can only be normatively correct if it accords to everyone the same weight as everyone else.

(3) *The claim to primacy.* The third element of the preliminary formulation is that the idea of equality (understood in the strong, that is, "modern" sense) is accorded a primacy in both normative fields, those of law and morality. Two different things are implied here. Firstly, something else must exist with respect to which the primacy of equality can be claimed. This is true of both normative fields; they do not consist only of the demand for equality and its concretizations and consequences. In the field of the law this has always been indisputable: legal-technical and pragmatic considerations clearly possess a decisive significance. Many legal propositions simply result from the fact that a ruling must be made, others regulate implementations, and others secure extensions. More significant, however, is the fact that in the field of the law other kinds of obligation are recognized and imposed than those of the equal consideration of everyone. This applies to individual legal acts like amnesty and pardon,[3] but above all to those legal propositions that give expression to the value-convictions of a particular form of life. In the field of morality, the significance of such nonegalitarian normative obligations can be seen in values like solidarity, loyalty, friendship, care, and sympathy, that is, in obligations that do not constitute relationships between everyone, but instead between particular individuals. In both law and morality, then, we are concerned with obligations that do not deal with equality, but with the peculiarity of the participants: a legal ruling can make something obligatory for all those that it concerns in order to express, defend or promote the particular form of life of a society. A moral obligation can prescribe or prohibit a mode of action in the name of qualities that are peculiar to these particular individuals. "Peculiarity" here is another word for individuality, be it the individuality of a common form of life or that of the life of an individual. Nonegalitarian obligations are obligations that follow from the consideration of individuality, and not from the equal consideration of everyone.

As opposed to such nonegalitarian obligations, modern law and modern morality proclaim a fundamental primacy of equality. Demands of equality should accordingly have priority over those demands that arise out of the consideration of individual peculiarities. That is, individual peculiarities should be able to ground normative claims or obligations only when they do not contravene the basic requirement of the equal consideration of everyone. The primacy of the idea of equality means that in the modern consciousness equality has become a normative *condition* of the consideration of individuality.[4] The claim that the idea of equality itself is not conditioned—that it is unconditional—is thus bound up with the thesis of its primacy. By according equality normative primacy over everything else, the modern consciousness thus claims, at the same time, that equality is not grounded in any other normative or practical standpoint; for then it would also be conditioned by this other normative standpoint. The modern claim of the unconditional priority of equality is therefore accompanied by the claim of its fundamental status. The idea of equality has primacy over the other normative obligation of the consideration of individuality; and the idea of equality does not require for its justification the reference to any other normative obligation.

The Thesis

This double claim at the center of the modern idea of equality is deeply problematic. For this claim rests upon a false understanding of both the (internal) constitution and the (external) position of the idea of equality, and thus, at the same time, upon a false understanding of the normative in both of its fields, those of law and morality. The claim of the fundamental status of equality falsely understands its inner constitution, and the claim of the priority of equality falsely understands its position in the fields of law and morality. In order to correct this doubly false self-understanding of the modern idea of equality, we thus need to question both its constitution and position—a theoretical questioning that also leads, in its consequences, to a practical limitation of equality. This questioning and limitation of the idea of equality contradicts the double modern claim of its priority and fundamental status by reversing its standpoint: it observes the idea of equality not from its own point of view, but from outside; it observes the idea of equality from the perspective of the other, nonegalitarian obligations that arise out of the consideration of the peculiarities of individuals.

To observe the idea of equality in this way thus means, firstly, to observe it as only one, necessarily limited, normative orientation among others. In the questioning and limitation of equality, we assume toward it a perspective in which we allow both its image and weight to be refracted by something else—by the other basic form of normative obligation. What we are concerned with here is such a refracted understanding of the idea of equality. That is, we do not want to revoke the modern idea of equality— or the modern centering of the legal and the moral around this idea—or take leave of it in favor of another central normative idea. Instead, we want first of all to attain another mode of observation of equality, and then also to track down other forms of its enactment. These modes of observation and forms of enactment are different because instead of starting out from the priority of equality, they argue for its relativity. They see the idea of equality as being in a conflictual relationship with the obligations arising out of individuality—a relationship which is not decided in advance in favor of the primacy of equality, but which instead always has to be enacted anew with regard to this conflictuality.

To question the idea of equality means to observe it from outside: in relationship with its other instead of in precedence to its other. What the idea of equality relates to or is relative to is not, however, extrinsic to it. This is the *second* and decisive aspect of the questioning of equality. In its first aspect, the questioning of equality confronts the claim of its priority with the claim of its relativity. In its second aspect, the questioning of equality is directed, over and above this, against the claim of its fundamental status, of its groundedness in itself. This objection is contained in the thesis that the questioning of equality from outside, when viewed correctly, is nothing other than its questioning from inside—its self-questioning. The questioning of equality enacts itself as a confrontation of equality with its other—one that takes place by means of a return to that which equality itself already contains. The idea of equality puts itself into question. For the normative orientation toward individuality, from the perspective of which the idea of equality is questioned from outside, arises in the inner enactment of equality itself. We relate to or, more precisely, assume this other normative orientation precisely when we are concerned with equality. The orientation toward equality is constituted in such a way that it already contains that which is later opposed to it, as a questioning and limitation, from outside. The modern idea of equality contains its antithesis as its presupposition. Following the language of Hegel, objects that are constituted this way can be called "dialectical."[5] The modern idea of equality and the normative obligation toward individuality are subject to an irresolvable dialectic: they only exist in their transition into their opposite. It is this thesis that the chapters of this book seek to develop; this chapter deals with its general structure, Chapter 2 relates it to some important authors, and the following chapters explicate its details.

The Antinomy of Reflection

The first and most obvious—but also the most superficial and inadequate—way in which the dialectical constitution of the idea of equality manifests itself is in the confrontation of two forms of reflection that pervade the history of modern ethics. Modern ethics as a whole, since the eighteenth century, can be characterized, using an expression of Niklas Luhmann, as a "reflective theory of morality."[6] What this means is that modern ethics is not only a form of enactment, and also not only a description or classification of the moral position; it is, rather, a theory, a (meta- or self-) reflection of it. If the idea of equality stands at the center of the moral standpoint according to the modern understanding, a reflection of equality is just as central to modern ethics. This reflection is central, however, in two antinomic forms.

In its first form, the ethical reflection of equality is concerned with the justification of equality. Ethical reflection means, first of all, the distanced observation of the practical enactments of equality as regards the question of their normative justifiability. The fact that this justification is the *first* form that the reflection of equality assumes in modern ethics follows from the central position of the idea of equality. The central position of the idea of equality in modernity and the modern emphasis on justification are directly connected with one another. This is rendered apparent by the new understanding of (normative) justification that lies behind this emphasis: only those normative rulings that can be justified with regard to everyone are considered to be grounded. However, these are precisely the normative rulings that consider everyone equally, that is, they are rulings of equality. According to the standard of the modern concept of normative justification, it is only the normative obligations of equality that are universally justifiable. It is this connection between "egalitarian" and "justified" that stands, in the first instance, at the center of modern ethics: it grounds the idea of equality in (nothing more than) the idea of justification. In modern ethics, to reflect upon the idea of equality means, at first, to ground it. For this reflection claims that the idea of equality itself already follows from the idea of justification. With this step, modern ethics moors the idea of equality, in a new way, in the "nature" of human beings:[7] it derives it from the "natural" capacity of rationality as the capacity of justification. The obligation of the equal consideration of everyone should follow from this, whether indirectly, because it demands "properly understood self-interest" (as in contractualism), or directly, because the idea of equal treatment follows from the rational capacity of human beings (as in Kantianism). To be rational means to be egalitarian: this is the core of modern ethics' program of justification.

In this equally historical and systematic first form, the "reflection of equality" means the justification of equality. The reflection of egalitarian practice involves here an uncovering and presentation of reasons. As against this, there stands, in modern ethics, a second form of ethical reflection—one that reverses the line of vision from the grounds to the consequences of equality. In Luhmann's outline of modern ethics this opposing movement of reflection does not come to the fore; he mentions it only tangentially, by referring to the "philosophy of inversion" that the Marquis de Sade proposed from his prison cell.[8] The motive for this omission is simple: Luhmann wants to present his own sociological reflection of morality as the only alternative to philosophical ethics' supposed fixation on justification. The inversion of reflection does not only take place, however, outside the undertaking of modern ethics, in the dungeons of the Bastille and the sociology seminars of Bielefeld; it forms a significant and continuous strand of tradition in modern ethics itself. This is how modern ethics answers the justification of equality by means of its questioning.

The program of a reflective questioning of the idea of equality attained its first coherent articulation in the last years of the eighteenth century, in the literature critical of the French Revolution. Schiller's fourth letter on aesthetic education provides a succinct example of this, first of all distinguishing between two "different ways in which men existing in time can coincide with man as Idea."[9] In another formulation, the two ways in which the "ideal man" of the egalitarian standpoint (and hence also of the state) can come to correspond with the "empirical man" of sensuous inclinations (and hence the human being in its peculiarity and individuality) are: "either by the ideal man suppressing empirical man, and the State annulling individuals; or else by the individual himself *becoming* the State, and man in time being *ennobled to the stature* of man as Idea."[10] Schiller follows this distinction with a methodological remark that throws light upon his understanding of ethical reflection: "It is true that from a one-sided moral point of view this difference disappears. For Reason is satisfied as long as her law obtains unconditionally. But in the complete anthropological view, where content counts no less than form, and living feeling too has a voice, the difference becomes all the more relevant."[11] Schiller calls "one-sided" a "valuation," positive or negative, of the moral orientation that only hears in it the voice of reason and thus considers it grounded. His characterization of the other kind of "valuation" shows what he means by this. Schiller calls this valuation "complete" because, in contrast to the first, it sees not only one side, but two sides and their difference: the difference between the egalitarian standpoint and another standpoint which Schiller describes as that of the "vivid sentiment" of the "empirical" or "individual" human being. Because the "complete" or "anthropological" valuation makes and does not forget this distinction, it makes a difference if the norm of equality is accomplished by means of the oppression or "refinement" of empirical human beings. The other kind of "valuation" is a form of reflection that is concerned with differences. This is also the way in which it views the standpoint of equality: as differentiated. The other kind of "valuation" is an ethical reflection which introduces the standpoint of equality into this difference, and which asks what significance this standpoint has with regard to that which is different from it.

As the history of the revolution compellingly demonstrated for Schiller, this significance can be a negative one. The implementation of the idea of equality can have disturbing consequences for other, nonegalitarian orientations and for obligations arising out of individuality. This implementation thus can be questioned from the perspective of these orientations and obligations; indeed, it may need to be restricted by them. This is how Schiller begins a tradition of the questioning of morality; a tradition that looks at the significance and consequences that morality has for the individuals subjected to it or, more precisely, for the individuals who subject *themselves* to it. It is a tradition which Hegel and Nietzsche took up in very different ways, continued, in a no less differing and, indeed, opposing manner, by contemporary authors like Adorno and Foucault, Taylor and Williams.

Modern ethics thus consists, in a manner different to that suggested by Luhmann, of two strands. Although both of these strands pursue an ethical reflection of equality, they lead to an entirely different attitude with regard to the idea of equality. They pursue the ethical reflection as a justification and questioning of the normative idea of equality. With a view to these two strands, we can speak of an antinomy of the ethical reflection of equality. The justification reflection derives the attitude of equal treatment from something indubitably given in the "nature" of human beings, from their reason. It thus claims the unconditional validity of the imperative of equality. By contrast, the questioning reflection relates the standpoint of equality to something indubitably desirable for human beings, the orientation toward individuality. It places the imperative of equality in relationship to something different and thus, as a consequence, relativizes it. Without a doubt, the programs of reflective justification and questioning pose an idea of equality whose coordinates do not coincide—and which can lead, moreover, to conflicting orientations.

The Dissolution of the Antinomy

This is the picture which determines the history of and the debates concerning modern ethics. The common understanding of the relationship between the two forms of reflection mentioned above is governed by their most extreme formulations. Kant as against Burke, Mill as against Nietzsche, Habermas as against Foucault: this appears to be an appropriate way to describe the two forms of the ethical reflection of equality and their relationship to one another, that is, as a relationship of mutual exclusivity. Even if all of this may appear self-evident at first glance, this picture is nevertheless superficial and therefore false. It is able to capture in the dialectical constitution of equality only the moment of mutual opposition between its two sides, and not the moment of their mutual interdependence, that is, the moment in which the opposing forms of reflection are simultaneously connected to one another. It is true that the two forms of reflection view the idea of equality from different perspectives, and can therefore lead to opposing attitudes toward it, that is, to the justification of equality and the affirmation of its priority, on the one hand, or to the questioning of equality and the affirmation of its relativity, on the other. Nevertheless, the two forms of reflection are inherently and indissolubly connected.

The nature of this connection becomes clear if we consider the argument by means of which the two forms of reflection proclaim their exclusivity. This argument is the same on both sides: each party claims that the other fails to understand the true meaning of reflection. According to this doubly false perspective, reflection can consist only in one thing, either justification or questioning, either deduction or problematization, either a descent into the roots or a step beyond the normative idea of equality. According to this view, the two ethical forms of reflection must contain two opposing and fundamentally different understandings of the nature and meaning of reflection. For the first party—the party of justification—reflection means a return into itself: a reflective becoming aware of a concealed but fundamental reason. For the second party, however—the party of questioning—reflection is a movement out of itself and a consideration from outside that registers a difference to something else. For the first party, the reflection of equality consists in the knowledge of a rational, essential content of equality (of reason *as* its essence). For the second party, it consists in the unfolding of an indissoluble conflict between equality and the other normative standpoint of the orientation toward individuality. It is for this reason that, for the party of justification, the questioning of equality from outside is nothing more than an empty skepticism or frivolous irony; whereas, for the party of questioning, the belief in reasons is only an intellectual dishonesty of backwoodsmen (Nietzsche's *Hinterweltler*).

This exposes the common mistake in the antinomian self-understanding of both forms of ethical reflection: the two parties have an opposing understanding of the reflection of equality only because they have the same, and equally unsatisfactory, idea of equality. Both parties share the same insufficiently complex understanding of the idea of equality. For both sides ascribe to the idea of equality a simple or homogeneous constitution: equality is here something which—according to the position of justification—has an essence (and in this essence its reason), and which therefore makes up, according to the position of questioning, only one side of an external difference. By emphasizing and elaborating only their

opposition to the other party, both programs of reflection overlook the opposition which already reigns in their object, in the idea of equality itself.
Both overlook the fact that the idea of equality already contains its other, the normative orientation toward individuality, in itself. This is what I
called above the dialectical constitution of equality. Only an ethical reflection which transcends the external opposition between justification and
questioning can do justice to this constitution. Such an ethical reflection
is able to bring to light the dialectical constitution of equality because it
connects the two reflective movements which come apart in justification
and questioning. The reflective movement outward and questioning from
outside *follows from* the reflective becoming aware and justification; the
reflective becoming aware and justification *turns into* the reflective movement outward and questioning from outside. When viewed from the perspective of the normative idea of equality, reflection as a questioning from
outside and reflection as a return to its own ground are not two different
undertakings, but instead two different, and even opposing, aspects of the
same undertaking.

This undertaking is a critical self-reflection of equality. It is a *self-
reflection* because its aim is the reflective becoming aware of something
which is already contained and presupposed in the idea of equality itself.
The reflection of equality takes place not from outside, as the position of
questioning seems to assume. This becoming aware is *critical* (in the literal sense of this expression) because it discovers and unfolds in equality
its difference with respect to individuality; the reflection of equality is not
the unveiling of the simple essence of equality, as the position of justification assumes. The questioning and justification of equality are therefore opposed to one another in the undertaking of a critical self-reflection
of equality, but they are both equally necessary. They are doubles which
are, at one and the same time, enemies and allies. We cannot do the one
thing without doing the other. The self-reflection of equality, and hence
the whole of modern ethics, is not a unified project; its unity is a movement through the opposition of forms of reflection. In the unfolding of
the connection and opposition of these forms of reflection, the dialectic of
equality unfolds itself.

This thesis of the internal connection between the opposing forms of
ethical reflection requires an elucidation, which will be given here (and in

Chapter 2) mainly from the perspective of the program of an ethical questioning of equality. The question to be asked concerns the version in which this program can be justified. My comments above should have made clear which version of this program cannot be justified: the program of a questioning of equality cannot be understood and defended as a reflection from outside, putting in question equality from a perspective alien to it. The questioning of equality must instead be understood as a movement of its own critical self-reflection, in which the dialectical constitution of equality unfolds itself. In this self-reflection, the questioning and justification of equality are linked to one another. Nevertheless, before the program of an ethical questioning of equality can be elucidated in such a way that it loses its external opposition to the program of justification (C), we need a more detailed determination of the standpoint of equality itself (B).

B. Determining Equality

So far, I have been discussing the reflection of equality using Niklas Luhmann's characterization of modern ethics as a reflection *upon* equality—as an attitude in which the idea of equality itself becomes an object in either a justificatory or questioning mode. The standpoint of equality, however, is already internally reflective. The "reflection of equality" does not only imply a reflection upon equality, but also a reflection *from* its standpoint. It is not the justification or questioning of equality which enacts itself in the reflection of equality in such an internal or immanent mode, but its determination. There is no standpoint and, a fortiori, no practice of equality which does not possess an internally reflective constitution; the standpoint of equality consists only in its own reflective enactment. If we call the reflection upon equality its ethical reflection, then the reflection from the standpoint of equality can be called the *egalitarian* reflection. The ethical reflection—as both the justification and the questioning of equality—is a reflection upon the egalitarian reflection.

Equalizing: Normative and Descriptive

To reflect primarily means to compare. It was in this way that Kant elucidated the notion of reflection in his theory of the concept, or of the conceptual determination of objects: to reflect upon an object—or simply to reflect an object—means to compare it with other objects in order to find out "what they have in common." More precisely, Kant determines reflection as the intermediary step between the "comparison," which is a mere listing of qualities of different representations, and the "abstraction," which is a mere registering of the correspondence of different representations, under the condition of the "isolation of all other qualities in which the given representations differ from one another." Reflection is the process between these two steps: the "consideration of the way in which different representations can be grasped in a single consciousness."[12] Reflection is that operation of comparison which not only lists the qualities of different representations, but also determines what is common to them, that is, their "unity," but without "isolating" this unity from the different representations from which it has been abstracted. Reflection is a transition from comparison to abstraction: it is a comparison which is oriented toward unity and an abstraction which is conscious of difference.

This characterizes the theoretical use of reflection in the conceptual determination of objects. Normative reflection, however—which constitutes the standpoint of equality—has a similar constitution. The reflexivity of equality (the reflexivity which is immanent to equality) must be understood as a more precise determination of its processuality. The modern idea of equality, as I said at the beginning, requires an equal or symmetrical consideration of everybody. This is, however, an ambiguous formulation. On the one hand, it can be understood in such a way that a decision or ruling has the normative *quality* of the equal consideration of everybody. On the other hand, the notion of the equal or symmetrical consideration of everybody can also be understood as the determination of a *process* by means of which the above-mentioned egalitarian decision or ruling is made. This second, processual meaning of equal consideration is the fundamental one; the equal consideration of everybody as a quality of decisions or rulings is produced by means of the equal consideration of everybody in the process of the generation of these decisions and rulings.

Following Kant, we could express this in the following way: a decision or ruling considers everybody equally if, and only if, it is made from a "universal standpoint," that is, if it is made from a standpoint which is not that of one of the many different individuals, but instead that of anybody. A decision or ruling which anybody can desire is a decision or ruling which equally considers any particular individual and therefore everybody. However, in the same way in which abstract concepts must be formed by means of comparison and reflection (according to Kant's formulation), the universal standpoint is not simply there to be taken as such. Like abstract concepts, the universal standpoint needs to be produced. This is the point of the processual meaning of the formula of the equal consideration of everybody. The universal standpoint—the decisions and rulings of which possess the quality of the equal consideration of everybody—needs to be *formed* by means of a process of the equal consideration of everybody; a process which begins from a particular standpoint which is different from all others.

Kant speaks of an "operation of reflection" not only in the case of the formation of concepts, but also in the case of the formation of the universal standpoint of egalitarian consideration; the egalitarian attitude only exists in the process of its formation by means of reflection.[13] The "operation of reflection" consists in the step from comparison to abstraction—both in the case of the formation of concepts and in the egalitarian attitude. This means that, in both cases, reflection leads to a position of unity and begins with an act of comparison. In the egalitarian attitude, however, the original comparison does not have a theoretical meaning, but instead a normative one. To compare means here to equate people normatively with respect to their relative weight in decisions or rulings. In egalitarian reflection, as we have seen, such an operation of regarding as equal always enacts itself from a particular and different standpoint. The operation of regarding as equal therefore means here regarding *oneself* as equal *to* everybody else. If I consider everybody equally in the egalitarian attitude, this means that I—that is, my desires, inclinations, and intentions as well as those of my friends, loved ones, and neighbors—possess for myself no greater weight than all others. When I assume the egalitarian attitude, I compare myself with others in such a way that I accord to all of us, myself and others, an equal weight. This is the primary normative meaning of egalitarian reflection: to attain an abstract perspective—"the universal standpoint"— by means of an operation of comparing myself with, and regarding myself as equal to, others. From this abstract perspective, we all possess an equal weight, and count equally as much as anybody else.

This normative meaning, however, does not exhaust the egalitarian reflection: the reflection of equality is not only a process of the equal *consideration* of others; it is also a process of their equal *determination*. This follows from the irreducibly descriptive content which is connected to the normative attitude of equality. Equality in the normative sense—to consider everybody as equal—also presupposes equality in a descriptive sense. This can be seen most clearly in cases in which the normative idea of equality obliges us to treat somebody in a different way than others: for instance, to allow him to have a greater amount of some good than others. For to consider everybody equally or each one as equal does not mean that everybody receives an equal share: equal attention, help, care, or even equal goods or resources. Equality does not mean equal distribution, and the equal measure of consideration does not require an equal amount of distributable goods. Instead, equal treatment often means treating somebody differently than others because in some relevant respect he is "in greater need" than them. In such cases, only a different and divergent treatment of others can fulfill the condition of equal treatment. This shows that equality and inequality are here, as in other cases, perspective-relative or, more precisely, description-relative expressions. The same mode of action which implies inequality on one level of description (for instance, in a description of allocated "goods"), implies equality on a different level of description (for instance, in a description of the "dignity" of persons).[14] When we normatively designate a certain mode of action as an equal consideration, this designation always has a descriptive content: it implies a characterization of the other with regard to the particular determination or quality which this particular mode of action has considered equally. The equal treatment of the other therefore presupposes that this other is described as equal in certain relevant respects; equal treatment requires equal description.

At first glance, it might seem appropriate to assign the descriptive content of the normative attitude of equality only to the secondary dimension of its "application": in this case, we only undertake an equal description of others if we try to realize the fundamentally normative attitude of equal consideration in certain concrete situations. This link between description and application is misleading—at least if we understand the notion of application in the conventional sense of norms and their application. According to this sense, the norm, that which is meant to be applied, exists prior to and independently of its application: it exists in a universal formulation which does not contain any reference to its applications. It is precisely this, however, which is not true in the case of the normative attitude of equal consideration. To formulate this as a normative attitude which gives a practical orientation already *means* to apply it: it already means to connect it with a certain description, with a certain descriptive content. For a formulation of the attitude of equality which is free of any descriptive content has no force of orientation whatsoever. The requirement that we consider everybody equally does not have any particular meaning if the empty place of this formulation remains unfilled. For this requirement, when viewed more closely, is a requirement of the equal consideration of everybody *with respect to a certain x.* As long as this *x* remains undetermined, we do not know what it prescribes or prohibits. And to determine it means precisely to give the attitude of equality—in the formulation used above—a descriptive content, that is, to point out the quality with respect to which we want to, or ought to, consider everybody equally; the quality which must be *possessed* by all those who we want to, or ought to, consider equally.

Person and Rule

This descriptive content of the normative operation of regarding as equal manifests itself in the fact that it is the consideration of *persons* which is at stake in the attitude of equality. The addressees of the attitude of equality are conceived as persons; the attitude of equality *makes* its addressees into persons. In this context, the concept of a person has a double meaning: it links together singularity and universality. The singularity of a person means here that every single individual counts for the attitude of equality; the addressees of equal consideration are individual persons. This means that they are considered here not because they are, for instance, members of groups or communities. And it means that they are not considered here in their *quality* of being members of groups and communities. This refers us to the second aspect of the concept of a person, that is, its universality. This second aspect implies that the consideration of individual persons in the attitude of equality conceives them, at the same time, as universal. The equal consideration applies to the individual in a universal description which, because it is universal, applies to everybody. The expression "person" means precisely this: that equal consideration applies to individuals to the extent that each of them represents the instantiation of a universally shared determination. The person who we consider equally is the individual—not in his particularity, however, but insofar as he can be brought under a universal description. Only persons who are equal, or who have been described as equal, in certain universal respects can be normatively considered as equal. The person is the mask of equality behind which individuals enter into the field of vision of the egalitarian attitude.

The double determination of a person as being, at one and the same time, singular and universal corresponds to the fact that the attitude of equality finds its formulation under the guise of rules. For the rules of equality manifest a double determination which precisely corresponds to that of a person: a doubling into formality and determinateness. The rules of equality are formal and therefore can refer to every individual. At the same time, the rules of equality are determinate because they can refer to every individual only under a universal description. The concepts of a person and a rule therefore manifest, once again, the normative-descriptive double determination of the idea of equality itself: they manifest the fact that the claim to consider everybody equally is always accompanied, not only in its realization but already in its formulation, by a determination and description of its addressees. Every determination of this kind (the determination of persons by means of rules) is abstract, but not, as a consequence, neutral: it does not speak from nowhere, but instead from an identifiable historical and cultural place; it articulates the locally shared assumptions about what makes everybody equal and what makes everybody a person. This is not an objection to any determination of this kind, and it is not a claim which considers every such determination as equally good. It reminds us, however, of the fact that when we give an *abstract* determination of individuals as persons we always also give a *specific* determination.

Repetition and Working Through

In each formulation, and all the more in each act of equal treatment, we presuppose a conception of what it means to be a person. Usually, these conceptions direct our understanding and our judgments without becoming explicit. This means that we rely upon a certain preunderstanding of the abstractly described characteristics of persons that become significant in the attitude of equality. Sometimes, however—and we will soon see in which cases—this descriptive content of our normative attitude becomes explicit and thematic: it becomes explicit if (and usually only if) a certain problem arises. For in such a case the unproblematically presupposed conception of a person comes to appear as a "prejudice" (Gadamer), and the formulation of the attitude of equality which has been proposed by means of it, in a (legal or moral) rule, comes to appear only as a "prima facie obligation" (Hare)—as a necessary starting point which nevertheless needs to be subjected to further examination. In our practice of equal treatment, we usually rely upon a certain conception of a person; occasionally, however, we need to subject these customary descriptions to a further examination. This examination makes up a central aspect of the process of reflection which is immanent to the attitude of equality.

A conception of a person implies the respects in which another person is equal to myself and all others. Each conception of a person is, therefore, the result of a process of abstraction. If abstraction is taken as a process then it is called, in the Kantian terminology introduced above, "reflection"; it consists in a process of "comparison" which is meant to discover what different objects have in common. This comparative process of reflection is usually forgotten in our customary practice of equal treatment; its result—that is, a certain conception of a person—has detached itself and now exists independently. For this reason this result appears as something natural. And it is this detachment of the result from its production which we revoke in a new examination of our customary conception of a person. To examine a customary conception of a person means to retrace the abstraction by means of which it has been formed. In this way the abstraction again becomes a process of comparative reflection. To examine a customary conception of a person therefore means nothing more than to repeat the process of reflection by means of which it has formed itself, and from which it has later detached itself by means of its familiarization. The point is to learn how to view the customary as abstract and detached—and to learn how to reconstitute the process of reflection by means of which it was once formed.

To repeat abstraction as a process, and hence to turn it back into reflection, means to enact it step by step from the very beginning. The beginning of reflection is "comparison," the comparison of different objects; the abstraction which has been reflectively enacted as a process begins with the grasping of the concrete. If in an abstract and universal description we call the particular human being who is equal to all others a "person," then in a concrete description—the point of which is to characterize the individual's peculiarity—we call this being an "individual." If, in the egalitarian attitude, persons are particular human beings, then individuals are particular human beings *prior to* and independently of this attitude: particular human beings such as they appear to themselves and others outside of the perspective of equality. As soon as we enter into an examining repetition of our conception of a person—and enact it once more, from the very beginning, in its process of formation—we do not already refer to particular human beings as persons, but instead only as individuals. At the beginning of every conception of a person we can find the (self-) descriptions of individuals. A new examination of our customary conception of a person implies its supervision—and possibly its revision—in the light of our understanding of individuals.[15]

In this examination of our conception of a person, the notion of a reflexivity which is immanent to the egalitarian attitude (and which does not simply question or justify it) has assumed a different meaning. At the outset, egalitarian reflection consists in an operation of regarding ourselves as equal to others; this operation has a normative meaning, the equal consideration of everybody; and a descriptive content, the description of everybody as equal. This is still an insufficient characterization, however, of the reflection which we enact in the egalitarian attitude. For this picture of a reflective generation of equality (in the normative as well as descriptive sense) suggests a fictional situation—one in which we are at the beginning only egotists, and in which we only later come to "take into account" others and hence consider and describe them as equals. In fact, however, the reflective generation of equality takes place in the form of its reflective *revision*—in the form of a reflective revision of customary egalitarian practices. This reflective revisionism follows from the "hermeneutical" fact that the practices of equal treatment, along with their modes of equal description, already exist—and thus do not need to be produced out of nothing.

Let me summarize these considerations concerning the normative-descriptive double character of egalitarian reflection: egalitarian reflection itself already implies, according to its very meaning, an examination of existing practices of equality which never ends because it is always newly enacted. This self-examination takes place in the name of the normative idea of equality. At the same time, however, as we have seen, this ever-new examination can only enact itself in such a manner that we repeat, once again and from the very beginning, the process of formation of our particular, "abstract" conception of a person. In the process of the revision of our egalitarian practice, we unavoidably become implicated in a different project: that of the understanding of individuals in their concreteness and difference. The attitude of equality cannot only consist of operations of equality. Equal treatment is the fundamental aim of this attitude. To be able to attain *this* aim, however, we always need to pursue another aim in the egalitarian attitude. To be able to attain the aim of equal treatment we need, at least preliminarily, to pursue the nonegalitarian aim (which does not necessarily mean the anti-egalitarian aim) and interpretatively do justice to others as individuals. For it is only through a certain understanding—one which does justice to individuals in their peculiarity—that we can succeed in an adequate description, and thus in a true equal treatment, of persons.

Understanding an Individual

It is true that the understanding of individuals from which the revision of our conception of a person starts enacts itself in the name of the normative attitude of equality. For this is the reason for such a revision: we experience the fact that, upon the basis of our customary conception of a person, a true equal treatment has become impossible. (I will show in the next section, using an example from political ethics, how we come to have such an experience—and I will also elucidate its content and consequences.) Nevertheless, the understanding of persons does not enact itself *from the perspective of* the normative attitude of equality. This is the point which proves decisive for the difference between the universal determination of persons and the understanding of individuals. The operation of describing somebody as a person and the operation of understanding somebody as an individual differ, first of all, with regard to their contents. To understand this difference in content as the external difference between equality and difference would, however, be misleading. The conception of somebody as a person does not consist in a mere listing of the qualities which he shares with others, nor does the understanding of an individual consist in a mere listing of the qualities which differentiate him from others. That which distinguishes the determination of persons and the understanding of individuals is, rather, the angle of vision from which we observe the qualities or, more precisely, the determinations and intentions of a particular human being. A person is the particular human being considered as anybody; the conception of a person ensues from the perspective of everybody. The issue at stake in the formation and application of conceptions of a person is the following: can the determinations and intentions of particular human beings be conceived in such a way that they represent concretizations of the abstractly described determinations and intentions which can be equally ascribed to everybody? When understanding individuals, by contrast, we consider particular human beings from their own perspective. The issue at stake in this context is how an individual conceives and understands his own determinations and intentions.

This is the reason why individuals cannot be understood as objectively and externally characterizable items—the qualities of which can simply be listed. To understand an individual means, rather, to understand his perspectively oriented mode of self-referentiality. Individuals are determined by the modes in which they disclose and disguise, conceal and reveal themselves in the course of their own life process. Individuals *consist* in their relation of self-disclosure and disguise. It is this that we try to grasp when we attempt to understand individuals: not what they are in themselves, but what they are for themselves, that is, which determination and meaning they give to the elements (and sometimes also to the whole) of their lives—especially from the perspective of the active enactment of those lives.

It is above all important in these practical contexts—in contexts of evaluative judgment, decision, and action—to know the relevance, that is, the value, which individuals accord to the elements of their lives. The self-reference of individuals is not only interpretative; it is also evaluative. Individuals can apply to the elements of their lives systems of value discrimination of various kinds and of various degrees of intensity; these can be, for instance, discriminations between important and less important, between good and bad, between indispensable and dispensable. Individuals differ not only because of the way in which they contentfully determine such discriminations, that is, because of what they consider valuable and valueless. They also differ because of the kind and intensity—because of the "language"—of their evaluative discriminations, that is, because of the *way* in which they enact their evaluations. The reference point of these evaluations is, however, always the life (and this does not necessarily mean the *whole* life) of an individual; what is at stake here is the accomplishment of this life. Individuals are determined by the perspectives of evaluative judgment regarding what is important, good, or indispensable for them in their lives. Just as there is no individual whose being-for-itself does not enact itself within the limits of an opposition between disclosure and disguise, there is no individual whose being-for-itself does not orient itself according to some form of such a self-referential, evaluative discrimination.

This claim of understanding—a claim to take up the perspective proper to an individual—is connected to a second, nonegalitarian concept of justice. Already in our everyday life, the concept of justice has two different uses. These can be understood as two different interpretations of the fundamental requirement of justice: that everybody ought to be given his due. The first interpretation is social: everybody ought to be treated according to his status in a group. (It is self-evident that the modern idea of equality is a particular version of this social interpretation of the requirement of justice: it requires the same status of everybody and it extends the group to all.) The second interpretation is individual: everybody ought to be treated according to his being as an individual. This second, individual interpretation manifests itself in the expression "to do justice to someone," which, as against the social interpretation, does not possess any comparative sense. Instead, it means to treat someone in a way that corresponds to him as an individual. To learn how to view the other from his own perspective is a form (and possibly the basic form) in which we practice justice in its individual understanding. This shows that the understanding of an individual possesses its own normativity: it succeeds if—and only if—it does justice to the individual; and it does justice to him if—and only if—it understands him from his own perspective, that is, as he is for himself.

This requirement of justice in the understanding of individuals is exposed to the threat of misunderstanding. The misunderstanding arises if we conceive the aim of just understanding (to understand someone in the same way in which he is for himself) in the sense of a mere doubling or repetition. To interpretatively do justice to somebody would then be to understand him in the same way in which he understands himself. The requirement of justice would be the requirement of the identity of two acts of understanding: my understanding of the other and his self-understanding. Such identity, however, is not only unattainable, it is also not a requisite of the attempt to interpretatively do justice. The claim of understanding—to grasp the proper determination of an individual—does not necessarily contain a requirement that the individual understood in such a way should explicitly ascribe to himself such a determination. In such a case, the understanding of this individual would merely repeat his own expressions, his own language.[16] It is precisely the attempt to interpretatively do justice which can, however, require a moment of violent construction: a construction which is violent insofar as it completes, transforms, or revokes the explicit self-understanding of the other. This is the case not only with respect to the determinations which we ascribe to an individual while understanding him; it is already the case with respect to the mere attempt to determine the other as an individual. For this is a nonneutral, noninnocent act. The concept of an individual used in this text, for instance, already implies the discrimination between different classes of objects (an individual is, for instance, not a text and not a thing); the concept elucidates this discrimination by means of certain structural qualities which need to be possessed by something or which we need to be able to ascribe to something that we consider as an individual (an individual is determined, for instance, by means of an interpretative and evaluative perspective upon himself). We have always already applied such discriminations to an interlocutor when we attempt to interpretatively do justice to him as an individual. An understanding which intends to do justice to an individual from his own perspective is also, therefore, a construction which can go beyond what manifests itself in his own perspective.

From this constructive, and even violent, characteristic of an attempt to do justice to individuals, there follows a negative claim with respect to the question as to the role that the understanding of individuals plays in the reflective examination of our conception of a person. This is the claim that the difference between the understanding of individuals and the equal description of persons is *not* the difference between a first mode of determination, which consists in a mere repetition and doubling of the concretely individual, and a second mode of determination, which operates by means of general concepts. Nor is this difference a difference between self-determination and determination by others, between truth and construction, between absence of violence and distortion. Instead, we can say that *both* modes of determination—determinations of individuals and determinations as persons—operate by means of concepts, and that *both* modes of determination enact themselves from certain perspectives. It is for this reason that both modes of determination can be equally adequate *or* inadequate, that is, both can be equally contentious. There is a conflict of interpretations in both fields: a conflict whose stake is the conception of a person which makes possible a true equal treatment and a conflict whose stake is the conception of an individual which orients us in our attempt to interpretatively do justice.[17] To reiterate, what distinguishes the concept of a person from that of an individual in this context is only the *point of view* from which their determination enacts itself: a person is determined from the perspective of his equality with all others; an individual, by contrast, from his own perspective upon himself. When we form a concept of a person we need to discover what everybody wants in such a way that everybody can want it equally. As against this, when we want to interpretatively do justice to an individual we need to discover what—and the way in which—somebody views and values from his own perspective. Nevertheless, both perspectives do not stand in an external relationship of mere difference. In the egalitarian reflection, they are interconnected. In the context of the struggle for the correct concept of a person, this manifests itself in the fact that this concept remains indissolubly connected to the understanding of individuals.

A Political Example

Let us observe more closely and by means of an example the interaction between the two aims of the egalitarian attitude—between the main aim of the equal treatment of persons and the auxiliary aim of the understanding of individuals; we will observe how they both interplay and conflict with one another. The point of the egalitarian attitude is the equal treatment of persons, which presupposes the equal description as persons. Whereas we usually accept such equal descriptions as given, they are in fact the result of a process. Taking up a suggestion of Kant, I have described this process as a transition from comparison-through-reflection to abstraction. This still turned out, however, to be an abridged description. The abstracting formation of a conception of a person which needs to be revised in a certain situation was already a revision of a prior conception of a person. The conceptions of a person are never simply given, they are always the result of processes of their reflective formation; this is one point. On the other hand, this reflective formation never takes place in such a way that the conceptions of a person are simply invented, as it were, using as a starting point the "concrete" determinations of "different" individuals. Conceptions of a person come into existence, rather, by means of a process of the reflective examination and transformation of already existing conceptions of a person. And it is in this reflective process—from one conception of a person to another—that the understanding of individuals plays its role: the role of an inducement and corrective.

We can demonstrate this process, which takes place anew over and over again, using an example of the inner dynamics which govern the fundamental norms of modern constitutional states. These fundamental norms give a legal form to the egalitarian attitude of the equal consideration of everybody. The meaning of equal citizenship (and always simultaneously its scope) is subject to the constant transformation of these norms. It also makes little sense, in this context, to understand these transformations in such a way that the principle of equality—which always remains the same—is simply "applied" in different ways. For the principle of equality exists in each moment only *in* its different and ever changing applications. More precisely, the applications of the principle of equality differ and change because of the conception of a person upon which they rely in every case. The history of equality is a history of our conceptions of what constitutes a person.

This already becomes evident in the event in which modern constitutional states have their origin, that is, in their emergence out of confessional civil wars. The modern constitutional states are determined, from the very beginning, by the fact of their being the form of political order which is capable of bringing about lasting peace between the parties of confessional civil war. One version of this thesis interprets the success of the modern state by emphasizing the act of the contractual establishment of an instance of sovereign power. Another version (which I am going to align myself with in this text) claims that the modern constitutional state succeeds in bringing about peace between the confessionally divided parties because these parties decide to regulate their relationship with one another by orienting themselves to the principle of equality. If we follow this second version—which explains the stability of modern constitutional states on the basis of their bringing about peace, and bringing about peace on the basis of equal consideration—we cannot understand it in such a way that the principle of equality, as a normatively orienting principle, has been discovered, or even invented, in this event for the first time. For it was precisely the parties to this conflict who were very well acquainted with the principle of equality (for example, in the version it had assumed in the Pauline epistles).[18] What was new was not the principle of equality itself, but the decision to use this principle for the solution of *this* conflict, for the regulation of *this* relationship. This decision is, however, simultaneously a discovery—it is possible only if a discovery is made at the same time, the discovery of a new conception of a person. The principle of equality owes to this discovery its newly acquired political existence and power. Without this new and simultaneous description of what a person is, there would have been nothing (or nobody) whose equal consideration could have led to the end of confessional civil war. This means that it was by means of a new conception of a person that the confessional enemies *became*, for the first time, the possible addressees of equal consideration. The orientation of the relationship between the confessional parties to the idea of equality, on the one hand, and the new determination of what a person is, on the other, are two simultaneous moves which can only be enacted together.

This new conception of a person can be most simply determined if we say that the members of the other confessional party are no longer viewed either as followers of dangerous heresies or as the victims of devilish insinuations, but are instead described as religious believers *just like ourselves*. By means of such a new description, the concept of a "believer" forms itself for the first time in a neutral, that is, nonconfessional, sense—in a sense which abstracts from confessional differences. In this semantic innovation, "faith" and "believer" become predicates which are different from those of "orthodoxy" and "orthodox believer"; these new predicates

allow us to see common features in a field where we used to see only differences, or even irreconcilable oppositions. Such an abstracting equal description is evidently the presupposition of the ability to consider others
as equals beyond the limits of confessional differences: the follower of one
faith views the follower of another—which he still considers a heresy—as
somebody who, despite the false content of his faith, is *also* a believer; as
somebody who deserves equal consideration because in this respect he is
equal to him and wants the same for himself (that is to practice his faith).
The equal consideration of everybody is connected, in this context, to this
new conception of a person as a believer. The "equal consideration of everybody" here means, therefore, the equal consideration of all believers.

The indissoluble link between the orientation toward equality and
the conception of a person explains both the fact that the idea of equality transforms itself with time and the mode of this transformation. For
although the orientation toward equality is always linked to a conception
of a person, it is not "indissolubly" linked to any particular conception.
If the conception of a person transforms itself, then the idea of equality
must also undergo transformation. This process takes place continually in
modern constitutional states. No new and abstracting description of persons can be final; it needs to be constantly examined and repeated anew in
the egalitarian attitude. For, on the one hand, each conception of a person
is abstract: it is introduced and justified by reference to the fact that it allows us to ignore the differences whose emphasis we begin to view as cata-
strophic (as, for instance, leading to confessional civil war). On the other
hand, however, no conception of a person is neutral: each conception of a
person which we are able to form in the egalitarian attitude, even if it remains abstract, is still a specific contentful determination; it understands
persons in a *certain*, and hence potentially contentious, and, in principle,
changeable, sense. To take up the example described here: the conception
of a person in question understands a person as somebody who has a religious faith (even if only, at the beginning, a Christian faith), although the
content of this faith is irrelevant. (Locke's and Lessing's concepts of toler-
ance are examples of these stages in the development of the modern understanding of equality.) Later on, this framework transformed itself in the
modern history of equality and engendered a determination of persons by
means of their "conscience"; it is no longer assumed of this conscience that

it can only arise out of religious allegiances and only express itself in religious forms (as, for instance, in Rousseau and Kant).

This new determination allows for an extension of the idea of equality in a double sense: the domain *in which* persons are considered equally becomes broader in scope (for instance, it also includes now the opinions and activities which have nothing to do with religious life); and, as a consequence of this, the circle of persons *who* are considered equally also becomes broader (this circle extends itself to nonbelievers, who—on the basis of the new concept of conscience—are no longer denied, for instance, the capacity to assume moral responsibility). Nevertheless, even this extended concept of a person is not neutral. This concept forms, rather, the basis for the exclusion of groups such as those of economic dependents, women, and nonwhite races—whose members are not accorded such a conscience. The further development did not (and still does not) simply consist in the attempt to do away with this constraint—in the attempt to claim that everybody is a person with a conscience who is therefore deserving of equal consideration. The further development consisted, rather, in an attempt to transform the *conception* of a person itself—in line with Nietzsche's and Freud's critique of the concept of conscience. The pressure for the revision of this conception arises here from the fact that the concept of conscience is viewed as being just as narrow, and hence just as exclusive, as the former definition of persons by means of a certain faith. And the transformation consists in the assumption that persons do not need to have any conscience in order to be able to be considered equally. This not only allows us to consider more persons; it also exerts a pressure that they be considered in different respects. An example of this double-sided development, which is still far from complete, is the determination of persons by means of their well-being—and by means of the attempt to register this well-being in ever longer lists of allegedly universally valid aspects.[19]

We will assume that something similar to this process has actually taken place in the modern history of equality, and that this process of transformation did not restrict itself to the philosophically articulated conceptions of a person, but instead became practically effective in the fundamental norms of modern constitutional states. It is of fundamental importance *that* the conceptions of a person—and, in line with them, the idea of political equality—transform themselves; of equal importance, however, is *the way* in which this process takes place. Each transformation of this kind is an answer to objections: it is with these objections that the process of the examination of conceptions of a person begins. At the beginning, however, these objections are never already suggestions of other, apparently better, conceptions of a person. They are, rather, the objections of individuals, that is, objections which are made in the name of that which a certain conception of a person implies for a certain individual. The revision of the conception of a person is usually initiated by the fact that individuals raise complaints about the violence, constraint, and oppression that is implied for them by the existing practice of equality—a practice which is itself erected upon the basis of a certain conception of a person. These complaints evaluatively judge the existing practice of equality from the perspective of individuals—and from the perspective of the consequences of this practice for their lives. "Violence" or "oppression" does not (yet) mean here nonegalitarian treatment; rather, they mean a treatment that makes impossible or denies what is important, valuable, or indispensable for an individual in his life.[20] It is with the understanding of this complaint—and, along with it, of the individual perspective from which it has been raised—that every process of the revision of an existing practice of equality begins: such a process begins when we make clear to ourselves why an existing practice of equality is experienced and objected to by certain individuals as being violent or oppressive.

In the understanding and explication of this complaint of individuals about an existing practice of equality, the conception of a person which forms the basis of this practice moves to the center. For instance, this practice can consider everybody as a religious believer. As we have seen, the proper sense of the description of everybody as a "religious believer" is that everybody can be equally considered under it. The complaint of individuals about an existing practice of equality must therefore be understood as an objection to this conception of a person, that is, as an objection that points out that certain things which these individuals want to do or be cannot be brought under their description as religious believers—for instance, because they do not follow any particular religious doctrine. According to the objection which raises a complaint, the conception of a person—which is linked here to the attitude of equality—is not really abstract. In other words, it is not abstract enough because it does not include and allow for the "concrete" determinations and intentions of *this* individual; on the contrary, it oppresses or denies them. The understanding of individuals thus becomes an understanding of the difference between what they are and want from their own perspective, on the one hand, and what they are allowed to be and want as equally considered persons, on the other.

It is with the presentation and understanding of this difference that the complaint of individuals translates itself into the demand for a transformation of the conception of a person: this conception should be reformulated in such a way that the complaining individuals are also included in it. It is precisely at this stage—and *only* at this stage—that the complaint of individuals about the violence which the existing practice of equality implies for them articulates itself in the name of a better practice of equality; up until this point, it was a complaint in the name of individuals and that which they are and want. In the example given above, this leads, in the first step, from freedom of belief to freedom of conscience, and, in the next step, also beyond this. By means of these steps the practice of equality transforms itself, sometimes even for the better, by becoming broader in scope: the conception of that which constitutes a person—and, as a consequence, the circle of those who count as a person—becomes less narrow and exclusive. If it is to remain free of contradiction, however, this sequence of steps cannot be completed with the idea of a final step. For every practice of equality is connected to a specific conception of a person—which, precisely because of its determinacy, can always be experienced and objected to by individuals as violent.

The crucial point, however, is that the attempt to interpretatively do justice to individuals plays a decisive role in the sequence of steps in which the attitude of equality transforms and expands itself—and thus in the reflective process that makes up the attitude of equality itself. The path from one practice to another, that is, from one conception of a person to another, is not direct; it is a detour through the individual. The step from freedom of belief to freedom of conscience, for instance, would not have to have been made, and strictly speaking would have been meaningless, if certain individuals had not complained that a practice of equality centered around the concept of the religious believer was oppressive for them. At first, we need to try to understand this complaint in the sense that we attempt to do justice to the individual who raises it; it is only later that we can examine, in the light of this complaint, the customary conception of a person which serves as a basis for the existing practice of equality. In the process of reflective revision which is immanent to the attitude of equality, it is the consideration of the individuals to whom we try to interpretatively do justice which serves as the motivating force.

C. Justification and Questioning

The View from Outside

The attitude of equality—as we saw in the last section—has an internally reflective constitution. For equal consideration can only be attained if the presupposed equal descriptions or conceptions of a person are constantly subjected to examination—and, if necessary, to transformation. This reflective examination can only enact itself if it starts from and operates by means of an understanding which does justice to others as individuals, that is, if it enacts itself from their own perspective. In its immanent reflexivity, the attitude of the equal consideration of everybody is therefore dependent upon the *other* normative attitude of the understanding which does justice to individuals. That is, it is dependent upon this attitude for the sake of its own success; the aim of equal treatment is the reason for the attempt to do justice to individuals. The attempt to do justice to individuals *serves* here the idea of equality. It is for this reason that I have called the process of reflection in which the attempt to do justice to individuals enacts itself a process which is "immanent" or "internal" to equality. This process of reflection refers to the attempt to interpretatively do justice to individuals, and thus to the other of equality—although in the orientation toward equality.

This distinguishes the reflection internal to equality from the two forms of an external reflection of equality which I described and distinguished at the beginning—the forms of a justification and a questioning of equality. These two opposing forms of reflection can be called "external" because they take into account that which serves as a basis for the egalitarian attitude; they are a perspective *upon* the egalitarian perspective. For in both justification and questioning, we reflect precisely upon that which we presuppose in the egalitarian attitude: the idea or, better, the *principle* of the equal treatment and consideration of everybody. In both the reflective justification and the reflective questioning of equality, we explicitly refer to the fundamental and constitutive assumption of the egalitarian attitude—which, precisely because it is fundamental and constitutive, does not become thematic *in* the egalitarian attitude; what constitutes a perspective is, at the same time, its blind spot. This is the fundamental difference between an internal and an external reflection: the determining or internal reflection enacts itself under the presupposition of the normative orientation toward the principle of equality. By contrast, the external reflection, in both its justificatory and questioning modes, orients itself toward this principle as such. The external reflection is a reflection of the internal reflection with respect to its own nonthematic presupposition. It is from this fact that the estrangement-effect of the external reflection results; it forces that which is always already presupposed to become alien and distanced.

Both the internal and external reflection—and the relationship between them—can only be adequately understood if we hold together these two propositions. The first proposition claims that, in its internal reflection, the practice of equality is irreducibly related to its other, to the attempt to interpretatively do justice to individuals. The second proposition claims that, in its external reflection, the internally presupposed principle of equality becomes thematic as such only when viewed from outside. The first proposition aims at an internal otherness *in* the practice of equality, the second proposition aims at an external otherness *with respect to* the principle of equality (and both dimensions of otherness unfold themselves in the processes of reflection: in the internal and external reflection of equality). The two dimensions of otherness are different; but these two dimensions—and their reflective enactments—cannot be separated from one another.

This means that the *external* reflection—in its estranging mode of the observation of equality—refers, in a different way, to precisely that otherness which is internal to equality. The external reflection offers a different reading of the doubling which is immanent to the practice of equality in its internal reflection. The doubling in the normative attitudes of equal treatment and the attempt to do justice to individuals comes to the fore, as we have seen, in the reflection internal to equality. In this reflection, however, this doubling remains determined by the orientation toward the principle of equality: the internal reflection undertakes attempts to interpretatively do justice to individuals *from the perspective of* the aim of equal treatment. By contrast, the external reflection reverses this perspective: its view is directed *toward* the aim of equal treatment. This view of equality, however, is not a view from nowhere. The external reflection looks at the aim of equal treatment, but it looks from the other side of the doubling which defines this aim in the process of egalitarian reflection itself, that is, from the requirement that we interpretatively do justice to the other in his quality as an individual. The external reflection can only attain and enact a view of the principle of equality in such a way that it uses the otherness internal to the practice of equality. The external reflection intervenes in the gap that opens up in the internal reflection of the practice of equality itself; its ground is the abyss which yawns between the two moments of this practice.

This determination of external reflection has a normative meaning. It is accompanied by the thesis that the external reflection is only understood and enacted in the right way if it is understood as described above. This thesis is directed against both understandings of the program of an external or "ethical" reflection of equality that I distinguished at the beginning—and their antinomic relationship that determines the history of modern ethics. Reflection is understood here either as a return into itself and an uncovering of the concealed ground, in which case it is a justificatory reflection, or as a movement out of itself and observation from outside, in which case it is a questioning and limiting reflection. In view of the doubling of normative attitudes that unfolds itself in egalitarian reflection, this opposition in the understanding of the ethical reflection of equality is untenable. The reflective return into the ground of equality implies the discovery of the constitutive relatedness of equality to its other, to the normative orientation toward the individual. In the same way, the reflective observation of equality from the perspective of its other implies the unfolding of a doubling which is already contained in equality. The return of equality into itself and the unfolding of its difference with respect to its other are not two opposing projects; when viewed in the right way, they represent two different *aspects* of an ethical reflection of equality.

Does this mean that there is no opposition between the justification and questioning of equality? Certainly not, for this would be a meaningless claim. What it does mean, however, is that the opposition between the justification and questioning of equality is not an opposition between two operations of reflection which are different in kind. There is only *one* "external" or ethical reflection upon equality. This reflection consists in the reversal of the perspective of internal or egalitarian reflection: the external or ethical reflection orients itself toward the principle of equality, and it does this from the perspective of the other normative attitude, that is, from the orientation toward the individual—without which there can be no practice of equality. This observation of the principle of equality has two different, and even opposing, effects: it justifies *and* questions equality at the same time.

The Ground of Equality

What is at stake in the egalitarian or internal reflection is the determination of equality, that is, the determination of what it means to consider everybody equally. Usually, we undertake such determinations on the basis of the unproblematically presupposed conceptions of a person. This picture is, however, as we have seen, incomplete and hence distorting. An essential part of the egalitarian attitude itself consists, rather, in the fact that we examine our conceptions of a person as to their compatibility with the internal perspective of individuals. This takes place in the egalitarian attitude in such a way that we react to the complaints of individuals about a customary practice of equality, that is, when we first try to interpretatively do justice to the complaining individuals and then attempt to transform our determination of equality in such a manner that the reason for complaint disappears. This is the aim of the egalitarian reflection: it strives to attain a new determination of equality that renders objectless the complaints of individuals about the previous practice of equality. Conversely, this also means that the newly attained determinations of equality are grounded in the complaints of individuals. The ground of the newly determined equality is the fact that we have considered the complaints of individuals.

This expression—the "ground of equality"—has a weak, an internal or relative, meaning in the egalitarian reflection. It refers here to a reason for a preference of one (new) determination of equality over another (old) one: the consideration of the complaint of individuals is the reason why it is correct to determine the principle of equality in this and not that manner. The orientation toward the principle of equality is already itself presupposed in the egalitarian reflection. It is for this reason that the justification of this orientation seems to be as yet unattained. Moreover, this justification needs to be enacted in such a way that it does not have recourse to the elements or attitudes which are put to use in the egalitarian reflection itself in the name of the determination of the principle of equality; for this would be circular. Instead, this justification must have been enacted in the egalitarian reflection, independently of the normative attitudes. The justification of equality which I have rejected above is of this kind. It claims that the idea of the equal consideration of everybody follows from the concept of practical justification itself: as soon as we really—and not only apparently or relatively ("hypothetically")—begin to justify a practical proposition, we simultaneously begin to justify a proposition of equality.

Now, it is possible to demonstrate that such a strong or absolute justification of the principle of equality, which strives to escape the circle of its own self-justification, is itself circular.[21] This does not mean, however, that only the weak, internal or relative, meaning of justification remains at our disposal. The justifications enacted in the process of the egalitarian reflection are never purely internal. They contain, rather, a justificatory force with regard to the principle of equality itself. The justifications internal to equality acquire this justificatory force because they are precisely the justifications which start out from the other of equality: the reason for the correctness of a certain understanding of equality is the fact that it considers the complaints of individuals. It is for this reason that, in the egalitarian reflection, the consideration of the complaint of individuals becomes the decisive evaluative criterion. The egalitarian reflection itself uses this criterion only in order to discriminate between different determinations of equality. This criterion, however, can also be used externally or absolutely, that is, with the aim of the justification of the idea of equality itself. Moreover, this external or absolute meaning, if viewed correctly, is already contained in the justification internal to equality: the argument that this new determination of equality is (relatively) *better* than the old one because it considers the complaints of individuals, already implies, for the same reason, that this new determination of equality allows us to find a mode of action or ruling which is *good* (in itself). In the external reflection, this is the justification which we are able to give for the principle of equality itself, and not only for one of its determinations: the principle of equality is correct because (and insofar as) it leads to the establishment of modes of action or rulings which are good—"good" in the sense that they consider the complaints of individuals.[22]

The same consideration of the complaints of individuals which plays, in the egalitarian reflection, the role of the source of the objection to and revision of the customary practices of equality, begins, in the ethical reflection, to play the role of the ground of the principle of equality itself. It is in this way that the internal and external reflection are connected in this context. The attitude of a consideration of the complaints of individuals that thus becomes the ground stands in need, however, of a closer elucidation, which can be given if we again take a step back. The consideration of the complaints of individuals is, as we have seen, a particular formation of the normative attitude which I have described as the attempt to do justice to individuals. The attempt to do justice to individuals assumes this particular form thanks to the role which it plays in the other normative attitude, the attitude of equality. This fundamental normative attitude of doing justice to individuals also exists, however, in other forms. The original form, that is, the form in which this attitude is for the most part practiced and philosophically investigated, is the form which exists in the framework of personal relationships—love, friendship, and community. The attitude of doing justice to individuals does not require, however, the effective existence of personal relationships; in the absence of such relationships, this attitude is not only possible but also necessary.[23] It is necessary, for example, in the reflective enactment of the fundamental normative attitude of equality. It is by means of this role in the process of the enactment of equality that the attitude of doing justice to individuals assumes a form different to the one which it has in the context of personal relationships.

This formal difference has two aspects. The first aspect already manifested itself when we were discussing the role played by the attempt to do justice to individuals in the egalitarian reflection. The attitude of doing justice to individuals acquires here a *negative* orientation: it becomes the consideration of the complaints of individuals. This attitude is fundamentally different to the attitude of doing justice to individuals in the context of personal relationships. In love, friendship, and community, doing justice to individuals consists in the positive enhancement of the intentions and undertakings of others. Of central importance here are attitudes of care, benevolence, and support—the aim of which is the good of others. By contrast, the attitude of doing justice to individuals which we must practice in the name of equality reacts to the negative experiences of others, to their suffering and its expression in the form of complaint. Both are attitudes of doing justice to individuals, for in both forms we orient our judgment toward the judgment of the other; we assume the perspective of the other. Nevertheless, whereas in love, friendship, and community we want that which the other wants—in the last instance, his own good—in the egalitarian reflection our will is determined by the others' resistance: we do not want for the other what he does not want for himself. The attempt to do justice to individuals implies here a reaction *with* the other *against* the same thing which *he* himself reacts against in suffering and complaint.[24]

The ground of this formal difference is the already mentioned independence of the attitude of doing justice to individuals in the egalitarian reflection. We do not assume this attitude because we are already connected to the other in personal and affective relationships, that is, because we love him, are friends with him, or feel ourselves somehow attached to him. In the egalitarian reflection, the attitude of doing justice to individuals becomes anonymous. This characterizes the second aspect of its formal difference: in the enactment of the egalitarian reflection, the attitude of doing justice to individuals as anonymous orients itself toward everybody who expresses himself in suffering or complaint—not only toward somebody to whom we feel ourselves personally attached. In the form in which it is related to equality, the attitude of doing justice to individuals is not only negative (in the already explained meaning of that term), but also (potentially) *universal*.[25] It is *potentially* universal because it does not orient itself to everybody at the same time. The attitude of doing justice to individuals is not capable of this; in each of its acts it is limited to particular individuals. Nevertheless, doing justice to individuals in the enactment of equality is universal in the sense that it does not exclude anybody who expresses his suffering by complaining about the existing practice of equality. Above all, however, there is a close connection between the two aspects of the form which the attitude of doing justice to individuals assumes in the context of equality: because it is (potentially) universal, the attitude of doing justice to individuals *can* only have a negative constitution. For everybody who expresses his suffering in the form of a complaint wants everybody else to consider it; when suffering, I want everybody else to want my suffering as little as I do. Nevertheless, it is certainly not the case that everybody who is looking for, or even realizing, his own happiness wants everybody else to care for his success; while looking for happiness, I do not want everybody else to want my happiness as I do. In the enactment of equality, the consideration of individuals does not orient itself toward their happiness, but instead against their suffering.

These two aspects—the negative and the universal—describe the form of doing justice to individuals which the ethical reflection upon equality manifests as its ground. The ground of equality is the consideration of the suffering of every individual that is expressed as a complaint; *in order* to be able to consider the complaint of each individual, we orient ourselves toward the idea of equality. The ground of equality is not, then, normatively neutral (as is assumed by the above-criticized attempts to derive equality from the notion of practical justification or reason). The ground of equality is, rather, the normative attitude which orients itself toward others as individuals. This normative attitude can also be questioned as to its justification. In contrast to the idea of justice itself, however, it becomes immediately clear that this justification cannot be attained by means of the concept of practical reason. What is less clear is whether any justification of this other normative attitude can be given which, at the same time, justifies the attitude of equality. What is decisive here, however, is that everybody who orients himself toward, and reflectively enacts, the idea of equality always already invokes this justification in considering the complaint of each individual. The justification of equality by means of this other normative attitude is not a philosophical thesis which can add anything to the egalitarian attitude. The justification of equality by means of the consideration of the complaint of each individual is already contained in the egalitarian attitude or, more precisely, in the egalitarian reflection itself. We view or *practice* the orientation toward equality in this way because we expect or hope that it will be able to do away with the suffering of every individual which is expressed as a complaint.

This explains the meaning of a "justification" of equality. We do not speak of "justification" here in the sense of a derivation which would help the attitude of equality to acquire a greater obligatoriness. The sense in question is that of the demonstration of a relationship of unilateral dependency—one which can be read in at least two ways. On the one hand, the consideration of the complaint of each individual is a *presupposition* of the idea of equality: those who do not assume this normative attitude, who do not try to interpretatively do justice to the other as an individual, will not—and will not even be able to—orient themselves toward the idea of equality. The consideration of the complaint of every individual is an attitude, and hence also a capacity, which is presupposed in the orientation toward equality. This is, however, already a normative thesis; it explains the consideration of the complaint of every individual as the presupposition of the correct, that is, reflective, practicing of the idea of equality. It is from this fact that the other decisive aspect of the dependency between the two normative orientations results: the consideration of the complaint of each individual formulates the *claim* in the light of which the idea of equality reflectively enacts itself. When we revise the existing orientations toward equality in the light of the complaints of individuals, we are looking for an order of equality in which the complaint of each individual is considered. It is this which we require of the equal consideration of everybody, and it is by these means that we want to attain it. At the same time, however, the equal consideration of everybody can only attain this order in an always preliminary and contingent form: the equal consideration of everybody cannot guarantee this order and can always, as a consequence, enter into conflict with it.

The Problem and Limit of Equality

Schiller and Burke, to whom I referred at the beginning of this chapter, founded a tradition of the questioning of equality in the name, and from the perspective, of the individuals who are affected by its rulings.[26] The issue at stake in this questioning is a reflection *upon* the egalitarian reflection that views equality from outside. Such a reflection investigates equality in a broader context, which Schiller calls "anthropological." At the same time, this external reflection is an *ethical* reflection because it asks a question not about the costs of equality for the proper functioning of economic or political systems, but about the consequences of equality for individuals (it considers the costs for the proper functioning of systems only insofar as they have consequences for individuals).[27] The questioning and limitation of equality is an ethical reflection because a different normative attitude manifests itself in it, the attitude of doing justice to individuals. The questioning and limitation of equality takes place in the name of the obligation which we have with respect to individuals.

This describes the normative status of the questioning of equality. As to its content, this questioning consists in a problematization of equality. Equality becomes a problem for this questioning because its realization can give rise to a conflict with the obligations arising from the attitude of doing justice to individuals. To do justice to an individual means to determine our actions with respect to him and in accordance with that which he wants in and for himself; it means to make his perspective of understanding and judgment our own. By contrast, the logic of the egalitarian attitude implies that—in the name of the equal treatment of everybody—it can contravene, render impossible, and even destroy what an individual wants in and for himself. To consider everybody equally does not exclude, that is, does not *prohibit*, causing an individual's suffering.[28] The fact that the egalitarian attitude causes an individual's suffering—precisely in its attempt to treat him equally—is a by-product of it, one which must remain outside its field of vision. In the ethical reflection of equality, however, this by-product of the egalitarian attitude moves to the center of consideration. The ethical problematization of equality consists in the lamentation of the suffering caused by equality. In this lament, this problematization practices justice with respect to individuals.

In its phenomenologically original form, this objection to equality is raised upon the basis of the experience of the suffering of a *neighbor*. The attitude of doing justice to individuals which justifies the objection to equality is itself justified here by recourse to the particular affective attitude which we assume with respect to certain others. The attitude of doing justice to individuals is here a *part* of the love, friendship, or community which connects us to others. *Because* we are affiliated to others in love, friendship, or community, we are obliged to do justice to them by means of the assumption of their perspective of observation and evaluation. When we perceive from this perspective the suffering of the other caused by the existing form of equal treatment, this affectively justified obligation to do justice to individuals leads to the contention of, and even resistance to, their equal treatment. In its phenomenologically original form, the questioning and limitation of equality therefore appears as a defense of the specificity of the relationship to others in love, friendship, or community. Part of this specificity consists in the fact that, in such relationships, we are bound to others—it is precisely this bonding which can sometimes bring us into opposition to equality.

It is from the perspective of the opposition to equality—into which the relationships of love, friendship, and community can bring us—that the program of a questioning and limitation of equality derives its phenomenological evidence; for these conflicts are notorious (in theory as well as in practice).[29] The choice of this opposition as a starting point and central example is confronted, however, by the danger of a fundamental and far-reaching misunderstanding. This misunderstanding concerns, first of all, the explanation of why (or by what means) the bonds that grow out of the relationships of love, friendship, and community can enter into opposition to equality. The main aspect of this misunderstanding concerns, however, the structure of this opposition itself: it is a misunderstanding of this opposition as one between two attitudes that stand in an external relationship to one another—and enter into conflict as a consequence of lamentable circumstances. This is also why this misunderstanding conceives the questioning and limitation of equality as something external, that is, as a questioning and limitation from outside which is not grounded in that which it questions and limits. The misunderstanding consists in an *externalistic* conception of both the structure of the opposition to equality and the status of its questioning.

This misunderstanding can be rectified if we once again look back at that conflict with equality which provides the original phenomenological evidence for the program of its questioning. In this conflict, the bonds arising out of the relationships of love, friendship, or community are opposed to the bonds of equality. This is explained by two characteristics of these relationships; the relationships of love, friendship, and community are determined by two fundamental aspects, the first structural, the second motivational. Love, friendship, and community constitute relationships in which we practice the attitude of doing justice to individuals with respect to others; this is their structural determination. The affective bond, by contrast, explains *why* it is that we assume this attitude with respect to *these* others. Moreover, it explains why it is that we do this with respect to these others *in precisely this way*, that is, with the practical consequence that, in a situation of conflict, we sometimes reject the requirements and duties of equality. As regards the structure of the opposition to equality, it is decisively important that both aspects—the motivational and the structural, the affective bond and the attitude of doing justice to individuals—are conceptually independent of one another. The attitude of doing justice to individuals—in which we experience and take seriously the suffering of others, and occasionally the suffering of others that is or can be caused by equality—does not presuppose the affective bond; it can and even ought to be practiced in the absence of such a bond. On the other hand, the affective bond with the other in love, friendship, and community is essential if we are to understand why it is, and with what consequences, that we assume this attitude. The normative content of the objection to equality stems from the attitude of doing justice to individuals; by contrast, the motivation for this objection, which can be more or less strong, stems from the affective bond. The fact that we also evoke the suffering of individuals as an argument against the attitude of equality follows from our attitude of doing justice to individuals; the fact that we do this in some particular case, with the consequence that we decide against the duties of equal treatment, follows from our affective bond.

This shows that we need to distinguish between a questioning and a limitation of equality more clearly than we have been doing so far. The *limitation* of equality concerns the field of practical decisions in which, in the case of conflict, the affective bond can be decisive: occasionally we limit the binding force of the requirements of equality by means of other binding obligations—those which constitute the relationships of love, friendship, and community.[30] This follows from the "strong" motivation which is connected to the attitude of doing justice to individuals in this context. In relationships of love, friendship, and community, affective bonds motivate us to assume the attitude of individual justice; as a consequence, we are also motivated to draw from this attitude far-reaching practical consequences. By contrast, the *questioning* of equality is a form of ethical reflection upon the egalitarian reflection. Our discussion of the two aspects in the relationships of love, friendship, and community should have made clear that it is the attitude of doing justice to individuals that plays the decisive role in this questioning. This attitude characterizes the normative content of the questioning of equality: it is a questioning, in the name of the suffering, that equality can bring about in individuals. The ground of the questioning of equality is none other than the interpretative doing justice to individuals—in which we assume their own perspective. Such doing of justice to individuals is, however, independent from the affective bonds in the relationships of love, friendship, and community.

If this is a correct description, if the motive for the objection to equality is in fact the affective bond, and its ground the attitude of doing justice to individuals, then the opposition to and questioning of equality can no longer be understood "externalistically" in the sense elucidated above. For the attitude of doing justice to individuals is not only independent of the existence of those affective relationships which are, like love, friendship, and community, unrelated to equality; the attitude of doing justice to individuals is, rather, as we have seen, a requirement which is internal to equality. This means that the questioning of equality, even though it follows from the other normative attitude of doing justice to individuals, is not external with respect to equality. This has often been overlooked in the tradition of the questioning of equality which constitutes the second strand of modern ethical reflection, for example, in Nietzsche.[31] The questioning of equality appears here, for the most part, as the confrontation of equality with a type of obligatoriness which is fundamentally alien to it. The reason for this has already been stated: it is the one-sided orientation toward the opposition between equality and love, friendship, and community. This unilateral orientation is accompanied by an externalistic misunderstanding according to which the opposition to equality *is grounded* in the force of affective meaning. The decisive normative ground of the opposition between love, friendship, and community, on the one hand, and equality, on the other, is not, however, the affective bond, but instead the attitude of individual justice. It is for this reason that the opposition to equality is not external with respect to it but arises out of it. If we take our lead from what has manifested itself in the discussion of the reflexivity internal to equality—as well as in the related discussion of the "weak" justification of equality—then we can see that the attitude of equal treatment and the attitude of doing justice to individuals are not related to one another externally. The attitude of equal treatment is, rather, itself irreducibly bound up with the attitude of doing justice to individuals. That which opposes equality by questioning and problematizing it is its own presupposition, its own ground.

We can characterize this more precisely, once again, by referring to the above-proposed formulation of the ground of equality. The ground of equality is the consideration of the complaint of each individual. This means first of all that, in the egalitarian attitude, we need to assume the other normative attitude of doing justice to others; this is an essential moment of the process of reflection which is internal to equality. Without the preliminary assumption of the attitude of doing justice to individuals, the presupposed conceptions of a person cannot be examined and true equal treatment cannot, as a consequence, be attained. The fact that the ground of equality is the consideration of the complaint of every individual implies, moreover, that the attitude of doing justice to individuals, in the enactment of egalitarian reflection, detaches itself from the affective bond with which it is intertwined in the relationships of love, friendship, and community. This is the moment of universalism in the ground of equality; using an expression of Walzer and García Düttmann, we can call it "reiterative" universalism. It is precisely here—in the egalitarian attitude—that we practice the individual attitude in a radical form which is detached from all pregiven bonds, that is, as an attitude of doing justice which is directed to every individual who expresses his suffering in complaint.

This radical, because universal, form of doing justice to individuals is motivationally weak in comparison with the form which is affectively grounded in the relationships of love, friendship, and community. This is also true with respect to both the entry into the attitude of doing justice to individuals and the practical consequences which we draw from it. This (relative) motivational weakness, however, in no way affects the sharpness of the normative opposition which can open up between doing justice to individuals and universal equal treatment. The sharpness of this opposition results precisely from the fact that it is not external to equality, but is instead grounded in it: because the egalitarian attitude needs to transform itself into the individual attitude in the name of equality, the former contains in itself that which can become autonomous from and oppose itself to the latter.[32] With respect to the program of the ethical questioning of equality, this means that this questioning is (nothing more than) an external presentation of the fundamental tension which is internal to equality itself; the ethical questioning of equality only draws the consequences of that opposition between normative attitudes which constitutes the reflective enactment of equality itself. It is for this reason that the questioning of equality is not an arbitrary act, but is instead well grounded in equality itself.

The justification and the questioning of equality—the two versions of its external or ethical reflection—appear in modern ethics in two complementarily distorted forms: they appear, firstly, as a program of the *strong* justification of equality by means of the reflective uncovering of its essentially rational ground; and they appear, secondly, as the *externalistic* program of the questioning of equality by means of its confrontation with the obligations of love, friendship, and community. Both of these programs misunderstand themselves because they misunderstand that toward which they are directed—that is, the attitude of equality. For if we understand the egalitarian attitude correctly—as a process of reflection which needs to refer to the other attitude of doing justice to individuals—then the justification of equality can no longer be understood in the strong sense; and the questioning of equality can no longer be understood in the externalistic manner. Equality cannot be justified in the strong sense because it can only be justified *by means of its other*. And the questioning of equality cannot be understood in the externalistic manner because equality questions itself *by its own means*.

We can formulate this most simply, perhaps, by saying that the questioning of equality cannot be the mere rejection of equality, and that the justification of equality cannot be its mere affirmation. The justification of equality does not end up with a mere affirmation of equality because it justifies equality by means of its other, the attitude of individual justice. The questioning of equality does not end up with a mere rejection of equality because the other attitude of individual justice—from the perspective of which it questions equality—is already immanent to equality itself. At the beginning, I proposed that we call this the (negative) "dialectic" of equality. This dialectic unfolds itself in the oppositional movement of ethical reflection between justification and questioning. Justification and questioning are opposed to, and turn into, one another. The dialectic of equality is not only a figure of ethical reflection, however, but also a figure of ethical practice. Our ethical practice consists in the enactment of the conflicts between the egalitarian and individual attitudes. The self-reflection of equality, the insight into its dialectic, is not without consequence for the practice of these conflicts: we enact these conflicts in a different way if we become aware that the conflicts *between* the egalitarian and individual attitudes fuel themselves on conflicts in the egalitarian attitude itself. It is true that even the self-reflective insight into the constitution of these conflicts can no longer open up the room for an autonomy in which we acquire, by means of reason, the freedom to avoid or even solve these conflicts; the conflicts between the egalitarian and individual attitudes are unavoidable and irresolvable. Nevertheless, it is precisely our insight into this which allows us to perceive forms of a *sovereign* treatment of this conflict; we can endure these conflicts in these forms because we no longer want to decide upon them.[33]

Genealogy, Deconstruction,
Critique: Three Forms of the
Questioning of Morality

The thesis of the negative-dialectical constitution of equality, the basic traits of which have been developed in the first chapter, makes up a central part of the moral philosophy which has been formulated by the so-called "older" critical theory—by Horkheimer and, later, by Adorno. At the same time, this thesis characterizes a moment which most sharply distinguishes the older critical theory from the "younger" one—in the first place, from Habermas. In the new discourse-ethical justification of morality developed by Habermas, the idea of equality should take a form which exempts it from the negative dialectic of its self-questioning and self-limitation. In the first instance, however, the thesis of the negative-dialectical constitution of equality is decisive for the understanding of the relationship between the older critical theory and two other forms of the questioning of morality: genealogy and deconstruction. Habermas's discourse ethics pertains to the first tradition of a reflection of equality which has been characterized above (p. 000)—the tradition of a justification of the idea of equality and its "categorical" validity in the field of law and morality. By contrast, genealogy and deconstruction, along with the older critical theory, form part of the second tradition which undertakes a questioning of equality with regard to its consequences. All three enterprises want to show what the idea of equality implies for individuals. Moreover, they want to show the ways in which this idea can shape, limit, and even impair the lives of individuals; this is the moral-philosophical commonality of critique, genealogy, and deconstruction.[1]

Nevertheless, the differences which exist between these three forms of moral questioning are fundamental. This is true not only of the phenomena which these forms analyze—and of the language which frames these analyses. Over and above this, these forms differ from one another in their fundamental conceptual construction. These differences in conceptual construction concern two moments. In the first place, critique, genealogy, and deconstruction differ in their determination of the consequences of equality *with respect to individuals.* This first difference between the three forms of the questioning of morality concerns their concept of an individual, and hence also the normative status which they accord to that reference to individuals which is presupposed in the questioning of morality. In the second place, critique, genealogy, and deconstruction differ in their understanding of the consequences of this questioning *with respect to equality.* This second difference between the three forms of the questioning of morality concerns their practical attitude toward the idea of equality—which decisively depends, in turn, upon their understanding of the internal constitution of this idea.

In this chapter, I will describe the differences between critique, genealogy, and deconstruction in these two dimensions; the aim of this description is a further elucidation of the model of a self-reflection of equality that was proposed in Chapter 1. This will only be a sketch; I will do no more than outline the schema of an argumentation, I will not try to develop specific arguments. Another sense in which this will be a sketch is that I will reduce all three conceptions to some fundamental characteristics; in each case, I will refer to one representative of each conception—the position of which will be outlined by means of an interpretation of one central text. The texts will be Nietzsche's *On the Genealogy of Morals,* Adorno's *Negative Dialectics,* and Derrida's "Force of Law." We can preliminarily describe the relationships between these three texts, authors, and conceptions by saying that in both of the dimensions mentioned above—the question concerning the consequences of equality with respect to individuals, and the question concerning the consequences of this questioning with respect to equality—these conceptions enter into two different constellations. *Both* Nietzsche *and* Adorno, for instance, understand the questioning of equality as a critique which is grounded in an ethics of individuality; this critique thus presupposes a normative concept of the individual. This programmatic self-understanding links critical theory to genealogy and distinguishes both of them from Derrida's deconstruction (A). As regards the second question, by contrast, both Derrida and Adorno stand on the same side, because both of them understand the concept of equality as internally heterogeneous; it is for this reason that they understand the questioning of equality not as its overcoming, but instead as its transformation. This distinguishes *both* critical theory *and* deconstruction from Nietzsche's genealogy (B). We can also describe this twofold constellation of genealogy, deconstruction, and critical theory by saying that Adorno's critical theory links together that which is compelling in the projects of genealogy and deconstruction. At the same time, however, Adorno can only be understood in such a way if recourse is taken to the reflections of Nietzsche and Derrida; in the absence of this assistance, Adorno's moral philosophy remains disoriented and unclear.

A. The Consequences of Equality: On the Logic of a Critique of Morality

The Value of Morality: Nietzsche

As Nietzsche writes in the preface to *On the Genealogy of Morals*: "on the day we can say with all our hearts, 'Onwards! our old morality too is part *of the comedy!*'" we will have achieved the "cheerfulness" which constitutes the "*gay science.*"[2] The overcoming of (egalitarian) morality, the undermining of the trust in it, is a decisive move in that process of recovery which Nietzsche frequently grasps, in his middle and later writings, by means of the employment of aesthetic metaphors: he refers, for instance, to the acquisition of an aesthetic "*freedom over things*" which also makes possible the "*ability* to stand *above* morality."[3] At the same time, however, Nietzsche repeatedly emphasizes that such aesthetical cheerfulness and freedom beyond morality is "the reward of a long, brave, industrious, and subterranean seriousness,"[4] the seriousness of "sincere," "true" knowledge. The overcoming of morality can only be achieved by means of an insight

into morality. It can only succeed if we advance into the "immense and al-
most new domain of dangerous insights"—a domain which is opened up
by means of a psychology which "shall be recognized again as the queen of
the sciences":[5]

if one has once drifted there with one's bark, well! all right! let us clench our teeth!
let us open our eyes and keep our hand firm on the helm! We sail right *over* morality, we crush, we destroy perhaps the remains of our own morality by daring to
make our voyage there—but what matter are *we*! Never yet did a *profounder* world
of insight reveal itself to daring travelers and adventurers.[6]

The overcoming of morality is, for Nietzsche, a gain which is promised to
"those who know," these "daring travelers and adventurers," as a reward for
the dangers which they assume; a profounder insight is the precondition of
a capacity to stand above morality.

Nietzsche's project of the overcoming of morality by means of an attainment of knowledge has repeatedly been understood in the sense of an
objectivistic and even scientistic reduction, that is, it has been understood
as a project which strives to expose the semblance of moral notions and
discriminations by opposing them to the "true" reality of immoral facts.
In the world of objectively ascertainable facts—and this is the point of
Nietzsche's critique of morality according to this interpretation—everything which constitutes our moral world, the difference between good and
evil, for instance, or the freedom of the subject to act responsibly, simply
does not exist.[7] This interpretation does not grasp, however, the issue which
is at stake in Nietzsche's questioning of morality. The fact that morality is
a semblance cannot possess, for Nietzsche, the force of an objection against
morality—what could possess this force is only the fact that morality is a
semblance unconscious of itself. The "moral problem" which Nietzsche
wants to expose is not the problem of the truth of morality, but the problem of its value: "we need a critique of moral values, the value of these values themselves must first be called in question—and for that there is need-
ed a knowledge of the conditions and circumstances in which they grew,
under which they evolved and changed."[8] Nietzsche's overcoming of morality follows from his "depreciation" of it;[9] it follows from a "depreciation"
which is connected to the fact that the value of morality is limited or weak
or, more precisely, to the fact that this value only has value *for* those who
are "humble" or "weak." Nietzsche does not criticize the world of morality
because it is not truly real, but instead because it is not truly valuable.[10]

Each question of value is, for Nietzsche, a question about purpose: "The question: what is the *value* of this or that table of values and 'morals'? should be viewed from the most diverse perspectives; for the problem 'value *for what?*' cannot be examined too subtly."[11] That which a thing serves or is good for, however, cannot be determined universally. The fact that it possesses a certain value because it serves something means that it possesses a certain value because it serves *somebody*. The question of value has a threefold structure: what is in question is the value which a thing has for somebody with respect to something; each question of value, as a question, "for what?" is, for Nietzsche, at the same time a question, "for whom?" It is precisely when the value of a thing has been claimed that "one can still always ask: what does such a claim tell us about the man who makes it?"[12] To ask the question of the value of morality means to ask what it means for somebody to orient himself toward the norms of this morality. It therefore means to ask what kind of person somebody must be if this morality is to have a certain value for him.

Now, this questioning of the value of morality from the perspective of a person can be divided, according to Nietzsche, into two stages: the first stage investigates the "the *history of the origins* of these feelings and valuations," and the second stage moves to "critique of ethical systems."[13] And the critique certainly results from the history of morality if the latter is carried out in a consistent manner; this takes place in the genealogy of morality. The history of morality leads the different forms of morality back to the "conditions and circumstances in which they grew, under which they evolved and changed." The question of the history of morality asks for whom, in which way, and for what aim a certain kind of moral prescription becomes valuable and useful. This does not exhaust, however, the genealogical question, which does not only concern the relative value of a morality for different persons, but also asks "*why have morality* at all when life, nature, and history are 'not moral.'"[14] In order to be able to answer this question, genealogy needs to give up the value-neutral perspective of a historian without claiming for itself the objective perspective of a metaphysician. The question concerning the general purpose of morality can only be answered by a genealogist if he takes it personally:

The lack of personality always takes its revenge: A weakened, thin, extinguished personality that denies itself is no longer fit for anything good—least of all for philosophy. "Selflessness" has no value either in heaven or on earth. All great problems demand *great love,* and of that only strong, round, secure spirits who have a firm grip on themselves are capable. It makes the most telling difference whether a thinker has a personal relationship to his problems and finds in them his destiny, his distress, and his greatest happiness, . . . Why is it then that I have never yet encountered anybody, not even books, who approached morality in this personal way and who knew morality as a problem, and this problem as his own personal distress, torment, voluptuousness, and passion? It is evident that up to know morality was no problem at all. . . .

I see nobody who ventures a *critique* of moral valuations.[15]

The questioning of morality, which Nietzsche wants to push to the limit of its overcoming, is a personal question in a double sense: it is a (historical and ascertaining) question about the person for whom a certain morality has a certain value; and it is a (critical and problematizing) question which is asked *by* a person—it is a question by means of which the genealogist makes morality one of his "personal" problems. The genealogist makes morality into one of those problems in which a decision is taken concerning "his destiny, his distress, and his greatest happiness."

By asking, in this personal manner, about the person for whom (egalitarian) morality has a meaning and value, the genealogist leaves behind the perspective of an observer and becomes a participant in the struggle concerning this morality—a "fearful struggle on earth for thousands of years."[16] Genealogy reconstructs the struggle for concerning egalitarian morality and is itself an active part of this struggle. This means that it is party to and takes part in this struggle, it discriminates and makes decisions, it becomes critique. Genealogy does not only ascertain for whom, for what kind of person, a morality has a certain value; over and above this, genealogy judges the value of morality, and it does so for the kind of person the genealogist himself is or wants to be. Nietzsche's questioning of morality, then, is not only nonobjectivistic (and instead personal), it is also nonrelativistic and instead normative: genealogy asks the question concerning the value which a morality possesses, if somebody wants "to make a whole *person* of oneself and keep in mind that person's *greatest good* in everything one does."[17] The determination of what it means, and how it is possible, "to make of oneself a whole person" is the central task of that "ethics of the individual" which Nietzsche already speaks about in his notes of the early 1870s.[18] This "ethics of the individual" is of a new kind, but it is no less normative than the ethics to which it appeals, that of Epictetus, Seneca, Plutarch, Montaigne, and Stendhal.[19] This ethics describes and propagates a personal, proper, and, in Nietzsche's words, "noble" life in "sovereign" freedom. It was mainly in the writings of his middle period that Nietzsche tried to elucidate this by means of an attitude of experimentalism: according to these writings, to be an individual in the normatively demanding sense—and to be oneself as an individual—means to become oneself by means of experiments with different opinions and forms of life. It is this conception of an ethics of the individual which compels Nietzsche's philosophy to assume a critical attitude: its "task," its "hard, unwanted, inescapable task," consists "in being the bad conscience" of its "time,"[20] because it confronts contemporary culture with the question concerning its meaning for the "personal" life of individual human beings. It is this—and not the objective knowledge of the true constitution of reality—which makes up that "*profounder* insight" which, according to the formulation of Nietzsche mentioned above, leads us to "sail right *over* morality": it is the insight of the ethics of the individual into the constitution of a "noble" and truly accomplished life. For the morality of equality which contemporarily prevails is grounded in an attitude of animosity toward the accomplished life of an individual person.

The Question of the "Right Life": Adorno's Critique of Culture

Adorno's critical theory coincides with Nietzsche's genealogy in this project of a critique of morality and culture, introduced in the manner of an ethics of the individual. According to the first sentence of the dedication of *Minima Moralia*: "The melancholy science from which I make this offering to my friend relates to a region that from time immemorial was regarded as the true field of philosophy, but which, since the latter's conversion into method, has lapsed into intellectual neglect, sententious whimsy and finally oblivion: the teaching of the good life."[21] The central ideas of this melancholy science are those of the "autonomy" and "happiness" of "individual existence." Both Nietzsche's and Adorno's critiques of culture are then, from the very beginning, related to a normative criterion which is not exhausted by the moral principle of equality—but rather forms the perspective from which this principle can be judged. That which Adorno refers to, in *Minima Moralia*, as "humanity" decisively consists in the accomplishment of relationships to oneself and to others—relationships which are not to be judged according to the criterion of equality: solidarity and tact in the relationship to others, for instance, and freedom and enjoyment in the relationship to our own nature.

Nevertheless, the accomplishment of these relationships is not merely "private"; it is not merely a question of the circumstances which would fit an individual or for which he would even take responsibility (and which cannot, as a consequence, be the object of a critical social theory). The individually right life depends, rather, upon the cultural situation of a society. This must not be understood, in Adorno, in such a way that the cultural situation of a society decides, that is, *determines*, whether there can be a right life for an individual. (Adorno repeatedly points out the contingency upon which individual happiness and accomplishment depend.)[22] What is truly decided in advance by the situation of a culture, however, is whether we can achieve—and if so, in which way—a correct *understanding* of the right life. Every individual must himself decide where to look for the accomplishment of his life. On the one hand, no individual can even begin to look for this accomplishment without referring to the patterns of accomplishment which are pregiven in, and initiate the individual into, a culture. These patterns mold a culture's understanding of the accomplishment of life; without having recourse to them, nobody can acquire an understanding of the accomplishment of his life. A culture does not, then, decide or determine whether our life is accomplished; it does, however, preform the way in which we understand the accomplishment of our lives.

The undertaking of a critique of culture—which is justified by its reference to an ethics of the individual—finds its grounding in this "hermeneutical" connection between the accomplishment of a life and cultural patterns. For it is as a result of this connection that the situation of a culture plays a decisive role in the accomplishment of individual existence. It does not play this role immediately, however, but instead in a mediated fashion: the situation of a culture is decisive for the accomplishment of an *understanding* of that which constitutes the accomplishment of our existence. What is probably the most famous sentence of *Minima Moralia*—the one which claims that "wrong life cannot be lived rightly"—can be understood to mean that the wrong life only knows the false images of the right one.[23] Or, more precisely, that the "wrong" culture can only form images or patterns of life which no longer enable individuals to attain a self-understanding which would allow them to lead a right and accomplished life. "We shudder at the brutalization of life, but lacking any objectively binding morality we are forced at every step into actions and words, into calculations that are by humane standards barbaric, and even by the dubious values of good society, tactless."[24] It is one thing to criticize a society because it does not accord to some, or even many, of its members the equal opportunity or chance to lead a good life; this is a critique of the inequality in this society. It is another thing, however, to criticize a culture because it does not put at our disposal the patterns or form the capacities which allow individuals to attain an adequate idea of the accomplishment of their individual existence; this is the inhumanity which Adorno's critique is directed against.

This simultaneously characterizes a fundamental commonality between Adorno and Nietzsche: both of them undertake a critical investigation of culture which—not only in its starting point, but also in its proper interest—depends upon the individual, upon the culturally determined accomplishment or failure of his existence. It is true that Adorno's "melancholy science"—in the mode of procedure which it assumes as the critique of the existing culture by means of an ethics of the individual—differs from Nietzsche's gay science. Whereas Nietzsche opposes to this culture an ideal of the accomplishment of life, Adorno traces the damage and suffering that it causes. What is common to both, however, is that, in criticizing the existing culture, they take their object "personally." This has the double sense mentioned above: both Adorno and Nietzsche are concerned to demonstrate what the existing culture means for persons, for individuals in their attempt to lead a right life. This only discloses itself before the eyes of a critic, however, when he attempts to lead his own right life. For Nietzsche and Adorno, critical knowledge of the existing culture is only possible as a life-experiment; one acquires an insight into the existing culture only if one "gropingly forms" one's "own life in the frail image of a true existence."[25] The normative perspective of Nietzsche's and Adorno's critique is characterized by the fact that it measures the existing culture according to the criterion of what it means for the individual accomplishment of a ("right") life.

Moral Autonomy and Individual Freedom:
Nietzsche and Adorno

Because it damages the right life of individuals, egalitarian morality is, for Adorno, one of the cultural practices which is deserving of critique by means of an ethics of the individual. This is the meaning of the
"critique of morality" which *Negative Dialectics* develops, by means of a
confrontation with Kant, in the first of its models.[26] In this text, Adorno
wants to show the extent to which "abstract morality,"[27] as he himself puts
it using a Hegelian expression, contains a "repressive aspect"[28]—that is,
the extent to which it possesses "coercive features."[29] In this way, Adorno
continues Nietzsche's diagnosis of the "self-ravishment" which the moral
order implies for individuals; for Nietzsche, the core of this order is constituted by the "delight in imposing a form upon oneself as a hard, recalci-
trant, suffering material and in burning a will, a critique, a contradiction,
a contempt, a No into it, this uncanny, dreadfully joyous labor of a soul
voluntarily at odds with itself that makes itself suffer out of joy in making
suffer."[30] This is how Nietzsche, and after him Adorno, situates the moral
subject at the center of the critique of morality—by asking how he who
subjects himself to the norms of equality behaves, or *must* behave, with
regard to himself. Both Nietzsche and Adorno accept Kant's elucidation
of morality in terms of autonomy. Neither Nietzsche nor Adorno consider moral laws "repressive" because they are imposed upon individuals
from outside. These laws are no *less* repressive, however, because individuals impose them upon themselves. It is precisely the free self-imposition of
moral laws which Nietzsche characterizes as the "self-ravishment" of morality—and which Adorno characterizes as its "repressive aspect." For both
Nietzsche and Adorno, moral freedom is, as autonomy, a compulsion.

Neither Nietzsche nor Adorno understand this thesis in such a way
that *all* freedom is compulsive *in an equal measure*. It is true that Nietzsche's
genealogy—and Adorno follows him in this—shows that there is no freedom without a breaking of natural compulsion (and that this breaking is
itself a compulsion).[31] Such a compulsion—one which is opposed to the
natural compulsion—opens up, for both Nietzsche and Adorno, the possibility of freedom. Furthermore, it is—or, more precisely, was—the *moral*
compulsion opposed to our own nature which proved, in the course of human history, to be a compulsion opening up the possibility of freedom:

The tremendous labor of that which I have called "morality of mores" (*Dawn*, sections 9, 14, 16)—the labor performed by man upon himself during the greater part of the existence of the human race, his entire *prehistoric* labor, finds in this its meaning, its great justification, notwithstanding the severity, tyranny, stupidity, and idiocy involved in it: with the aid of the morality of mores and the social straitjacket, man was actually *made* calculable.

If we place ourselves at the end of this tremendous process, where the tree at last brings forth fruit, where society and the morality of custom at last reveal *what* they have simply been the means to: then we discover that the ripest fruit is the *sovereign individual*, like only to himself, liberated again from morality of custom, autonomous and supramoral (for "autonomous" and "moral" are mutually exclusive), in short, the man who has his own independent, protracted will and the *right to make promises.*[32]

This moral compulsion was necessary, and even justified, because it led to the "consciousness of power and freedom" of a sovereign individual capable of governing himself. If this supramoral autonomy is achieved, however, by means of the compulsion which is exercised by moral autonomy, then this compulsion loses its justification; the moral compulsion then becomes unnecessary and hence unjustified. In both Nietzsche's and Adorno's critique of morality, compulsion and freedom are not merely opposed to one another, nor are they merely identified. No freedom can arise and exist without compulsion, but not all freedom is equally compulsive. Both Nietzsche and Adorno discriminate between two different forms of freedom, *both* of which are based upon compulsion—but *both* of which can nevertheless be distinguished, when compared with one another, as freedom and compulsion. The central thesis of Nietzsche's and Adorno's critique of morality—that moral freedom is compulsion—can thus be taken to mean that this freedom is compulsive with respect to individual freedom in the determination and enactment of an accomplished life. Morality is, for both Nietzsche and Adorno, a cultural practice which obstructs the accomplished or right life—it teaches individuals to understand freedom as moral autonomy, that is, to understand it in such a way that they are no longer able to practice that "sovereign" freedom which is necessary for an accomplished or right life.

When Nietzsche and Adorno attempt a more detailed and precise description of these obstructing consequences of morality—a description which concerns, in the first instance, *what* they obstruct—their analyses certainly differ. Whereas, for Nietzsche, morality results in the nihilistic "diminution and leveling of European man,"[33] which puts an end to the "creative power and masterfulness" of "the higher man,"[34] these representations are, for Adorno, "the wishful image of an uninhibited, vital, creative man."[35] Adorno describes the "rule over one's inner nature" that accompanies these wishful images not as an objection to morality, but, on the contrary, as precisely its own consequence.[36] Nietzsche tries to exorcise that which obstructs morality by means of images of heroic greatness and power; Adorno, by contrast, by means of images of reconciled togetherness.[37] Once again, however, Nietzsche and Adorno articulate here a common motive. For, in one essential respect, they similarly determine that feature of individual freedom which is weakened or oppressed by moral autonomy: its expressive moment.

Moral freedom, that is, the idea of a free relationship to oneself— which forms the basis of both the idea and practice of morality—is the idea of a subject who stands behind or above his own act, who is responsible for his act because he could have acted in this or that way. The idea of a free self-subjection to the moral law presupposes that we "believe in a neutral independent 'subject.'"[38] For without this belief—and this is Nietzsche's argument—the demand which the moral law puts to "strength," that is, the demand that "it should not express itself as strength, that it should not be a desire to overcome, a desire to throw down, a desire to become master, a thirst for enemies and resistances and triumphs," cannot be justified.[39] In order to be able to criticize "strength" and subject it to the requirement of self-limitation, "popular morality" speaks of moral responsibility and freedom, "as if there were a neutral substratum behind the strong man, which was free to express strength or not to do so."[40] This is the fiction, however—and this is how Adorno takes up Nietzsche's objection—of an "absolute volitional autonomy,"[41] one which contradicts the fundamental conditions of free action in reality: "True practice, the totality of acts that would satisfy the idea of freedom, does indeed require full theoretical consciousness. . . . But practice also needs something else, something physical which consciousness does not exhaust, something conveyed to reason and qualitatively different from it."[42] This something else, "intramental and somatic in one,"[43] is that which Nietzsche calls "force," and Adorno "impulse"; action (or practice) is a self-expression of forces or an effect of impulses. This is why *free* action cannot be considered in the way in which it appears in the idea of moral autonomy, that is, as an action which has its ground in the decisions of an instance—a substratum or subject—which is situated *behind* its own forces or impulses. Free action cannot be constituted in this way because action possesses no such instance. If all action is a self-expression of forces or an effect of impulses, then free action must also be irreducibly expressive—it does not dispose over forces, but instead allows them to express themselves.[44] True freedom—without which no accomplishment in life is possible for individuals—requires a retraction of the "moral" splitting into the act and the actor into the "neutral substratum" and its freely choosable modes of action; it requires the self-effacement of the subject as an instance of autonomous control. This explains why the cultural model of moral autonomy inevitably fails, and even threatens, the practice of individual freedom. The predominance of morality forms or practices a self-relationship which weakens and atrophies that capacity of freedom which allows our forces and impulses to express themselves. It does this to such an extent that it can impair the accomplishment of individual life.

Two Cases: A Critique of Deconstruction

The critique of egalitarian morality—as regards the "subjection" which it imposes upon individuals in the conditions of its predominance—is a central motive of the deconstructive version of the questioning of morality. Derrida points out, for instance, that the application of egalitarian norms is accompanied by an always exclusive delimitation of the circle of their addressees—precisely because it forces us to conceive these addressees as "subjects" in the sense criticized by Nietzsche and Adorno. If we criticize an action as an infringement of such norms, then we presuppose that "the other, the victim of the language's injustice, is capable of a language in general, is man as a speaking animal."[45] This notion of "man" is not, however, invariant: "there was a time, not long ago and not yet over, in which 'we, men' meant 'we adult white male Europeans, carnivorous and capable of sacrifice.'"[46] This does not only mean that our current notion of a human being is distinguished from other possible understandings. It is distinguished, above all, from other possible *self*-understandings of the addressees of egalitarian norms. From the perspective of the norms of equality, these addressees are "subjects" (or "human beings"); but they are not necessarily "subjects" for themselves.

Although Derrida occasionally seems to come close to the critique of egalitarian morality in the name of the accomplishment of the lives of individuals—a critique whose basic contours are agreed upon in Nietzsche's genealogy and Adorno's critical theory—he understands this questioning in a fundamentally different way. Deconstruction is not a normative, that is, individual-ethical, critique of egalitarian morality; it applies to egalitarian morality *and* its individual-ethical critique. Methodologically, deconstruction always means deconstruction of critique; deconstruction is anticritical. As against this, the following reflections will attempt to defend—by means of a critique of deconstruction—that form of questioning of morality which has been demonstrated in the work of Nietzsche and Adorno.

Firstly, however, we need to briefly recapitulate Derrida's fundamental theses concerning equality, which precede this controversy between deconstruction and critique (which I will take up in the following section). The issue which is at stake in Derrida's text can be preliminarily elucidated by means of the example of his central objection to "juridical ideology."[47] This objection claims that justice (as law) and violence are not opposed to one another, but instead systematically connected; it claims that justice as law stands in a "more internal, more complex relation with what one calls force, power or violence" than in the widely shared assumption that law *serves* a certain social power. Violence—and this is Derrida's thesis—is instead situated at the *origin* of justice as law, in its "very moment of foundation or institution." For from the perspective of its institution, it becomes clear that law is based upon impositions which cannot be made good upon by means of any "justificatory discourse" or "metalanguage." "Violent" means here, first of all, "unjustifiable."

According to Derrida, however, this possesses a double, and even opposing, meaning. Firstly, the law would be justifiable or derivable if it followed from pregiven and universal rules. It is underivable, however, because in each of its decisions it is governed by the "demand" that we address ourselves "to the other in the language of the other."[48] Justice thus demands the interruption of the derivation from pregiven rules; it can only arise from this interruption. This is the first sense of Derrida's claim that violence is situated at the origin of law: law arises from a demand of justice which concerns particular others, and this demand "violently" interrupts the (existing) law. Derrida also calls the law violent, however, in a second, directly opposite sense, that is, because it cannot satisfy the demand of justice with respect to the particular other—a demand which violently interrupts legal justification and derivation: "To address oneself to the other in the language of the other is, it seems, the condition of all possible justice, but apparently, in all rigor, it is . . . impossible."[49] To the extent that it comprehends justice in the form of universal norms of equality, the law contravenes the demand of justice with respect to the particular other. It is in this context that "violence" possesses its primary, everyday meaning as an injury which is done to the other. According to Derrida, however, this also has to be understood as an interruption of the context of justification. The only difference is that we are not concerned here with the justification of a decision on the basis of a universal norm, but, rather, with the justification of a decision in reference to its addressee—the particular other. A decision would be just if it grounded itself solely in the other to whom it applies; with respect to this other, the universal norms of law—which refer to everybody—prove to be violent.

In Derrida's "Force of Law," this ambiguity of the concept of violence is not the result of an unclear explanation; it constitutes, rather, the central thesis: that justice as law is not situated beyond violence, but consists of two different acts of violence, the violence of the interruption of universal norms in the name of the individually particular, *and* the violence of the molding of the individually particular by means of the universal norms of equality. The thesis that law consists in these two operations implies, for Derrida, in more precise terms, that they are opposed at the same time as they turn into one another. Derrida does not call both operations "violence" in order to claim that they are the same; he wants to claim, rather, that they are inseparable from one another. Neither of these "acts of violence" can exist without the other: there is no (violently molding) institution of the universal norms of justice in the absence of their interruption by the act of doing justice to the particular other. And there is no (violently interrupting) act of doing justice to the particular other in the absence of its molding by the universal norms of justice. As soon as one form of violence attempts to realize and establish itself, it turns into the other.

In "Force of Law," Derrida describes this movement of transformation under the heading of an "aporetic" connection between the universal forms of legal equality and an act of doing justice to individuals which is oriented toward the particular other.[50] This central deconstructive thesis of an aporetic constitution of justice can be understood, however, in two different ways. According to the first version, this thesis is a precise formulation of the internal heterogeneity of both morality and law; I will return to this version in the following section. According to the second version, which I will discuss here, the (specific) deconstructive thesis of the aporetic constitution of justice is intended to justify the (general) deconstructive thesis of the impossibility of normative critique. It is in this way that Alexander García Düttmann has interpreted deconstruction. From his point of view, "critique" (only apparently paradoxically) implies "dogmatics"— it implies "the dogmatics which is in no way a distortion of critique, but which is instead situated in the judgment, in the decision, at which critique as discriminating critique aims."[51] Before we draw any further conclusions, we can say that—according to this diagnosis—every operation of critique understands the discriminations which it introduces asymmetrically; it distinguishes between something positive, which it holds on to and defends, and something negative, which it rejects or dissolves. The very claim that such discriminations and decisions, between something positive and something negative, *can* be effectively enacted is already denominated by deconstruction as the "dogmatism" of critique. As against critique, deconstruction claims that there is a logical symmetry between the two sides: both sides discriminated by critique, the positive and the negative, are subject to the same movement of transformation into their opposite.

On the basis of the arguments outlined above, it is obvious that both Nietzsche and Adorno undertake a critique of equality in precisely that sense which deconstruction has put into question. For both Adorno and Nietzsche want to show that the orientation toward the idea of equality has consequences which destroy or undermine a central dimension of the accomplishment of individual life. This presupposes, however, that the idea of the accomplishment of individual life puts at our disposal a normative criterion which can be used against the idea of equality. Critique is *constituted* precisely when the normative criterion of an accomplished individual life is brought to bear against the idea of equality. This critique is undertaken, in different ways, by both Nietzsche and Adorno: Nietzsche undertakes it positively by drawing up images of an accomplished life;

Adorno undertakes it negatively by providing reports of a damaged life. In both cases, critique presupposes that there is an approach to the individual which does not distort him—while this is what can happen when we orient ourselves toward equality. To put it more simply, critique presupposes that there is an approach to the individual—at the very least, the approach of the critic—which can be understood as a *fulfillment* of the very same normative criterion which renders equality deserving of critique. In the absence of this premise, a critique of equality is impossible. It is precisely this premise, however, which deconstruction construes as "dogmatism." This is the fundamental argument of deconstruction against a normative critique of equality: there is no approach to the other which can claim to successfully do justice to his individually good life—and which can thus be brought to bear against the distortions introduced by the orientation toward equality.[52]

This fundamental deconstructive argument against critique is based, however, upon a confusion: it confuses a hermeneutical problem with a normative one; it confuses a problem of the philosophy of language with a problem of ethics. Both Derrida and García Düttmann arrive at their diagnosis of an indissoluble aporetics of justice—a diagnosis which forms the basis of their objection to the so-called dogmatism of critique—by means of an immediate derivation from an insight of the philosophy of language. This short-circuit can be found for the first time in Derrida's early confrontation with Lévinas. Writing about the linguistic determination of the other, Derrida claims here that it "can only indefinitely tend toward justice by acknowledging and practicing the violence within it. Violence against violence. *Economy* of violence."[53] This formula—violence against violence—can obviously be subsumed under Derrida's later thesis of the aporia of justice. In Derrida's early text, this formula acquires its meaning by means of a rejection of Lévinas's idea of "discourse." Lévinas understands "discourse" as the mode of expression which takes place in the face of a human being. Lévinas says of this expression that it is "not disclosure but revelation: a coinciding of the expressed with him who expresses, which is the privileged manifestation of the Other, the manifestation of a face over and beyond form."[54] The fact that no "disclosure" occurs by means of this discourse means, for Lévinas (as against Heidegger), that it is a discourse in which no determination (of something as something) takes place. According to Derrida, however, this critical decision and distinction—between a determining speech and a pure discourse—is impossible. If we agree with Lévinas and call determining speech violent, then we ought to say that *all* language is equally violent, in which case violence would become "transcendental"—"the origin of meaning and of discourse in the reign of finitude."[55]

Although Derrida's objection to Lévinas's idea of a pure discourse—a discourse which is absolutely free of determination (and distortion)—might appear convincing, it does not go far enough. For Derrida still agrees with Lévinas in maintaining that justice would only be truly attained by a behavior toward the other in his "discourse," that is, by a behavior toward the other which does not determine (and which cannot, as a consequence, distort). This is the concept of justice which Derrida's "Force of Law" takes as its starting point, if only in order to show that it cannot be satisfied by any particular behavior toward the other.[56] This demonstration is also convincing, at least as far as it goes: it is a demonstration of the internal absurdity of that concept of justice which Derrida shares with Lévinas. The absurdity of this concept manifests itself, once its validity is presupposed, in the fact that two cases which crucially need to be distinguished have to appear as identical. This becomes evident in the passage whose opening claim I have already quoted above:

> To address oneself to the other in the language of the other is, it seems, the condition of all possible justice, but apparently, in all rigor, it is not only impossible (since I cannot speak the language of the other except to the extent that I appropriate it and assimilate it according to the law of an implicit third) but even excluded by justice as right (*droit*), inasmuch as justice as right seems to imply an element of universality, the appeal to a third party who suspends the unilaterality or singularity of the idioms.[57]

On a closer reading, the quoted text shows that Derrida only vaguely connects—by means of the expression "even"—two completely different cases. The first case is constituted by the fact of a perspectival refraction—one which implies that I can only see the other and his perspective from my own perspective. This fact intersubjectively brings to light the as-structure of all determination. The fact that the language of law (and morality) brings particular cases, and their modes of expression and description, under general norms of equality is, however, an entirely different phenomenon, underivable from the first case. It is true that we *can* describe both cases by saying that there is something at work in them which obstructs the possibility of our doing justice to the particular other. In the two cases, however, both the moment which obstructs our doing justice to the other and the meaning of this doing justice are completely different. In the first case, to do justice to the other means to approach him in a manner which is free from *all* perspectival and hermeneutical determination; in the second case, it means to approach him in a manner which orients itself toward his *particular* perspective and mode of determination.

If the two cases can be distinguished in this way, then the operation of critique also retains—as against the deconstructive intention—its justification. For it is precisely the difference between these two cases which makes possible Nietzsche's and Adorno's practice of an individual-ethical critique of equality. The deconstructive claim that we are incapable of distinguishing between injustice and justice—as a result of our being unable to decide between them—can only be upheld with regard to the first of the two interrelated cases described by Derrida. This claim is only valid if we comprehend our doing justice to the other in the Lévinasian sense, that is, if we comprehend it as an understanding of the other which does not determine him; and this cannot, as Derrida himself correctly contends, be "carried out with all necessary rigor." The individual-ethical critique of equality which is proposed by both Nietzsche and Adorno orients itself, however, toward the second case. This critique is directed against the impairment of justice by means of the universal norms of equality; and it understands justice not in the sense of immediacy, as in Lévinas, but instead as something which aims to draw attention to, and not do away with, "the one-sidedness or particularity of one's own speech." This aim *is*, however, fulfillable—and the simple fact of the orientation toward this fulfillability does not compel critique to make ideological compromises. The criterion of this second case therefore allows us to critically distinguish and decide between two things: on the one hand, a practice of the successful doing justice to individuals, and, on the other, the obstructions and limitations which can—in the course of this practice—come to accompany the orientation toward the universal norms of equality.

We can now see that, in order to be able to reproach critique for its dogmatism and dispute its justification, deconstruction has to blur the categorical difference between two cases or modes of obstruction of the particular other, and thus, at the same time, two different meanings of the idea of individual justice with respect to this other. Conversely, the justification of the normative critique of equality practiced by Nietzsche and Adorno is grounded in the difference between these two cases, which carries a two-fold implication. Firstly, it implies that both critique and genealogy demonstrate the *specific distortion* which is connected with the subjection to the norms of equality. Deconstruction, by contrast, is only focused upon the distortions which are connected to all determination as such.[58] Secondly, it follows from the difference between these two cases that both critique and genealogy—as a consequence of their normative concept of individuality—demonstrate the *specific aspect* of the impairment which is brought about by the norms of equality. As against this, deconstruction views every determination as an obstruction and distortion of the "being-for-it-self" which is inherent to all objects, and not only to individuals. (García Düttmann speaks of the "unjustifiable being-there" of things which escapes all determination.)[59] When taken together, both aspects show the price which deconstruction has to pay for its avoidance of critique. Deconstruction wants to undermine the binary logic of critical decision; but it is only able to do this by simultaneously misrecognizing those distinctions which are of fundamental importance for the understanding of justice.

B. The Consequences for Equality: Models of the Explanation of Morality

Morality as "Expression": A Critique of Genealogy

Nietzsche derived the requirement of an overcoming of the moral idea of equality from the critical demonstration of the consequences which egalitarian morality can have for individual freedom:

Today . . . when only the herd animal receives and dispenses honors in Europe, when "equality of rights" could all too easily be changed into equality in violating rights—I mean, into a common war on all that is rare, strange, privileged, the higher man, the higher soul, the higher duty, the higher responsibility, and the abundance of creative power and masterfulness—today the concept of greatness entails being noble, wanting to be by oneself, being able to be different, standing alone and having to live independently.[60]

A *life* of such greatness above all presupposes, however, the abandonment of those ideas of equality by means of which the "*autonomous* herd" denies to the individual "every special claim, every special right and privilege."[61] It is true that an accomplished or "great" individual life needs to pass through egalitarian morality, and is only achievable as its "self-overcoming."[62] Once it is achieved, however, this life turns against egalitarian morality; individual life can only succeed as amoral.

According to a widespread opinion, this anti-egalitarian attitude is a necessary consequence of every critique of equality which is developed upon the basis of an ethics of the individual. The example of Adorno shows that this opinion is mistaken, however. For it is quite apparent that Adorno did not draw from his individual-ethical critique of egalitarian morality—a critique which agrees with Nietzsche in both perspective and content—the same consequences as Nietzsche himself. If, in Nietzsche, this critique justifies a rejection of morality from outside, from "beyond good and evil,"[63] then, in Adorno, it justifies the project of an internal or *self*-overcoming of morality. The outline of this project can be taken from a formulation which Adorno gives in a passage of *Negative Dialectics* that refers to the idea of just or equal exchange; in a derivative sense, this formulation is also true of the moral idea of equality.[64] On the one hand—and here once again Adorno takes up his own critique of equality—this idea forms part of the predominance of the "principle of identification." If for this reason, however, "we denied the principle abstractly—if we proclaimed, to the greater glory of the irreducibly qualitative, that parity should no longer be the ideal rule—we would be creating excuses for recidivism into ancient injustice."[65] This is the difference between an "abstract" and a "critical" negation of equality: "When we criticize the exchange principle [or the moral law] as the identifying principle of thought, we want to realize the ideal of free and just exchange [or 'the egalitarian idea,' which lives on as 'substance' in the universal moral law].[66] To date, this ideal is only a pretext. Its realization alone would transcend exchange [or egalitarian morality]."[67] The consequence of Adorno's critique of morality is that the transcendence of the moral law of equality is its own true realization. The "skepticism of the rancor involved in the bourgeois egalitarian ideal that tolerates no qualitative difference,"[68] that is, the skepticism which Adorno shares with Nietzsche, does not lead, in Adorno, as it does in Nietzsche, to an abstract rejection of the moral idea of equality in favor of an order of rank and privilege. It leads instead to the demand that egalitarian morality be realized by means of its own transcendence.

What is the precise meaning, however, of this formulation of the realization of morality by means of its own transcendence? This sounds "paradoxical enough," as Adorno himself concedes in a similar context.[69] Before we can elucidate an answer to this question, we need to understand why it is that Nietzsche and Adorno draw such opposing consequences from their parallel critiques of egalitarian morality. For this is not the result of an arbitrary decision; it follows from their different understandings of the targets of their critiques. We have seen that Nietzsche and Adorno agree upon (the method and content of) a critical questioning of the *consequences* which morality has for the lives of individuals. Moreover, it has become apparent that Nietzsche and Adorno contradict one another in the attitude toward morality which they derive from their critiques. What is decisive for both critiques, however, is their *concept* of morality; it is here that the lines of their agreement and opposition cross. Nietzsche's and Adorno's concepts of morality overlap in their determination of the *form* of morality; it is for this reason that they also offer similar descriptions of the consequences of morality. Nietzsche's and Adorno's concepts of morality are opposed to one other, however, in their determination of the *ground* of morality; and it is for this reason (and not because of arbitrary preferences or political prejudices) that they come to adopt opposing attitudes toward morality.

The form of morality which Adorno and Nietzsche determine in completely parallel ways is that of a universal, that is, absolutely valid, and internal, that is, self-imposed, law—one which prescribes the equal consideration of everybody. This determination of the form of morality, however, cannot render comprehensible its existence. In order to do this, it is necessary to investigate the origin and descent of this form. Both Nietzsche and Adorno view the moral law of equal consideration as a systematically secondary phenomenon that stems from a motive which is *different* to the moral "intention" which it manifests: "we believe that the intention is merely a sign and symptom that still requires interpretation"[70] which has to uncover what the moral ideal "means; what it indicates; what lies hidden behind it, beneath it, in it; of what it is the provisional, indistinct expression, overlaid with question marks and misunderstandings."[71] In explicit opposition to the rationalistic programs of justification which attempt "to derive the duty of mutual respect from a law of reason,"[72] and which therefore withdraw from this obligation every possible ground,[73] both Nietzsche and Adorno trace the moral law of equality back to something different, to something which only expresses itself in this law in a distorted form. The moral law stems from something different and, at the same time, attempts to conceal it.

Nevertheless, Nietzsche and Adorno determine that from which the law of equal consideration stems in strictly opposing ways; this is what constitutes the decisive opposition between their attitudes to morality. We can preliminarily understand these contradictory basic determinations in terms of their content. Whereas Nietzsche views morality as an expression of resentment, Adorno regards it as an expression of the impulse of solidarity. At the same time, however, this implies a structural opposition which Adorno characterizes much less clearly—and which he subsequently comprehends much less distinctly in its consequences. This structural opposition is that between an internally homogeneous and an internally heterogeneous concept of morality. If we refer back to the reflections which deconstruction proposed in its confrontation with Lévinas, we can elucidate why it is that—and how—the concept of egalitarian morality needs to be understood as internally heterogeneous. Whereas critique and genealogy stand on the same side, and oppose deconstruction, in their determination of the consequences which equality can have for individuals, critique and deconstruction, in opposition to genealogy, aim at the same program of the analysis of the ground of equality. It is because the understanding of the ground of equality is decisively important with regard to the attitude which we assume toward it that critique and deconstruction—in opposition to Nietzsche—also agree in their refusal to understand the questioning of equality as its dissolution or replacement.

Resentment: Nietzsche

In Nietzsche's view, the morality of equality is grounded in resentment: "The slave revolt in morality"—in which the morality of equality rises to predominance—"begins when *ressentiment* itself becomes creative and gives birth to values."[74] This is the central thesis of Nietzsche's explanation of morality, in which we can distinguish two steps. The first step traces the proclaimed moral intention of love, or at least respect, toward the other back to the motives of revenge and hatred. For there would "be more justification for placing above the gateway to the Christian Paradise and its 'eternal bliss' the inscription 'I too was created by eternal *hate*'— provided a truth may be placed above the gateway to a lie!"[75] Nietzsche justifies this apparently paradoxical thesis by means of a structural analysis of the "mode of valuation" which founds the morality of equality. The "slave revolt" which has called this morality into existence implies, for Nietzsche, an "inversion of the value-positing eye," which consists, from now on, in the "need to direct one's view outward instead of back to oneself": "While every noble morality develops from a triumphant affirmation of itself, slave morality from the outset says No to what is 'outside,' what is 'different,' what is 'not itself'; and *this* No is its creative deed."[76] According to Nietzsche, the requirement that we consider everybody equally is grounded in the hate-filled denial of those who, in the course of their lives and with complete "innocence" (albeit "the innocent conscience of the beast of prey"),[77] endanger, constrain, or obstruct the lives of others. These men, Nietzsche claims, are the "strong"—they are "rounded men replete with energy and therefore *necessarily* active."[78] They are feared, hated, and finally proclaimed to be "evil": the "man of ressentiment . . . has conceived 'the evil enemy,' 'the Evil One,' and this in fact is his basic concept, from which he then evolves, as an afterthought and pendant, a 'good one'—himself!"[79] The morality of equality is seen to emerge out of resentment because it is constituted, in its ground and center, as a turning against the dangerous other who is conceived as evil.

This is only the first step, however, in Nietzsche's elucidation of the morality of equality on the basis of resentment; it is only in its second step that this elucidation is completed. The morality of equality is negatively related to the individual freedom of the other not only because it fears, hates, and explains it as evil, as "mean and dangerous." This negative relation results, rather, from the fact that the hatred against the individual freedom of the other is grounded in (or implies) a self-understanding which mutilates our own individual freedom. In resentment—the ground of morality—fear and hatred of the other and fear and hatred of ourselves belong together; the denial of the other as evil corresponds to the resentful man's "denial of himself, of his nature, naturalness, and actuality."[80] The resentful man finds himself forced "to make necessary and orderly feelings into a source of inner distress."[81] The moral man does not or, more precisely, *cannot* desire the accomplishment of his own life; he therefore fights the life of the other.

This explains why Nietzsche's individual-ethical questioning of morality has to conclude with morality's dissolution. In this questioning, Nietzsche investigates the obstructing consequences which the morality of equality has with respect to the good life of individuals—consequences which result from the fact that this morality initiates these individuals into a false understanding of freedom, that is, into an understanding of freedom which renders the accomplishment of life impossible. In his conceptual determination of morality, which I have briefly recapitulated, Nietzsche wants to show, moreover, that these consequences of morality are, at the same time, its true ground. The morality of equality does not only *lead* to a weakening of the individual freedom that is necessary for an accomplished life; it is precisely *grounded* in the "morbid" desire to weaken individual freedom, to condemn and poison the accomplished life as guilty. According to Nietzsche, the morality of equality is, as a whole, an absent-minded expression of, and a self-concealing attempt at, the enhancement of a weakened and failed life. In Nietzsche's picture of morality, there is a seamless correspondence between ground and consequences. This is what is meant by the designation of this morality as "homogeneous." Contrary to first impressions, egalitarian morality, for Nietzsche, consists only of the morbid or degenerate will, which—precisely because it is, on the one hand, too weak to desire the accomplishment or even greatness of individual life and, on the other hand, unable to desire nothing—desires the weakness, smallness, restriction, and damage of this life; at first with regard to itself and then also with regard to the other.[82] The morality of equality is simply the most efficient means for the implementation of this desire.

The Impulse of Solidarity: Adorno

This homogenizing picture of morality is what Adorno most decisively opposes. At the same time, however, he takes up a reflection which Nietzsche repeatedly outlines but never, for a good reason, thinks through to all its consequences—consequences that are devastating for Nietzsche's concept of morality. We are concerned here with Nietzsche's determination of the true love of our neighbor or enemy. As we have seen, the morality of equality is comprehended in Nietzsche in such a way that, contrary to appearances, it needs to be understood as a morality of hatred. Nietzsche completes this argument by claiming that the virtue of love for our neighbor or enemy—once again contrary to appearances—cannot be thought on the basis of this morality of equality. It is only for the noble ones, that is, only by means of the rejection of the norm of equality, that "genuine 'love of one's enemies' is possible—supposing it to be possible at all on earth. How much reverence has a noble man for his enemies!—and such reverence is a bridge to love."[83] In arguing that the love of our enemy is not possible in the morality of equality, Nietzsche is claiming that this morality hates the enemy as evil—as a result of the fact that the man of this morality hates himself (and of the fact that the external evil enemy is only an incarnation of this self-hatred). The noble man, by contrast, is able to love his enemy; he does not have to hate his enemy because he does not hate himself. In this reflection upon the love of our enemy or neighbor, Nietzsche is claiming that a accomplished self-relation—which is only found in a strong or noble life—is the condition of the ability to enter into a positive relationship to the strong or noble life of others, that is, into a relationship in which we are not forced to hate these others as evil enemies. This connection between a (accomplished) self-relationship and a (positive) relationship to the other is most clearly expressed in a passage from *Dawn*:

> *Do not let our demon pass into our neighbors!*—We accept for the moment that good will and good action make up the good man; we can only add: "presupposing that he is first disposed *towards himself* with good will and good action!" For *without this*—if he flees from himself, hates himself, harms himself—he is certainly not a good man. He then rescues himself from himself only *in others*: if these others wish to see that they do not fare badly in this, and as long as he also apparently desires this for them!—But precisely this: to flee from and hate the ego and to live in others, for others—has just as thoughtlessly been called up to now reliably *"unegoistic" and consequently "good."*[84]

In his reflections upon benevolence and love, Nietzsche refers to modes of behavior which were not taken into account in his opposition between the modes of evaluation of slave and master moralities—and which indeed represent, in the light of this opposition, a genealogical paradox. These are modes of behavior which consist in the "need to direct one's view outward instead of back to oneself"; rather than being reactive and hateful, however, this "view outward" is a view of affirmation—it is an affirmation of the other which is made possible by an "affirmation of itself."[85]

This understanding of the love of our neighbor—which arises from a accomplished self-relation—shows the way in which Adorno attempts to describe those moral attitudes which ought not to succumb to the same verdict as the moral law of equality, that is, should not be judged as weakening and damaging an accomplished self-relation. At the center of the chapter on Kant in *Negative Dialectics*, Adorno describes "the sense of solidarity with what Brecht called 'tormentable bodies.'"[86] Moral action is action which arises from the feeling of solidarity. With this claim, Adorno brings to light—in the determination of the ground of equality—the same insight which he had previously brought to bear against it: no action can be explained solely on the basis of a free and reasonable decision; it requires, rather, an additional somatic "impulse" (see above, pp. 000 ff.). In the specific field of morality, this general action-theoretical argument implies that no action which we qualify as "moral" can be understood according to the rationalistic picture of the application of a moral law. Moral action does not follow from an "abstract" principle, but instead from a "somatic impulse" or "spontaneous . . . stirring."[87] This is also what is implied by the final sentence of Adorno's chapter on Kant: "the individual is left with no more than the morality for which Kantian ethics—which accords affection, not respect, to animals—can muster only disdain: to try to live so that one may believe himself to have been a good animal."[88] Moral action is the action of a "good animal." It is the action of a subject which does not—in order to obey the law—detach itself, and imagine itself as being free, from its own "forces" or "impulses"; that is, the action of a subject whose freedom consists precisely in its capacity to let its own "forces" or "impulses" express themselves. It is only in this way, in agreement or even "reconciliation" with his own forces and impulses, that man can be good.[89] "Men are human only where they do not act, let alone posit themselves, as persons."[90]

In its return to the moral impulse, moral action transforms itself not only in its structure—it cannot be explained in terms of a law which it applies—but also in its content. For if the normative content of the moral law is equality, then the normative content of the moral affect or impulse is the "solidarity with 'tormentable' bodies." In Adorno, then, the concept of solidarity takes the place of that which was formulated by Nietzsche as the idea of the noble and strong love of the enemy. Both notions characterize an affirmative relation to the other which is not mediated by the orientation toward a norm of equality—a norm which *can* at least imply, according to the critical insight of both Nietzsche and Adorno, a "denial" of the freedom of the individual. At the same time, however, Nietzsche's noble love of the enemy and Adorno's impulse of solidarity are distinguished by means of a feature which also throws a different light upon their relation to the norm of equality. For the "affirmation" of the other that Nietzsche takes into consideration is itself based, when he describes it as the love of the *enemy*, upon an approbatory judgment: Nietzsche's "affirmation" only applies to those others who possess an equal rank.[91] In Nietzsche, the practical attitude of the "affirmation" of the other depends upon this judgment of him which affirms that he possesses an equal strength or nobility. Adorno's feeling of solidarity, by contrast, does not imply a judgment (which does not mean that it does not determine; see above, pp. ooo ff.). What is decisive here is that which Adorno calls the "somatic moment" of the feeling of solidarity: "The somatic moment tells our knowledge that suffering ought not to be, that things should be different. 'Woe speaks: 'Go.'"[92] By means of its somatic character the feeling of solidarity is mimetically constituted. It is a mimesis of the other's adverse reaction to his suffering and pain. Solidarity is, in Adorno, an affirmative relationship to the other—but it is a somatic-affective affirmation of the other's somatic-affective refusal of his suffering and pain. Solidarity is *sym*pathy, then, in the literal sense: it is our reenactment of the other's suffering. Because it is mimetic, such a reenactment or imitation is immediate, that is, it is not mediated by any reflective judgment. Our solidaric sympathy has a judgmental content—it contains a judgment that the suffering of the other should not exist—insofar as it simply repeats the judgment of the other (according to which *his* suffering ought not to exist). Mimesis implies that nothing is added in the transition from the other's perspective upon himself to our perspective upon him. Our taking on of the suffering of the other, and hence of his judgment, ensues in an unexamined manner. In Adorno's feeling of solidarity, the other becomes the last reference point of our judgment—and rather than being judged again, this reference point is simply taken up without examination.[93]

This characterizes the opposition between Adorno's feeling of solidarity and Nietzsche's noble love of the enemy; at the same time, however, it also characterizes the opposition between Adorno's feeling of solidarity and the morality of equality. For in the morality of equality, the affirmation of the claims of the other is also mediated by a judgment. This judgment does not concern the other's rank; rather, it concerns the justification of his claims or complaints in accordance with the criterion of the equal consideration of everybody. The morality of equality replaces the mimetic assumption of the other's objection to his suffering with an examination and judgment of the justification of this objection. This is why Adorno characterizes the morality of equality as the result of a "ruthless rationalization" of the fundamental moral feeling of somatic-mimetic solidarity:

It is not in their nauseating parody, sexual repression, that moral questions are succinctly posed; it is in lines such as: No man should be tortured; there should be no concentration camps—while all of this continues in Asia an Africa and is repressed merely because, as ever, the humanity of civilization is inhumane toward the people it shamelessly brands as uncivilized.

But if a moral philosopher were to seize upon these lines and to exult at having caught the critics of morality, at last—caught them quoting the same values that are happily proclaimed by the philosophy of morals—his cogent conclusion would be false. The lines are true as an impulse, as a reaction to the news that torture is going on somewhere. They must not be rationalized; as an abstract principle they would fall promptly into the bad infinities of derivation and validity.

We criticize morality by criticizing the extension of the logic of consistency to the conduct of men; this is where the stringent logic of consistency becomes an organ of unfreedom. The impulse—naked physical fear, and the sense of solidarity with what Brecht called "tormentable bodies"—is immanent in moral conduct and would be denied in attempts at ruthless rationalization. What is most urgent would become contemplative again, mocking its own urgency.[94]

This description certainly brings to the fore Adorno's thesis that the morality of equality distorts and, as a consequence, inverts the sentiment of solidarity. This diagnosis presupposes, however, another thesis, which is not explicitly formulated by Adorno, according to which the morality of equality is grounded in the very same feeling of solidarity which it simultaneously distorts and inverts. When Adorno claims that the morality of equality arises from the sentiment of solidarity by means of its "ruthless rationalization," this claim contains both theses: the morality of equality reformulates and justifies the impulse of solidarity in a universal form—universal laws—and, precisely by doing this, it "denies" this impulse. This is how Adorno outlines an alternative genealogy of morality. For according to this picture, the law of morality does not stem, as in Nietzsche, from the resentful triumvirate of fear, hatred, and self-torture; it follows, instead, from the rationalization of the impulse of solidarity. This genealogy of the moral law—which traces it back to the sentiment of solidarity—does not only imply an alternative to the content of Nietzsche's genealogy, but also an alternative to the homogeneous structure of his concept of morality. For Nietzsche, as we have seen, the ground and the form of morality are identical: the moral law is nothing more than a form of expression of the resentment which grounds it. In Adorno's analysis, by contrast, the relationship between ground and result is twofold: the moral law is both *grounded* in something different and, at the same time, *obscures* it (which also means that the moral law obscures its groundedness in something different). From the perspective of Adorno's analysis, then, morality consists of two moments which are tensionally opposed to one another: the "somatic principle" of solidarity and the "abstract principle" of the equal consideration of everybody. Rather than being simple and homogeneous, morality is doubled into itself and even contradictory.

On the basis of Adorno's insight into the internal heterogeneity of morality, we can now understand the formula by which I earlier contrasted Adorno's and Nietzsche's critiques of equality. Adorno's formula of a "transcending" of the law of equality does not imply its undermining or abolishment, but instead its "realization." The attitude toward the law of equality which this formula outlines follows from the individual-ethical critique of the consequences which this law can have for the accomplished life of individuals. This explains why the law of equality cannot be everything—why it needs to be "transcended." In contrast to Nietzsche's homogeneous concept of morality, however, morality does not only consist here of the law of equality that damages the life and freedom of individuals. This form of morality cannot even be understood if it is not viewed as the expression of an impulse which is situated at the ground of morality—and which, as the impulse of solidarity, is oriented precisely toward individuals and the accomplishment of their lives. For this reason the transcending of the moral law of equality is, at the same time, its realization: the transcending of the moral law of equality is the realization of the impulse of solidarity with suffering individuals. More precisely, the transcending of the moral law of solidarity is *only justified*—and does not, as Adorno claims in his objection to Nietzsche, "create excuses for recidivism into ancient injustice"—*to the extent* that it simultaneously realizes morality, that is, to the extent that it realizes the impulse of solidarity with suffering individuals. This is the double thesis which is implied by Adorno's apparently paradoxical identification of the realization and transcending of morality: to realize morality means to transcend it; for to realize morality means to follow the impulse of solidarity with suffering individuals—even if this impulse leads us into opposition with the moral law of equality itself. Conversely, to transcend morality means to realize it; for to transcend morality means to oppose the moral law of equality in the name of solidarity with suffering individuals.

The Right of Law and the "Economy of Violence": Derrida

With his reciprocal elucidation of the realization and transcending of morality, Adorno has given the individual-ethical questioning of morality a completely different normative status than Nietzsche—even if there is a strong correspondence between the procedures and consequences of their questionings. Whereas Nietzsche's individual-ethical critique of morality vaguely oscillates between private complaint and objective value-theory, Adorno for the first time gives this critique a clear *normative* status.[95] Adorno elucidates the individual-ethical critique of morality, which grounds the requirement of its transcending, as a critique which is carried out from the perspective of morality itself. Because the individual-ethical critique questions the moral law of equality in the name of the accomplished lives of individuals, it is an act of solidarity with those individuals who suffer from the impairment of their lives. This transcending of the moral law of equality by means of the moral ground of solidarity necessarily remains incomprehensible, however, if it is not accompanied by the inverse, and even opposing, movement of a transcending of the impulse of solidarity by means of the law of equality.

This is manifested in Adorno's moral philosophy by the tendency toward reconciliation mentioned above. Adorno seems to believe that the transcending of the moral law of equality can succeed without any loss—precisely because it realizes the moral ground of solidarity. This semblance of a possible reconciliation is based, however, upon an unsatisfactory explication of the internal difference between the ground and form of morality. It is upon the basis of this explication that Adorno rejects Nietzsche's theory of resentment. Adorno explains the step of rationalization—the step from the impulse of solidarity to the moral law—in a way which he would certainly have called "undialectical"; this is the price he has to pay for his idea of moral reconciliation. In this picture of the emergence of the moral law, rationalization can only be "ruthless"; it does not look back upon that which it has left behind. In other, primarily aesthetic, contexts, Adorno has opposed to this ruthlessness another rationalization which remembers that from which it arises in a "second reflection." Adorno's formula for this is a "remembrance of nature." However this reflective transformation of rationalization might be understood, it has to presuppose the recognition of the "necessity" of rationalization itself—despite all of its negative consequences. It is precisely this insight which is lacking in the long passage cited above. Adorno claims here that moral propositions are only "true" as impulses. If these impulses are rationalized into "abstract principles," however, then they enter into "the bad infinities of derivation and validity." In making this claim, Adorno not only forgets what both the *Dialectic of Enlightenment* and *Negative Dialectics* say about the process of rationalization—that liberation is possible, that is, only by means of this process. He also forgets what Max Horkheimer wrote in the moral-philosophical chapter of the *Dialectic of Enlightenment* concerning the limitations of sympathy:

And Zarathustra preaches thus: "I see so much goodness and so much weakness. So much justice and compassion, so much weakness." In fact, there is an aspect of compassion which conflicts with justice, to which Nietzsche of course allies it. It confirms the rule of inhumanity by the exception which it practices. By reserving the cancellation of injustice to fortuitous love of one's neighbor, compassion accepts that the law of universal alienation—which it would mitigate—is unalterable. . . . It is not the softness but the restrictive element in pity which makes it questionable; for compassion is always inadequate.[96]

This is also true of the feeling of solidarity. Because it only applies to particular individuals, the impulse of solidarity is also limited or insufficient. Like sympathy (and unlike Nietzsche's noble love of the enemy), this impulse can take everybody as its object; the mimetic identification of solidarity can apply to everybody who reacts against his suffering and pain. Like sympathy, however, the sentiment of solidarity cannot apply to everybody at the same time. This universal application can only be attained by an action which corresponds to the modern understanding of the criterion of justice, that is, with the criterion of the equal consideration of everybody.

The "dialectical" picture of a differentiated and, indeed, heterogeneous morality—which Adorno tries to draw up in opposition to Nietzsche's homogeneous concept of morality—can be completed only if this insight of Horkheimer's is understood correctly. For Adorno one-sidedly emphasizes the normative deficiency of the moral law with respect to the feeling of solidarity. Horkheimer completes this insight, however, with the opposing thesis of the normative deficiency of the feeling of sympathy or solidarity. If we once again look back at the deconstructive investigation of the "aporias" of justice (see above, "Two Cases: A Critique of Deconstruction"), then this investigation can be understood as an attempt to think this reciprocal deficiency of the moral law and the feeling of solidarity. Deconstruction emphasizes the ambivalent character of rationalization by means of which the moral law is produced: in addition to being ruthless and obscuring, this moral law is normatively justified and, indeed, necessary. "Rationalization" here means the grounding of an action or decision upon the basis of a universal law or rule. According to Derrida, this is a necessary condition of the justice of an action or decision. It is true that "no existing, coded rule can or ought to guarantee absolutely" the decision of a judge—a decision which Derrida takes as an example for the elucidation of this problem—if this decision is to be just; "but we also won't say it [that the judge is just, free, and responsible] if he doesn't refer to any law, to any rule or if, because he doesn't take any rule for granted beyond his own interpretation, he suspends his decision, stops short before the undecidable or if he improvises and leaves aside all rules, all principles."[97] Derrida does not completely clarify the reason for this. According to one read-ing—which corresponds with the one criticized above—the just decision has to refer to a rule because *every* decision enacts a determination, and because every determination operates by means of concepts, that is, rules. In Derrida, however, we can also find a second reading which understands the universality of a rule, upon which the justice of a decision depends, in a specifically normative sense. The universality of a rule does not only imply, then, its applicability to many different cases, but also its acceptability for everybody. This means, in turn, that this rule considers everybody equally. Every just decision has to refer to a universal rule, then, because without a justification on the basis of a such a rule there can be no decision which considers everybody equally.

It is by means of this reflection that Derrida points out—in a simi-lar way to Horkheimer—the structural limitations of an attitude of doing justice which is directed toward others as particular individuals; this also applies to Adorno's impulse of solidarity. Because this attitude is directed toward the particular, it can only apply to *individuals*, and not to every-body. It is true that Adorno's impulse of solidarity does not exclude any-body. On the contrary, because the attitude of mimetic solidarity does not depend on any value judgment, it *can* take everybody as its object. In each particular case, however, this attitude can do this only by attempting to do justice to some particular individual, without being able to *simultaneously* do justice to all others.[98] This is the normative deficiency of a nonjudg-mental attitude of doing justice to particular individuals. The strength of this attitude is its weakness: its mimetic and nonjudgmental adoption of the perspective of others either forces it to limit itself to a particular indi-vidual—without its being able to give a reason for this limitation—or it leads it into a solidaristic adoption of completely different, and even op-posing, perspectives, without its being able to ground a decision between their different claims. This deficiency of the groundless limitation or deci-sion cannot be dispensed with in a normative attitude which attempts to do justice to the particular other. We require instead—and this is Derrida's argument—a "rationalizing" reference to the universal rules of equal con-sideration. In this way, an attitude like that of mimetic solidarity—which Adorno sets *against* the moral law—produces, by means of its limitation, the formulation and application of this law. The impulse of solidarity is the ground of the egalitarian moral law in a double sense: it makes the egalitarian moral law *possible*, for without it there is no morality at all, and it makes it *necessary*, for it cannot, precisely because of its limitation, make up the whole of morality.

In this reflection upon the normative deficiency of attitudes like Adorno's feeling of solidarity, there is nothing which would compel us to retract any element of Adorno's critique of the moral law. For the fact that the normative attitudes of solidarity and sympathy are *also* deficient does not imply that the moral law is *not* deficient. Derrida's attempt to think the indissoluble link between the necessity and violence of the moral law can be construed as the precise point of his elucidation of the internal heterogeneity of the moral or legal spheres—an elucidation which Adorno envisages but does not fully develop. The image which Derrida employs in order to capture this heterogeneity is expressed in the above-mentioned formula of "violence against violence." If, as against the tendency criticized above, we do not assume that this formula has a general hermeneutic meaning—that is, if we do not assume that it is a formula of the aporia of all determination—and if we understand it instead in its specifically normative content, as a formula of the aporia of justice, then we can see that it points to the different but simultaneous reduction which the two heterogeneous moments of morality imply for one another. On one side, the violence of the moral law—the violence which Adorno comprehends as a "ruthless" rationalization of the feeling of solidarity into a universal rule—is opposed by this very same feeling. On the other side, the "violence" of the feeling of solidarity—the violence which Horkheimer describes as its "inhuman" limitation to the particular other—is opposed to the moral law. More important than the reference to this doubling of violence, however, is the way in which Derrida understands here the *concept* of violence. For in both cases, Derrida not only understands violence as a violence against a normative claim; he also understands it as a violence which operates *by means of* or *upon the basis of* a normative claim. Violence means, for Derrida, the violence of the normative.[99] Both moments, the moral law and the feeling of solidarity, are "violent," then, with respect to one another; and not only because they reciprocally interrupt and limit one another. These two moments can constitute a reciprocally interrupting and limiting violence only because they both articulate a normative claim which is equally justified—even if in different ways. Derrida's (early) linguistic formulation of a "violence against violence" can therefore be understood in the context of the internal heterogeneity of morality and law—in such a way that it points to Derrida's only apparently contradictory (later) formula of the "aporia of justice." On this view, violence does not suspend justice, but instead arises from it: as a violence which opposes one normative claim, that justice be done to the particular other, to another normative claim, that justice be done to everybody at the same time.[100]

Derrida concludes from this insight that no ideal of the freedom from violence—an ideal which also implicitly grounds Adorno's idea of reconciliation—can be formulated in the name of normative claims: "*within history*—but is it meaningful elsewhere?—every philosophy of nonviolence can only choose the lesser violence within an *economy of violence*."[101] This is not to be understood in the sense of a quietism; it grounds, instead, the program of a movement between the "aporetical" dimensions of law and morality—dimensions which violently suspend one another. It is only this figure of a double movement—in which both normative claims violently suspend and overcome one another—that allows the structural heterogeneity of morality and law to fully unfold itself. For it is certainly true of this movement—as Derrida emphasizes in "Force of Law"—that it cannot, for conceptual reasons, be oriented toward the utopian or messianic "horizon" of its own end.[102] To put an end to this movement would mean to give preference to the violence of one normative claim over that of the other, thus concealing its violent character (whether in a situation of the equality of everybody or in an attitude of solidarity with respect to individuals alone). If the reinterpretation of violence as law forms the core of all ideology, then the recognition and processual unfolding of the economy of violence is concerned with the rejection of a double ideology: it rejects the ideology of equality just as much as the ideology of affective-impulsive solidarity.

Against this background, Adorno's formula of the realization of morality by means of its transcendence can be read, alongside Derrida, as a figure of morality's internal movement—as a figure of the movement *in* which morality as such consists: equality and solidarity need to transcend themselves because neither of them can be normatively sufficient. And equality and solidarity reciprocally realize one another because they only transcend themselves in this movement into their other or opposite. In this ("negatively dialectical") movement constitutive of morality Nietzsche's and Adorno's critique of equality makes up a decisive moment; in the absence of this critique, the movement of morality would come to a standstill in favor of the ideology of equality. At the same time, however, the critique of equality needs to be understood (and enacted) as a moment *in* this movement, as a moment of the negative dialectic of morality. Nietzsche fails to do this and, as a result, understands his critique of the repressive consequences of equality in such a way that he rejects, along with these consequences, the very idea of equality. According to Adorno's and Derrida's understanding, however—at least in the reading which has been outlined in this section—the critique of the repressive consequences of equality possesses as much validity as the insight into its normative necessity. Both moments have to be held together. Adorno and Derrida achieve this task by means of a political practice of writing. In this practice, the struggle for equality does not simply stand alongside its suspension in the name of individuality; these two moments are stringently related to one another, rather, precisely because they are opposed.

Ability and Faith: The Possibility of Justice

A. Philosophy and Deconstruction

Philosophy begins with wonder and ends with the achievement of insight. The insight philosophy ends with is an insight into the good. The time of philosophy lies between this beginning in wonder and this end in the achievement of insight. The determination of the beginning of philosophy is here conjoined with the determination of its end. Philosophy begins with a wonder that is itself already an insight: an insight into the lack of insight, the insight, that is, that we do not yet know something sufficiently (namely, ourselves). In philosophy, this is what it means to begin with a "problem."[1] Philosophy ascertains that this lack of insight is responsible for at least some, and perhaps the most persistent, of the contradictions in which we see ourselves caught up in our practice. Conversely, the philosophical achievement of insight should help to dissolve the contradictions that rend and obstruct us. The insight that philosophy seeks to achieve in order to solve the problems of our practice is therefore intended to lead or contribute to the good—to the accomplishment of this practice. To do this, philosophy's insight must also be an insight *into* the good. It must be an insight into that which constitutes the accomplishment of our practice.

In order to achieve insight into the accomplishment of practice, philosophy must first of all proceed descriptively—by going over the differences separating that which can be accomplished from that which, because it merely happens, can neither be accomplished nor fail. Furthermore, philosophy must differentiate basic forms of accomplishment within the field of that which can be accomplished or fail. Above all, however, philosophy must try to answer the question as to how and by what means the accomplishment of practical performances is *possible*. Philosophy is an investigation of the possibility of accomplishment. The concept of possibility here has not only a logical but a practical meaning. To philosophically demonstrate the possibility of accomplishment does not only mean to show that the diverse forms of the accomplishment of practices do not contradict either themselves or other evidences. To philosophically demonstrate the possibility of the accomplishment of our practices means much more: to determine the sources and potentials that *make* this accomplishment possible, that is, through which it is possible for *us* to bring about the accomplishment of our practices. This is why the philosophical question concerning the possibility of accomplishment leads to the capacities by means of which we *can* make practices be accomplished.[2] These are capacities to perform certain operations fundamental to our practices, like the capacity to make certain distinctions, draw certain connections, and pass certain judgments. Philosophy first of all makes suggestions about how these capacities can be described in a general, although nonempty, manner. In the process, moreover, it draws up a picture of how it can be understood that we actually possess and are able to exercise these capacities—what it means and what is required to be a being with such capacities. In this second move, philosophy is always more than a merely reflexive exercise that asks which capacities must be assumed if there should be accomplished practices. Rather, philosophy attains a claim, however "weak," to justification or foundation. By explaining not only which capacities we must have for our practices to succeed, but also how we can actually have these capacities, philosophy also assures us of the possibility of the accomplishment of our practices.

If we determine philosophy, in the manner suggested, not just by its object and procedure but its *meaning*, it should be immediately clear that deconstruction does not obey such an understanding. Furthermore, to put in question the outlined philosophical program—and with it the outlined program of philosophy itself—is not only an essential effect but an essential claim of the deconstructive undertaking. This is the point of Derrida's early self-description of deconstruction as "ultratranscendental." It is also the point of his summary of deconstruction's analyses—in his text dedicated to Austin—when answering the self-posed question "Are there signatures?" "Yes, of course, every day. The effects of signatures are the most ordinary thing in the world. The condition of possibility of these effects is simultaneously, once again, the condition of their impossibility, of the impossibility of their rigorous purity."[3] According to this formulation, deconstruction does not put in question the fact that the act of signature can succeed. What it puts in question is that there are conditions of possibility of this accomplishment that are not at one and the same time the conditions of its impossibility—of the impossibility of its rigorous purity. Deconstruction thus puts into question the successful implementation of the program that constitutes philosophy in its movement between wonder and insight into the good. This questioning of the program of philosophy takes place, however—and this is why deconstruction is called "ultratranscendental," in order to distinguish it from a "precritical" position—from the inside out.[4] Rather than renouncing the implementation of this program, deconstruction shows the contradictions and aporias that it must encounter in attempting to implement itself.

A widespread interpretation of deconstruction reads its questioning of the philosophical program from the perspective of the afterthought that Derrida added to his thesis that the conditions of possibility of accomplishment of a certain practice (here, of signatures) prove themselves to be the conditions of its impossibility: namely, the impossibility of the "rigorous purity" of this practice. According to this interpretation, Derrida relativizes his thesis with this afterthought, so that it no longer talks of the conditions of impossibility of (the accomplishment of) a certain practice in general, but *only* of the impossibility of its "rigorous purity." The "rigorously pure" accomplishment of a practice would be one that is deducible by application from the rules of that practice, which in turn presupposes that these rules can be represented in a theory in a complete and orderly, that is, systematic, manner. The capacity to perform a "rigorously pure" practice, or to secure the "rigorously pure" accomplishment of a practice, would thus have to consist in a first capacity to develop such a theory as the system of its rules, followed by a second capacity for the application of such a system of rules by way of subsumption or deduction. According to this interpretation, Derrida's deconstructive diagnosis of an internal logic of inversion of conditions of possibility into conditions of impossibility relates only to this "theoretistic" picture of our practical abilities. According to this interpretation, Derrida's deconstructive diagnosis would not, therefore, put the program of philosophy as such into question, but—in conjunction with authors like Wittgenstein and Davidson—merely one (albeit prominent) mode of its undertaking.[5]

In what follows, I want to try to go a step beyond this interpretation of deconstruction. My thesis will be that deconstruction does not merely put into question the "theoretistic" understanding of practical ability deeply embedded in our philosophical tradition. Deconstruction, rather, puts into question the very "confidence in ability [*Könnensbewusstsein*]" from which philosophy assumes its point of departure. Deconstruction thus puts into question how philosophy—in its program outlined at the beginning—introduces the concept of practical ability, namely as that which makes possible accomplished practice. According to this alternative interpretation, deconstruction refers to no less than the presupposition of philosophy itself or as such that it is our ability that makes possible the accomplishment of practices.

B. The Aporias of Making Possible: A Reading of "Force of Law"

Jacques Derrida's treatise "Force of Law: The 'Mystical Foundation of Authority,'"[6] with reference to which I want to explain the outlined perspective on deconstruction, was written as a contribution to a conference entitled "Deconstruction and the Possibility of Justice." From the beginning of his treatise, Derrida understands the title of this conference in the practical sense explained above. Accordingly, the question concerning the "possibility of justice" does not ask whether justice *is* possible in an objective sense. We would then ask under what conditions there can "be" justice, just as we ask under what conditions a particular plant thrives or the suicide rate rises. Derrida's question, however, concerns the understanding of how justice can be *made* possible—it concerns the conditions and modes of the "establishment" of justice. Derrida therefore views justice not as a state or event for which the occurrence of certain other states or events provides the necessary—or, at any rate, nonexclusive—conditions of possibility. Justice is, rather, a goal or telos that performances strive for. The question of the possibility of justice is thus concerned with the conditions

that a specific kind of conduct or behavior—primarily that of decision—
has to fulfill "to be just": "To be just, the decision of a judge, for example,
must not only follow a rule of law or a general law" (23). How must the
judge act and decide, indeed, how must he *be*,[7] what must he be able to do
and realize so that his action succeeds, so that his decision is just?

In his "practical" interpretation of the title of the colloquium, Derrida thus begins with a philosophical investigation in the sense elucidated
above: an investigation of what we have to do (and be able to do) in order
for a practice to be accomplished in a particular respect—here, that of justice. The fact that Derrida begins with such a philosophical investigation
does not mean, however, that he merely wants to suggest a better way of its
realization. He wants, rather, to show (in the sense of the "ultratranscendental" self-understanding of deconstruction) the fundamental difficulties
that must be encountered by every attempt to realize such a philosophical investigation—and thus by every philosophical "theory" of the practice of justice. In "Force of Law," Derrida determines these difficulties by
employing the concept of paradoxicality—to demonstrate "logico-formal
paradoxes" is, according to Derrida, one of the "two ways or styles" of deconstruction (21)—and, more importantly, the concept of "aporia." The
fundamental determination of this concept reads: "An aporia is a non-
road" (16). Where there is an aporia, there is no way; there is no way for us,
or it is not possible for us to carry out the movement by means of which we
would be capable of succeeding in our aim. An aporia indicates, therefore,
the impossibility of performances that guarantee accomplishment. Moreover, it should be noted that Derrida understands the mode of givenness
of an aporia as "experience." Derrida writes that the problems "covered by
the title *Deconstruction and the Possibility of Justice* . . . are not infinite simply because they are infinitely numerous. . . . They are infinite, if we may
say so, in themselves, because they require the very experience of the aporia" (16). This experience, however, is paradoxical: it is an experience of the
impossibility of experience.

The philosophical investigation of that which makes justice possible, then, comes up against an aporia—an experience of there being no
way (out). At the center of this aporia stands the characteristic structure of
"difference" that obtains between justice and law, a structure that separates
and at the same time connects them: "Everything would still be simple if
this distinction between justice and *droit* were a true distinction, an oppo-

sition whose functioning was logically regulated and permitted mastery" (22).[8] Derrida then unfolds this "untrue" distinction into three further aporias—all of which are encountered by the philosophical investigation of the possibility of a just decision. The first aporia is that of the *rules* of decision: the just decision must apply a rule and must not merely apply a rule. The second aporia is that of the *act* of decision: the just decision must be made decisively and is only possible in the consciousness of undecidability. The third aporia is that of the *time* of decision: the just decision is required right away, immediately and always remains to-come. Two different, but not exclusive, readings of these aporias are possible.[9]

According to their first reading, the aporias describe a conflict: a conflict in the normative content of the concept (or idea) of justice, and, as an immediate consequence of this, a conflict in the acts and performances that make justice possible. To be just *means*, then, something double, conflictual, and justice thus demands of us that we do two things at the same time—things which cannot, however, be done at the same time. On this first reading, the aporia that deconstruction draws attention to is a practical conflict. The features that outline such a practical conflict can be found in Derrida's description of all three aporias. This is clearest with regard to the first aporia, which consists in the fact that, in order that it can be just, a decision must "be both regulated and without regulation" (23). The second aporia is similarly expressed. It makes a conflictual demand on our behavior by telling us that justice can only be achieved if we make a conclusive decision and if we suspend this decision (cf. 23 ff.). The third aporia, which relates to the temporality of justice, obeys least of all this reading as practical conflict. Here this reading runs up against its limits, and this suggests an aspect of the aporia of justice that Derrida draws attention to that can no longer be understood as a practical conflict—as a conflict in the practical requirements of a just decision. Derrida understands this aspect as the tension between the always "precipitate" act of decision, which wants justice to occur here and now, and the countermovement of a postponement that "irreducibly" leaves justice to-come.[10]

The third aporia runs up against the limits of the first model of interpretation—the model of practical conflict—because the two sides of this aporia do not occupy the same level or are not of the same kind. As a practical conflict, the aporia is made up of two normative claims that only constitute the idea of justice when taken together. These claims lead to two requirements of our performances, of our mode of decision, that cannot be fulfilled at the same time. In Derrida's third aporia, however, one of its sides is no longer determined by a mode of just behavior, for one side of this aporia no longer formulates any requirement or form of the self-con-duct of a subject. The being-to-come of justice, which according to the third aporia opposes the always "precipitate" act of decision, relates rather to the curve of movement in which the *prevalence* [*Walten*] of justice be-comes independent with regard to the subjective *enforcement* [*Vollzug*] of justice. This divergence from the model of practical conflict does not only reveal, however, the exceptional character of the third of Derrida's aporias, that which distinguishes it from the other two. It indicates, at the same time, the possibility of another reading of all three aporias. This second reading, in contrast to the first, emphasizes the fundamental asymmetry of the sides aporetically opposed to one another. Accordingly, what is ar-ticulated in Derrida's aporias is not a practical conflict, but a conflict of the practical, that is, not a conflict *in* the practice of just decision, the conflict in that which we must do in the attempt to decide justly, but the conflict *with* practice, the conflict with the attempt to bring about justice through our own conduct, a conflict to which just decision, like all normative acts, is exposed.

The asymmetry that—according to the second reading outlined here—obtains in the aporias that Derrida draws attention to consists in the fact that these aporias do not refer to the practical difference between normative orientations but rather to the functional difference between that which makes possible and that which is made possible. The aporias that Derrida exposes between law and justice follow from the claim that the one is the *condition of possibility* of the other. By drawing attention to the aporias between law and justice, deconstruction thus puts into ques-tion the very relation of making possible that a philosophical investiga-tion, according to its program outlined at the beginning, must endeavor to discover between law and justice. The work of deconstruction consists in showing that that which makes possible cannot, at the same time, make possible—that is, in showing a simultaneous making possible and making impossible. It is this that constitutes the aporia in the relation between law and justice.

The aporetic simultaneity of making possible and making impossible applies to the relation between law and justice in two different ways. This means, to begin with, that *both* sides of this relation must be understood as claiming to make possible the other: the law claims to make possible justice, and justice claims to make possible law. In both cases, however, "making possible" means something different. They therefore also run into an aporia in different ways. The difference between the two relations of making possible is insufficiently comprehended, then, when we merely distinguish "the undeconstructibility of justice from the deconstructibility of *droit*" (15). For the object of deconstruction is not "the law," but the law *as* (that is, in the functional position of) the making possible of justice. What is deconstructed is the law's capacity to make possible. To this extent, however, that is, in this same *function* of making possible, justice is also deconstructible—even if the deconstruction of justice means something different than the deconstruction of law, just as the claim to make possible means something different with regard to justice and law. Let us now consider this double movement of deconstruction more closely.

The *first* relation of making possible that is deconstructed is the making possible of justice by means of the law; the law is that which makes possible justice. This means that, in order to do justice to the other, this "singularity that is always other" (25), we must behave in "conformity with the law" (25), in accordance with the form of legal decision. Derrida explains this relation of making possible the justice of a decision through its legal form by means of the connection between justice and justification. He refers to the law as that which makes justice possible because (or insofar as) the decision that conforms with the law can serve as a paradigm of the well-grounded decision. The premise of this combination of justice and law—namely, that a just decision must be a well-grounded decision—results from the consideration that a just decision is defined by the fact that it is not arbitrary. A just decision cannot be governed by the caprice or partiality of the subject who decides, but only by objective, "relevant" points of view. These, however, are reasons. The combination of law and justice that Derrida carries out is based on the assumption that the law can (at least in some respects) be understood as a publicly binding order of reasons, by means of which the justice of a decision can be guaranteed.

At the same time, however—and the aporia results from this second feature—the law makes justice impossible precisely insofar as, according to the suggested reading, the decision that conforms with the law is a paradigm of the well-grounded decision. Indeed, the law *makes* justice impossible because it ignores that the justice of a decision *is*, as Derrida reiterates, "the impossible": "Justice is an experience of the impossible" (16). In accordance with the practical meaning of "possibility," this thesis—which forces the difference between law and justice into the aporia—states, in its general version, that justice is simply not something that can be *made* possible by means of something else. Or, more precisely, as regards the combination of law and justice: the justice of a decision cannot be made possible or guaranteed by means of the reasons that are cited for it. To the extent that the law attempts to do exactly this, that is, to the extent that it believes that it can make possible that which cannot be made possible, it is itself responsible for the *im*possibility of justice. Deconstruction draws attention to precisely this aporia of making justice possible through the law. On the one hand, the law is that which makes justice possible, because—according to the suggested interpretation—only a decision that safeguards itself with reasons, that is, that follows from or is deducible from reasons, can be just. The justice of a decision cannot, however, be deduced from the reasons for the decision; no reason can enforce or guarantee justice. It is for this reason that the attempt to make justice possible through the law—or the trust in this possibility—in fact makes justice impossible.

The decisive argument in the demonstration of this aporia is obviously Derrida's reference to what he also calls the "presumption of a determinant certitude of a present justice" (25). A "presumption" / "présomption" (according to the *Petit Robert*: "opinion fondée seulement sur des signes de vraisemblance") is an inference in the midst of a lacking body of evidence, an inference that exceeds that which can be deduced or proved in the strong sense and thereby claimed as certain. The word *présomption* combines, as Alexander García Düttmann has said, "the conceit of assumption—this faith!—and the conjecture of presumption and supposition."[11] A presumption thus is an act of faith whose "ghostliness deconstructs from within any assurance of presence, any certitude or any supposed criteriology that would assure us of the justice of a decision, in truth of the very event of a decision" (24–25). Derrida once again formulates here, in a general way, his objection to the attempt to guarantee the justice of a decision by means of its relation to a (legal) order of reasons. It is an objection to the "faith" in the criterial connection between the formal determination of a decision and its normative quality. We cannot deduce the justness or unjustness of a decision from the way in which it was made or from the reasons by which it was attained. The certainty of justice is a faith because it is a *présomption*—something that can be supposed only on the basis of the modes and reasons of the decision.

This deconstruction of the certainty of a decision into a "faith" (which cannot be taken to imply a simple dissolution of either certainty or justice) has immediate consequences for the practical relation of the making possible of justice by means of a decision that conforms to the law. For the faith in the connection of criteria (the legal form of the decision) and normative judgment (the justice of the decision) is itself a practical faith, a faith in practice. It is the faith that the justification of a decision leads to justice. More precisely, it is the faith that *we* can *bring about* the justice of a decision by means of its justification, that is, that the justice of a decision is something that we can guarantee by means of our behavior. However, not only can we not do this, rather, to believe that justice can be made possible in such a way actually means to make justice impossible. Because the justice of a decision cannot be guaranteed by means of its good reasons, a decision or mode of decision that thinks itself capable of this will make justice impossible. It reduces the justice of a decision to something that can be deduced from its mode. Derrida is opposing such a reduction when he writes that only a decision that has gone "through the ordeal of the undecidable" can be just, and that this ordeal can never become "past or passed, it is not a surmounted or sublated [*aufgehoben*] moment in the decision" (24).

In the second reading reconstructed here, the deconstructive demonstration of aporias relates to the relation of making possible. According to this reading, the relation of making possible is aporetic because that which makes possible or, more precisely, its claim to make possible, at the same time makes impossible that which is made possible. In the special case of the making possible of justice through law, this aporia assumes, as we have seen, the following form: the fact that the law makes justice possible has to be understood in the sense of practical faith (a faith in and during practice), namely, the faith in it being possible for us to bring about justice by behaving in a particular way, by making our decisions in conformity with the law or oriented toward universally binding reasons. The "faith" that obtains here ties together practical ability, that is, the ability to make decisions in this mode or form, and normative accomplishment. This faith is constitutive of the orientation toward justice, for without it there would be no practice of justice. If we did not believe that we could bring about justice by means of something that we are capable of, we would give up our participation in practice. We would (as Derrida writes) "simply be spectators" (26), and thereby abandon the idea of justice itself. Conversely, however, and this leads to the aporia, it is precisely this faith in practice that brings about an attitude making justice impossible. Justice is impossible—this observation of deconstruction means that it is impossible for us to bring about justice. Justice is not something that we are capable of ensuring or guaranteeing by means of (the form of) our practice.[12] Only a practice of decision that knows this, and incorporates it into its form by becoming conscious of the connection between justice and undecidability, can be just. The aporia consists, then, in the fact that we must simultaneously possess and relinquish faith in our practices.

Let us now also take a quick look at the other relation of making possible that, according to Derrida's deconstructive demonstration, obtains between justice and law. The first relation of making possible—the one we have been considering up to now—consists in the fact that, in order to achieve justice, we must behave in conformity with the law (in the sense explained); so we can furthermore say that to be capable of behaving in conformity with the law is the condition of possibility of justice. The other, converse relation of making possible runs as follows: in order to establish a legal order we must behave justly; so we can also say that to be able to behave justly is the condition of possibility of law. This thesis is directed against the "conventionalist" and, consequently, "nihilistic" picture that both Montaigne's theory of obedience to the law and Stanley Fish's legal-theoretical pragmatism submit to on their "surface." According to this picture—as Derrida says, quoting Montaigne—laws enjoy "good standing, not because they are just, but because they are laws" (12).[13] In contrast to this justification of law(s) in themselves, in their mere existence or functioning, the question as to that which makes them possible leads, according to Derrida, to a form of conduct that makes itself answerable to the normative claim to justice. The observation that justice makes law possible relates precisely to this: only an action that is oriented toward the normative opposition of "just" and "unjust" makes possible the establishment of a legal order. *There is* law only for beings who (can) orient themselves toward the normative opposition of "just" and "unjust."

The point of Derrida's highly "active interpretation" of both Montaigne's formulation and Fish's concept of force consists, then, in the following thesis: this tracing back of the law to an action that orients itself toward the normative distinction between "just" and "unjust" also cannot be understood only in the sense of the practical relation of making possible—or, even more, of grounding or foundation. If laws are not comprehended as just because, as Montaigne would have it, they have credit at their disposal as laws; but if, conversely, against Montaigne, laws have credit at their disposal and function as laws because they are held to be just, precisely then the continuation of Montaigne's formulation applies according to which laws are based upon a "mystical foundation [or ground] of authority" (12). According to Derrida, a ground or reason can be called "mystical" when it eludes discursive understanding ("Here the discourse comes up against its limit" [13]). Insofar, however, as a ground or reason consists precisely in its discursive place or role, a mystical ground or reason is no ground or reason at all. A mystical reason is a "violence without ground" (14). This is the aporia that Derrida maintains regarding the relation of making possible between justice and law: just behavior makes a legal order possible by forming its foundation; and, at the same time, as a violence without ground, just behavior makes such an order impossible.

We can, once again, understand this aporia in the sense of the first reading outlined before, that is, as a practical conflict. The aporia would then state that just behavior comprises a normative orientation toward a "singularity that is always other" (25). This normative orientation toward singularity must lie at the basis of every legal order, but no legal order can satisfy it so that it always again is set off *against* the prevailing legal order. However, in Derrida's explanation of the aporia of making law possible through justice, this conflict between universal and particular, between equality and singularity, is not the decisive argument. For Derrida grounds the aporia not by means of the content of the normative orientation toward justice (the orientation toward the "singularity that is always other," which stands in conflict with the legal idea of equal treatment). He grounds it, rather, by means of its *form* or, more precisely, its *force*. Derrida formulates this as follows:

The very emergence of justice and law, the founding and justifying moment that institutes law, implies a performative force, which is always an interpretative force: this time not in the sense of law in the service of force, its docile instrument, servile and thus exterior to the dominant power, but rather in the sense of law that would maintain a more internal, more complex relation with what one calls force, power or violence. (13)

The way of behavior that founds the law and is normatively oriented toward justice is determined by its "relation with what one calls force, power or violence"—a relation which is not an exterior taking into service, but rather affects the inner constitution of this behavior. The aporia of making law possible through justice must, then, according to Derrida, be understood as the expression of an aporia of force or power. This follows from the fact that justice as a normative ground is itself a force or power. Justice can only be the ground of law, or make law possible, by being a force or power. Through such grounding, however, justice as force makes that which is made possible by it, namely law, impossible. For the law that is set into play by the force or power of justice is always interrupted again by it.

This deconstructive emphasis on the essential surplus of the force and power of justice over the law that it institutes should not be understood vitalistically. It would, conversely, be better to interpret vitalism, and its persistent appearance in modern philosophy, from the perspective of this deconstructive emphasis on the aporetic logic of force. This emphasis itself, however, is only properly understood when it is related not to force as a determination of the natural or living, but as a determination of the normative. The force or power that Derrida speaks of here is the force or power of justice, that is, in more general terms, the force or power of the normative. The aporia of this force or power refers to the double character of the normative as something that simultaneously institutes and exceeds. One way to make this comprehensible would be to relate this double character to the normative in the sense of a claim or requirement. Derrida's thesis would then be that the claim or requirement of the normative—here, of justice—is in principle irredeemable. The problem with this interpretation is not only that it explains justice as an idea that is in principle unrealizable—and that this is a view that Derrida explicitly disavows. Rather, the problem with this interpretation is above all that the explanation of the surplus force of justice in terms of the irredeemability of its requirement already presupposes that which it was intended to explain.

It is therefore reasonable to look for another explanation. This explanation should understand the surplus force of justice not as the force of its, in principle, unfulfillable claim, but, on the contrary, as the force of the experience of the fulfillment and reality of justice. Justice has force (or is force) insofar as we experience it here and now, in a particular situation and at a particular time, as real or reigning. I want to suggest that this be described as the *evidence* or *experience* of justice: the evidence of the experience that a particular action was just; the evidence, that is, not that justice was brought about by an action, but that justice in fact prevailed in a situation. As the first aporia of making justice possible through law showed, this evidence of (the experience of) justice cannot be a certainty *based on* reasons. The evidence of (the experience of) justice is not guaranteed by an action or judgment that fulfils particular conditions. It is precisely because of this, however, that the evidence of (the experience of) justice can provide no secure foundation *for* our actions and their normative structure. The evidence that justice reigns here and now tells us nothing about how we can reiterate justice at another place and time. The evidence of (the experience of) justice is, then, simultaneously force and foundation: as force it drives us ever onward; as foundation it is directed toward the order that it sets into play. If the practice of justice must be understood as rooted in the evidence of (the experience of) justice, then this practice is, at the same time, an expressive act of the realization of a force and an intentional act of the foundation of an order. This is the aporia that Derrida outlines in the relation of making possible between justice and law: as a productive foundation the evidence of justice makes law possible; as an expressive force the evidence of justice makes law impossible. Only an action that is grounded in the evidence of justice can bring about a legal order, but since the evidence of justice itself is not groundable, it also cannot ground an action capable of bringing about a legal order.

C. "Faith" and "Axiomatics"

Although the two aporias of making possible that Derrida draws attention to are different they also have something, that is, they have one side in common: they are both aporias that relate to the understanding of normative practice as productive (or producing). The aporia of making justice possible through law relates to the idea that an action can guarantee justice when it is safeguarded by generally shared reasons. Justice is, rather, always to-come—not because it lies in the future, but because it eludes the present certainty that it has been produced by oneself. The aporia of making law possible through justice relates to the idea that action can found or institute a legal order when it is grounded in the evidence of justice. The evidence of justice is, rather, an always surplus force that cannot provide a secure foundation for the result that it produces. Both aporias thus relate critically to a conception of normative practice that Derrida describes as being governed by the "subjectal axiomatic of responsibility, of conscience, of intentionality, of property" (25). It is the aporia of this conception of normative practice that Derrida draws attention to in "Force of Law."

What significance does the deconstructive demonstration of the aporias of the "subjectal axiomatic" have, then, with regard to the practice of justice? Must not this significance again be understood to refer—in accordance with the program of philosophy outlined at the beginning—to the way in which deconstruction is concerned, for its part, with accomplished practice, and more precisely, with the determination of the conditions of possibility of accomplished practice? This could certainly only be true of deconstruction in a characteristically paradoxical form, as when Derrida describes "a kind of non-passive endurance of aporia as the condition of responsibility and decision."[14] For if we understand this aporia, in the sense explained, as an aporia of making possible, Derrida maintains here that the insight into the aporia of the conditions of accomplishment is itself a condition of accomplishment. We could put this less paradoxically by saying that a accomplished performance, as decision or practice, is made possible insofar as we no longer think of it as made possible by us. The feature by means of which deconstruction breaks from the program of philosophy—the putting in question of its conviction of the making possible of accomplishment—could then be understood as precisely the feature by means of which it can claim to first fulfill this program, that is, the program of philosophy to contribute to the accomplishment of our practice by enlightening us about its form.[15] In contrast to this, the traditional philosophical conception of this accomplishment that accords with the "subjectal axiomatics"—because of the way it understands the making possible of this accomplishment—precisely does not make it possible. According to the "ultratranscendental" conception of deconstruction, the possibility of accomplishment would consist in a "non-passive endurance" of the aporias of making possible accomplishment.

In order to be able to ascertain whether, and in what fashion, the deconstructive demonstration of the aporias of making possible (accomplishment) itself makes (accomplishment) possible, we require a further determination of the conception of practice against which this demonstration is first of all directed—the conception that Derrida describes as "subjectal axiomatics." This axiomatics is not arbitrary, otherwise there would not be any aporia here. It is not a mere fiction, but instead formulates a fundamental feature of our self-understanding in and for practice. In the reconstruction of the deconstructive demonstration of aporias, we have seen that this axiomatics is rooted precisely where two aspects of our practical self-understanding are combined with one another. The first aspect is the constitutive connection between actions and normative claims, according to which we can realize our normative claims by means of our actions. The other aspect is the constitutive connection between certainty and reasons, according to which we can obtain normative certainty by means of reasons. In the case of just behavior, these two aspects are combined with one another thus: when I know which reasons for a decision can guarantee that I will have decided justly, then I also know how I must behave in order to guarantee that I will have behaved justly. For the reasons here—as Derrida, with Hart,[16] shows with regard to the form of law—are generally binding rules, that is, they are generally framed commands, the obedience or transgression of which can be clearly decided. If just decision could be analyzed in this way, then we could realize justice with the appropriate means of behavior, that is, the realizability of justice could be guaranteed by appropriate means. Derrida's claim is to have shown why this is not the case.

If we understand in this way what Derrida calls "subjectal axiomatics," it is immediately clear that it is a bundle of convictions that we cannot easily give up without giving up the idea of a reasonable normative practice itself. Although it is unclear what it might mean to "give up" this idea, it is clear in any case that this is not the aim of a deconstruction of "subjectal axiomatics." Deconstruction examines, rather, the validity and content of this axiomatics. As regards the validity-status of "subjectal axiomatics," deconstruction shows that, properly viewed, it is a "faith." Derrida relates this first of all to the certainty of the justice of a decision. In truth, this certainty is a "faith" or presumption because, contrary to its claim, it cannot be criterially grounded. Consequently, however, the certainty that we can bring about justice by means of our conduct is also a mere "faith," a "problematic" inference lying somewhere between presumption and assumption (García Düttmann). As regards the elements of the "subjectal axiomatics," this means that the combinations that it makes—between certainty and reasons and between normative claims and actions—are not conceptual (axiomatic) determinations, but unsafeguarded inferences in accordance with probability. The consideration of particular reasons makes a just decision more or less probable; acting in a particular way makes a just conduct more or less probable. But then the whole "subjectal axiomatics" itself possesses this status of a mere faith somewhere between presumption and assumption. This axiomatics is neither a conceptually true insight nor an arbitrary or pragmatic invention, but rather an inference, "fondée sur des signes de vraisemblance." It ensues from certain evidences or references in the performance of practice. These references consist in the practice-constitutive expectation and experience—an expectation that is an experience and an experience that is an expectation—that we can bring about and change something by means of what we do. If we did not believe this, we would not be able to act. The "subjectal axiomatics" is the false expression of this practice-constitutive faith.

The "de(con)struction" [*Abbau*] of axiomatic certainty into a presumed faith does not only affect its validity, however. When the certainty that we can guarantee our normative claims and certainties by means of actions and reasons turns out to be a faith, then the content of what we believed to be certain also changes. Not only are certainty and faith not the same attitude, they also do not have the same content. If talking of "faith" here includes a consciousness of not being able to know, then this also implies—as a consciousness of not being able to know whether being able to successfully perform—a consciousness of not being able to successfully perform. To believe, that is, not to know, that we can bring something about by means of our own conduct also means, then, to understand our own bringing about differently. Faith and knowledge thereby lose their simple opposition and begin to change places. To claim to know that we can bring something about by means of our own conduct means to believe that this is a product whose accomplishment can be guaranteed through action. To believe that we can bring something about by means of our own conduct means, however, to know that its accomplishment also essentially depends upon something—"circumstances"—that we are not ourselves capable of bringing about. The faith in being able to bring something about by means of our own conduct is, then, as faith, paradoxically always also a faith in an effect that is not our own doing.[17] This faith is not, however, a foundation or presupposition. It has to be understood as a structural characteristic of a normative practice, that is, of a practice that is oriented toward the idea of its accomplishment.

This once again brings to the fore the peculiar tension between deconstruction and philosophy—in the sense of the program of philosophy outlined above. Deconstruction shows that, in order for us to make possible the accomplishment of our practice, we must not think of this accomplishment as being made possible only by us. This deconstructive insight would exceed the boundaries of philosophy (and would thus no longer be a philosophical insight), if it were understood to detach the accomplishment of our practice from our practice itself—and if it were understood to comprehend this accomplishment as an occurrence transcending practice, that is, as a transcendent occurrence in which we can only have faith. Ability and faith—the ability to make justice possible and the faith in its approach—do not, however, stand in a simple opposition. Deconstruction proves, rather, that faith, *this* faith, is an aspect of ability, an aspect that is not added as a supplement to other determinations of ability, but instead determines the *mode* of our ability. In endeavoring after ability, deconstruction encounters faith and, with it, the limits of ability.

PART II

EQUALITY AND INDIVIDUALITY

3

Equality and Coercion:
A Hermeneutic Limit of
Modern Self-Reflection

A. Equality, Coercion, Reason: Hegel's Transformation of the Romantic Complaint

The suspicion that the specifically modern understanding of moral and legal equality is marked, in its innermost core, by a new establishment of coercion, violence, and domination, is as old as the (Kantian) articulation and the (revolutionary) institutionalization of this understanding. According to this suspicion, the standpoint of equality is inherently characterized by an estrangement and externality with respect to life relations. From the perspective of these relations, the possible implementation of equality can only appear as something threatening and destructive. It is for this reason that, ever since the first romantic articulation of this suspicion, there has been a balancing of the individual and social costs of the establishment of equality—costs which are obvious despite the undeniable developments and gains made possible by it. For the most part, however, this balancing of costs is unreflective in a double respect: it complains about losses without demonstrating the value of that which has been lost, and it demands the avoidance of losses without determining the possibility and subject of this avoidance. This is why the romantic balancing of the costs of modernization is so often connected with regressive and utopian motives.

Hegel's critique of romanticism starts with discontent over these regressive and utopian features of the romantic complaint. But Hegel explicitly agrees with the central diagnosis of this complaint: using the example of Kant's and Fichte's grounding of the idea of equality in the framework of the theory of autonomy, Hegel demonstrates that the modern idea of equality implies for each particular individual the necessity of "limiting and dominating" his "sensuousness,"[1] and that it implies for the political government of society the establishment of a relationship of "*coercion*."[2] Because the principle of equality implies limitation, domination, and coercion, Hegel calls it a "principle of unethical life."[3] At the same time, however, Hegel does not aim at a mere repetition of the romantic complaint, but rather at its transformation into critical knowledge. According to Hegel, the condition of this transformation consists in the possibility of our understanding the problem of the coerciveness of the principle of equality as a problem which concerns its rationality: the critique of the immanent coerciveness of equality forms part of a critique of reason.

This is true in a double sense. Firstly, the critique of the immanent coerciveness of equality is a critique *of* the form of reason which realizes itself in the standpoint and reflection of equality; the coerciveness of equality is therefore grounded in the specific understanding of rationality upon which it is based—Hegel describes it as "the non-essential abstraction of the one."[4] Secondly, however, the critique of the immanent coerciveness of equality is not only a critique of reason, but also a critique *through* reason. Accordingly, to criticize the immanent coercion which the principle of equality exercises as a consequence of its deficient or one-sided mode of reason implies an increase in reason—a process of rationalization. Hegel describes the enactment of this process of rationalization as the central task of philosophy. What is decisively important here, however, is the fact that philosophy can only enact this rationalization by taking as its starting point—and by incrementally transforming—precisely that deficient, and even unethical, form of reason which is already realized by the reflection of equality.[5] The process of rationalization, the development toward a "higher" or "greater" reason, can only enact itself as a *self*-reflection of the reflection *of* equality and its reason.

This self-reflection of the reflection of equality, which attains a greater reason, is characterized by the fact that it achieves an insight into the coercive character of the reason which is already realized in the reflection of equality itself. Hegel's central claim—according to which the rationalizing self-reflection of equality is capable of sublating, that is, of reformulating and transforming into critical knowledge, the romantic complaint about equality—is derived from this fact. This claim implies that the reflection of equality is itself able to attain an insight into the coercion which it imposes, and this means that it has become self-reflective. The possibility of the demanding idea of a rationalization of equality by means of its self-reflection rests upon the fact that there is a correspondence between enactment and knowledge, act and insight.

Hegel's *Science of Logic* has often been read—especially with regard to its highest concept, that of a dialectic sharpened into a method—as the working out of a procedure whose application should guarantee the success of such a self-reflective rationalization, precisely because it leads to a standpoint of perfect self-transparency. Even if this reading of Hegelian logic might be true,[6] it does not apply to Hegel's social philosophy and its analysis of the *social* actuality of reason. From the very beginning, this analysis contains a critical demonstration of the coercion which is connected with the social implementation of the "law" of equality. From Hegel's Jena writings onward, however, this analysis also and above all contains an insight into the fact that, in the absence of regressive or utopian escapes, this law cannot transform itself by means of any process of reflection in such a way that its violence and coercion are dissolved. The coercion of equality is indissolubly bound up with "absolute conflict" (Hegel), especially in the normative framework of modern societies.

The first clear formulation of this insight, in the third paragraph of the essay on natural right, is represented by the "image" of a "tragedy in ethical life." The reflections which follow are intended as an elucidation of this image. Rather than offering an interpretation, I will attempt to indirectly throw light upon it by discussing some aspects of the theory of Niklas Luhmann—a theory which might seem to be based, at first glance, on entirely different premises. For despite all the differences between their fundamental concepts, Luhmann is concerned with a problem which is closely related to that of Hegel: the social conditions or, more precisely, the social limits of the realization of the idea of a self-reflective rationalization in modern societies. In order to elucidate this problem, I will proceed by firstly outlining Luhmann's diagnosis of a modern dilemma of rationality (B). Secondly, I will investigate the application of this diagnosis to the principle of equality using the example of its social implementation in the modern welfare-state (C). Finally, I will ask what consequences this implementation has with regard to the understanding and possibility of the self-reflection of equality; I will also briefly take up Hegel's image of tragedy (D).

B. The Problems of Rationality
in Modern Societies: Luhmann's Diagnosis

Hegel's transformation of the romantic complaint situates the demonstration of the immanent coerciveness of equality in the perspective of a program of its rationalization—a program which he understands as a self-reflection of the reflection of equality. In this self-reflection, the attitude of equality should, firstly, attain a theoretical insight into its coercive moment and, secondly, draw practical consequences from this insight. Hegel thereby applies the traditional idea of the rationality of *persons*, the idea of a self-determination based upon self-knowledge, to the idea of different practical *perspectives*—here, the perspective of equality. Niklas Luhmann's system-theoretical "reconstruction" of the "idea of rationality" follows Hegel in this application.[7] According to this reconstruction, the idea of rationality contains "a truly utopian program": it contains the requirement that we "reflect" upon the functioning of this idea of rationality in its diverse consequences, and it contains the requirement that we control this functioning in accordance with the result of this self-reflection.

The acceptance of the traditional idea of rationality makes up only one side, however, of Luhmann's system-theoretical reconstruction. This acceptance is bound up with a skeptical diagnosis of the chances of the realization of this idea: a diagnosis of its "quasi-impossibility." According to this diagnosis, the idea of rational self-knowledge and self-determination entangles itself, under the conditions of modern societies, in the indissoluble "dilemma" of its simultaneous necessity and unrealizability.[8] In Luhmann's view, it is precisely this fact which denies to modern societies the possibility of retaining the traditional concept of reason, even if they hold onto the traditional program of rationality. For "reason" is the promise of a *guarantee* of the realization of that which the program of rationality demands.

Luhmann elucidates his diagnosis of a dilemma of rationality—which is directed against the optimism of the concept of reason—by determining the concept of rationality as "system-relative."⁹ "System-relativity" does not mean an "abandonment of rationality . . . , but instead a reconstruction of the concept."¹⁰ For to relativize rationality in relation to social systems does not mean to reduce it to their functioning. Rationality is "system-relative," rather, because the "facticity" in which—and this means under the conditions of which—it operates is the facticity of social systems.¹¹ The concept of rationality therefore needs to be adapted to the facticity of social systems in two respects: rationality is applied to the processes of the self-*reproduction* of social systems; and rationality is established by means of the processes of the self-*reference* of social systems. Social systems are, then, at the same time, both object and subject; they constitute the what and the who of every possible rationalization.

The system-relative concept of rationality allows us to give a more precise formulation of Luhmann's diagnosis of a dilemma of rationality. It claims that there is a gap between two aspects of the rationality which is understood as system-relative, a gap which cannot be closed in modern societies: social systems need more rationality than they are able to produce. In modern societies, for structural reasons, no adequate potential of the rationality of social systems corresponds to their demand for rationality.

In order to understand this thesis, we need to first of all elucidate the amount of rationality which is required by the facticity of social systems, in order to see how the latter fails to satisfy the former. That which the idea of rationality *requires* can already be inferred from its relativization with respect to systems. For Luhmann does not only use this relativization in order to pursue a (social-) ontological motive—that of an adequate determination of the "facticity" which is presupposed by all rationality, as the rationality of systems. He also uses it in order to pursue a critical motive. It is true that, according to Luhmann, rationality is "no norm, no value, no idea, which confronts real systems." Nevertheless, the concept of rationality characterizes the "standpoint of the critique of all selections"—a standpoint which allows us to "suspend" a "conclusive judgment" as to the mode of operation of systems.¹²

From the perspective of such a concept of rationality, everything which pertains to systems can be subjected to a detailed critique—including the concept of rationality toward which they orient themselves. A good example of this is provided by Luhmann's discussion of the concept of the rationality of action.[13] According to Luhmann, the concept of the rationality of action—because it takes actions, and not systems, as the basic elements of the social—is not only based upon a false social ontology; it simultaneously gives up the very critical potential which characterizes the concept of rationality. For the concept of the rationality of action only relates to those particular strategies of systems which are described in terms of aims and means, and which can thus be rationalized in the two dimensions of value-rationality and purposive rationality. No concept of the rationality of action, however, allows us to determine whether it is actually rational to proceed in this way, that is, by applying "purposive strategies." The concept of the rationality of action naturalizes this procedure and thereby renders impossible any judgment concerning its own rationality. By contrast, the very meaning of the concept of systemic rationality implies a reopening of the possibility of such a judgment: what is at stake is the judgment concerning the (system-relative) rationality of rationality itself (for instance, of the rationality of action).

The critical sense of the concept of system-rationality consists, then, in the attainment of an attitude of "distance" (Luhmann) that opens up the very space for judgment. This distance concerns everything which takes place in systems and is understood as rational. It is for this reason that the idea of rationality requires the self-reflection of a system; more precisely, this idea describes nothing other than "the most demanding perspective of the self-reflection of a system."[14] Luhmann elucidates this achievement of the idea of rationality in more detail by introducing it as the third stage of the self-reference of systems to their own difference from the environment. The first stage of this self-reference is constituted by the basic self-reference which always already "accompanies" (as autopoesis) the mere reproduction of systems: every new operation of a system refers back to its previous operation, and to something in it "with which it identifies itself."[15] The second stage is that of the reflection by means of which a system presents itself to itself in its difference from the environment: by means of reflection, and especially in the course of their differentiation, systems form a specific semantics which "can represent the relationship between system and environment within the system."[16] But "this alone does not deserve the name of rationality. Rationality is only attained when the concept of difference is used self-referentially, that is, when the unity of difference is reflected upon."[17]

This claim can be most easily understood—if we avoid any further discussion of the theory of autopoetic systems—by means of a consideration of the causal-theoretical translation which Luhmann gives to it: "If we translate this idea into a causal-theoretical language, then it states that, if the system wants to behave rationally, it has to control its effects upon the environment in their repercussions for itself."[18] The rationality of systems, as the "most demanding" mode of their self-reflection, consists in an expanded, that is, decentered, self-reference—it consists in the self-reflection of a system with regard to the retroactive influences which it exerts upon its other, its environment. This self-reflection includes both a theoretical and a practical moment. Firstly, the rationality of systems requires an expansion of their self-understanding, made possible by an insight into their environmental consequences. Secondly, this rationality also requires an expansion of the self-control of systems, made possible by a calculus of the environmental consequences which act back upon systems. If the self-reference of systems becomes *explicit* in this progression from the first to the second stage, from "self-reference" to "reflection," then in the progression from the second to the third stage, from "reflection" to "rationality," it becomes *eccentric*. Rationality is an eccentric self-reference: a self-reflection with respect to the other.

Eccentric self-reflection—as the "most demanding perspective" of the self-reference of systems—characterizes what is required by the idea of the rationality of systems. This exceptional mode of the self-reference of systems—with respect to the problems of their self-reproduction (in their difference from the environment)—is certainly required by the idea of the rationality of systems. This allows us to formulate more precisely Luhmann's diagnosis of a modern dilemma of social rationality. This diagnosis describes a mismatch between the rationality which is necessary for the self-reproduction of systems and the rationality which is possible in their self-reference: "With the extent of environmental transformations which proceed from systems, and with an expansion of the temporal horizon and of the interdependencies which are taken into account, there is an increase . . . in difficulties [of the establishment of rationality], and, in modern society, these difficulties culminate in claims which can hardly be fulfilled, in quasi-impossibilities."[19] In modern societies, the *problems* of the self-reproduction of systems, which arise because of the retroactive influences of the environment, and the *potentials* of the self-reference of systems, which are made possible by eccentric self-reflection, are incommensurate.

This excessive demand upon the rational and eccentric self-reference of social systems does not only apply to their practical potentials of self-control, but already to the theoretical potentials of a self-understanding which is expanded by means of an insight into their environmental consequences. Luhmann supports this claim with two reasons: the quantity and the complexity of the effects upon the environment. Firstly, Luhmann claims, the "enormous" influence of a system upon its environment—which itself provokes countereffects upon the system—already exceeds, as a result of its quantity, the system's power of comprehension. Secondly, however, it is the *complexity* of this influence which individual systems cannot live up to. Luhmann demonstrates this using the example of the effects which are produced upon the environment by the complex and combined operations of many social systems—effects which individual systems cannot perceive, however, as a product of such operations.[20] These effects cannot be "brought into" the "social process of communication," then, *as* effects which are produced upon the environment by the combined operations of social systems, that is, they cannot be brought into the social process of communication *as they are in themselves.*

The problems of quantity and complexity already demonstrate, then, the kind of limit the attempt to establish rationality runs up against: the establishment of a self-reference of social systems which is decentered with respect to its effects upon the environment reaches the limits of perception, that is, cognitive limits. Over and above this, the problem of complexity also demonstrates that this limit is not only to be understood as quantitative, with respect to the amount of knowledge, but also as qualitative; this limit is related here to the *kind* of knowledge or perception which the social systems of modern societies can attain of their own effects upon the environment. More precisely, this limit of perception manifests itself in the fact that systems are incapable of perceiving their effects in the environment *as* what they are *in* the environment; the cognitive limit of perception is, then, a hermeneutic limit—a limit of different hermeneutical "as-zones." This is why this limit does not only appear when there is a difference in complexity between system and environment. This cognitive or hermeneutical limit between system(s) and environment(s) always exists, rather, because of the particular form which this difference assumes in modern societies. The functionally differentiated society, which is no longer integrated by any center and no longer controlled by any apex, is determined by a difference between a perceiving system and a perceived environment which can manifest itself in severe hermeneutical dissonances. The limits of perception which become perceivable in these dissonances simultaneously point out a limit and dilemma of rationality. For they point out that the causal entanglements of the self-reproduction of systems in principle reach further than the cognitive capacities of their self-reflection—however eccentric the expansion of this self-reflection might be. What the self-reflection of systems aims at—environmental effects *before* they begin to react back upon systems in an uncontrolled manner—cannot be attained, for there is a hermeneutic limit which divides systems and environments: "The principle of differentiation of modern society makes the question of rationality more urgent—and, at the same time, more insoluble."[21]

Let us briefly summarize the result of Luhmann's reflections concerning the fate of social rationality under the conditions of modern difference. Luhmann describes this fate in his diagnosis of an indissoluble dilemma of rationality. On the one hand, this diagnosis undertakes an elucidation of the "truly utopian program" of the eccentric self-reflection of social systems with respect to their environmental consequences. On the other hand, however, this diagnosis contains a justification of the claim that this program can never be finally realized: under the conditions of modern differentiation, it runs up against an insurmountable hermeneutic limit. In the process of the dissolution of the privileged site from which both the internality of systems and the externality of the environment could be grasped with equal transparency, that is, in the process of the "hermeneutic" differentiation of modern societies, the reason which is in principle guaranteed success becomes a rationality which is in principle endangered by its "quasi-impossibility."

If we relate this diagnosis of the modern dilemma of social rationality to the problem of the immanent coerciveness of equality which was outlined at the beginning, we can see that it leads to the following thesis: if the idea of equality, in the process of its social implementation, brings about coercion and violence, then the idea of rationality—according to both

Hegel's and Luhmann's elucidation—implies that the standpoint of equality expands itself, in a process of self-reflection, by means of an insight into these violent and coercive consequences, in order then to avoid them by means of corresponding transformations. According to Luhmann's own diagnosis of the dilemma, however, such a rationalization—which enacts itself by means of a self-reflection upon its own violent consequences—is unrealizable. The self-reflection of equality can never achieve such an expansion of its self-understanding because an insurmountable hermeneutic limit obstructs an adequate perception of its consequences, that is, a perception of these consequences as coercion and violence. The project of a rationalization which enacts itself by means of a self-reflection upon its own consequences fails because of the cognitive limits which cut through modern differentiated society.

In the following two sections, I want to subject this thesis, which results from the application of the diagnosis of a dilemma of rationality to the self-reflection of equality, to a closer examination. I will proceed in two stages. Firstly, I want to show how Luhmann's diagnosis adequately characterizes a central problem of the rationalizing self-reflection of equality. I will do this by critically discussing Luhmann's analysis of the rationality problems of the modern welfare-state (C). Secondly, I want to show how Luhmann draws from his diagnosis a mistaken conclusion concerning the form and possibility of the rationalizing self-reflection of equality. In order to do this, I will briefly outline the way in which such a self-reflection is still possible—even under the conditions of the modern dilemma of rationality (D).

C. The Welfare-State as an Example of the Dilemma of Rationality

In order to be able to judge the suggested application of Luhmann's skeptical diagnosis to the idea of equality, we first of all need to understand the effects which this idea has upon the environment—effects which justify their romantic evaluation as "coercive." We can do this if we take as a starting point Luhmann's analysis of the modern form of the political in the welfare-state. In explicit opposition to Luhmann, I here understand the welfare-state as the agent of the social realization of equality. For Luhmann, by contrast, what realizes itself in the welfare-state is not a neutral or egalitarian attitude, but instead a claim oriented toward the improvement of life situations—which are combined and transformed into "leading values."[22] At the same time, Luhmann has exemplarily described, in relation to the paradigm of the welfare-state, the "consideration of the side effects of programs of action and the limits of their possibilities."[23] In order to be able to gain an insight into the "side effects" of its "programs of action," which follow inescapably from its own "leading values," the welfare-state needs to distance itself *from* its own values and "sensitivize" itself *to* its own effects.[24] The welfare-state acquires rationality only by means of an eccentric "transcending of the type of processing of information which characterizes it as a welfare-state."[25]

Although Luhmann clearly formulates the program and the problems of a self-reflection of the welfare-state, he simultaneously obscures them by misunderstanding the process of abstraction which they require. For Luhmann misunderstands the welfare-state's consequence-sensitive abstraction from its own values as a methodological abstraction from all normative standpoints in general. It is for this reason that he connects the demand for rational self-reflection to the demand for the overcoming of all normative discourse in a "hard pedagogics of causality."[26] It is true that this misunderstanding—one which confuses self-reflection with functional analysis—remains unproblematic as long as we are concerned with those side effects of the welfare-state which primarily need to be analyzed in functional terms (above all, the much discussed consequences which its expansion has for the systems of economy, education, and law). This misunderstanding becomes problematic, however, when it leads to a foreclosure of all the consequences which cannot be adequately grasped in these terms. These are the consequences, pointed out by Luhmann, but not investigated any further, which the welfare-state has, not for other social systems in its own intrasocial environment, but instead for "psychical systems" in its extrasocial environment—or, in more traditional terms, for the life of individuals. Even to be able to adequately describe these consequences, we need to describe them as consequences *for* individuals. For the individuals themselves, however, these consequences are effects which, according to the formulation once given by Luhmann himself, concern the "possibilities of individualized, personal life-conduct";[27] they are effects which are measured according to the criterion that "a humanly sat-isfying life, the 'good life' (Aristotle), remains possible."[28] The good life is that which is at stake for the individuals themselves, and it is still under-stood—and this is relevant for the self-reflection of the welfare-state—ac-cording to the historically specific interpretation which "was formulated . . . circa 1800 under the headings of freedom, independence, individual and world, art, love."[29] If the eccentric self-reflection of the welfare-state is (also) concerned with the whole spectrum of its effects upon the good life of individuals—effects which go partially unnoticed—then, contrary to Luhmann's methodological misunderstanding, such a self-reflection can-not consist in the wholesale abandonment of the normative perspective; instead, it needs to bring into play the normative *counter*perspectives to the welfare-state's own normativity.

As an example of such a theory which investigates the welfare-state with regard to its normative consequences for individuals, Luhmann him-self mentions "neo-Marxism."[30] This is not, however, the only possible example. There are at least two other normative analyses of the harm-ful consequences which the welfare-state's social establishment of equal-ity has for the individual conduct of life. In order to distinguish these two analyses from neo-Marxism, we can refer to them as "neo-Aristotelian" and "neo-Nietzschean." In the elucidation which follows, I will refer to the neo-Marxist analysis of Jürgen Habermas, the neo-Aristotelian analy-sis of Charles Taylor, and the neo-Nietzschean analysis of Michel Foucault. These three analyses offer a different description of both the content and the means of the welfare-state's impairment of the life-conduct of indi-viduals.

Habermas's neo-Marxist analysis concentrates on the side effects which the welfare-state brings about by means of the "medium of power" which it uses in a "seemingly innocent" fashion.[31] For "the legal and ad-ministrative means through which welfare-state programs are implement-ed are not a passive medium with no properties of its own. On the con-trary, they are linked with a practice that isolates individual facts, a practice of normalization and surveillance"—which directly affects individuals be-cause it implies limitations of the "autonomy" of their conduct of life.[32] The aim of the welfare-state is to create for everybody equal possibilities of a self-determined life; the welfare-state corrupts this aim itself, however, because of the means of state power which it uses in order to pursue it. For by using legal and bureaucratic procedures, the welfare-state claims a power of definition with respect to something which can only be defined by individuals themselves, that is, that which constitutes their self-determined lives.

Whereas the neo-Marxist analysis concentrates on the autonomy-threatening consequences of the welfare-state's means of power, according to the view which is shared by the two other analyses of consequences—the neo-Aristotelian and the neo-Nietzschean—it is the social implementation of equality *itself* which already implies a move of devastating abstraction; this move can lead, according to Taylor, to "terrible costs,"[33] and its "dark side" consists, according to Foucault, in the "submitting" of "forces and bodies" in "the disciplines."[34] At the same time, however, Taylor and Foucault see the good life of individuals as being threatened by two entirely different aspects of the social implementation of equality. Taylor describes the social implementation of equality as the establishment of an atomistic model of society in accordance with which the good becomes privatized and the public empty. The "terrible costs" of equality consist in the dissolution of those communal practices which are supported by common values and which provide the only possible framework for the enactment of the good life of individuals. Foucault, by contrast, describes the social implementation of equality as the establishment of a self-understanding which is committed to the aim of rational self-control. On this view, the "dark underside" of equality consists in the obstruction of the transgressive and experimental processuality of authentic life.[35]

In contrast to neo-Marxist analysis, then, the welfare-state does not have threatening, or even devastating, consequences for the autonomy of individuals, simply because these individuals are incapacitated by its legal-administrative means. According to the neo-Aristotelian and neo-Nietzschean analyses, the welfare-state already has threatening, or even devastating, consequences for the good life of individuals—in the two dimensions of communal practice and transgressive processuality—because of its very orientation toward equality.

All three analyses can be understood in such a way that, according to the above-cited program of Luhmann, they transcend the "type of information processing which is characteristic of the welfare-state" by "increasing" its "sensitivity" to its side effects. It is for this reason that the three analyses of consequences need to be examined with respect to their content: we need to find out whether the side effects which they describe do in fact arise (in this way). As regards Luhmann's skeptical diagnosis of rationality, however, I am interested here in a different aspect: I am not interested in the content of these analyses of consequences, but instead in their *locus*. The question that Luhmann's diagnosis of a dilemma gives a skeptical answer to concerns the chances of the ("eccentric") self-reflection of social systems with respect to their consequences for the environment. As we have seen, Luhmann justifies his skeptical answer by pointing out that social systems are incapable of forming an adequate perception of their own consequences for the environment—that they run up against insurmountable hermeneutic limits. How does this thesis apply to the perception of the above-mentioned consequences brought about by the welfare-state? Can the welfare-state's establishment of equality sensitivize itself to the consequences which it has for the good life of individuals? As regards the consequences pointed out in the neo-Aristotelian and neo-Nietzschean analyses, the answer to this question will have to be no. The reasons for this become clear if we recapitulate how the neo-Marxist analysis transforms the question of the self-reflection of the welfare-state into the question of its democratization, and if we recapitulate why it is that this analysis gives an affirmative answer to this question.

The neo-Marxist analysis describes the possibility of a self-reflection of the welfare-state by orienting itself toward the (practical as well as theoretical) idea of its democratization. Democratic processes here are, on the one hand, the media of the participation of individuals in the formulation of the aims and measures of the welfare-state. At the same time, however, these participatory processes can be understood in such a way that it is only by means of them that the welfare-state is able to adequately *perceive* the individuals. For when individuals become the "authors" of the welfare-state, by means of democratic participation, they can themselves bring to light the consequences which it has for the conduct of life of individuals as its "addressees."[36]

This does not apply, however, to all the consequences which the welfare-state has for the conduct of life of individuals. This becomes clear when we consider the function which this sensitivization to the threatening consequences of the welfare-state exercises in the welfare-state itself:

the function of the presentation of counterreasons. What is at stake in the welfare-state is equality. This is why the welfare-state only considers the consequences which threaten the life-conduct of individuals as counterreasons when they can simultaneously be understood as impairments of equality. In their role as democratic authors of the welfare-state, individuals can only accept as counterreasons those experiences (of impairment) which are bound up with their role as addressees of the welfare-state and which can be translated into the language of equality.

The question of the possibility of the self-reflection of the welfare-state can be formulated, then, as a question of the possibility of articulating, in the processes of democratic participation, the threatening consequences *of* the welfare-state as counterreasons *in* the welfare-state. On the basis of this formulation, it becomes possible to understand the above-mentioned difference between, on the one hand, the neo-Marxist description of the consequences of the welfare-state and, on the other hand, the neo-Aristotelian or neo-Nietzschean description. Whereas the impairments of the autonomy of individuals can be accepted in the welfare-state as counterreasons, that is, in the name of equality, this is *not* true of the impairments of the good life of individuals in their communal practice or transgressive processuality. For equality and autonomy are correlative: equality is exercised with a view to (the possibility of) the autonomy of the conduct of life; and autonomy (as capacity, and not in every concrete enactment) is secured and made possible by equality. The idea of equality is not correlative, by contrast, with those demanding conditions of the good which I have briefly described above as communal practice and transgressive processuality. Rather, their relationship is heterogeneous:[37] equality can impair the communal practice or transgressive processuality of the good life of individuals; and the communal practice or transgressive processuality of this good life cannot be claimed in the name of equality. In the process of self-reflection of the welfare-state, in the form of its democratization, the impairments of the autonomy of individuals can therefore be recognized as counterreasons against the means of the welfare-state. For in the language of its aim—the claim to equality—the welfare-state itself disposes of a vocabulary which allows it to formulate its consequences for the autonomy of individuals in exactly the same way in which these consequences are presented to the individuals themselves. In the process of the self-reflection of the welfare-state, in the form of its democratization, the impairments of the communal practice or transgressive processuality of life *cannot*, by contrast, be recognized as counterreasons. For if the conduct of life of individuals in their communal practice or transgressive processuality is *impaired* by the implementation of equality, it is always *condemned* by the reflection of equality. The reflection of equality cannot accept the dimensions of communal practice and transgressive processuality which it impairs as good counterreasons; and this means that the reflection of equality cannot even adequately *perceive* these dimensions as specific aspects of justification. With respect to the consequences of equality which have been demonstrated in the neo-Aristotelian and neo-Nietzschean analyses, we can thus reiterate the general thesis which has already been formulated above: the self-reflection of the welfare-state runs up against an insurmountable hermeneutic or perceptual limit.

D. Summary: Self-Reflection as Remembrance

In the second section (B), I discussed the way in which Luhmann grounds his skeptical diagnosis of a dilemma of rationality in the hermeneutic differentiation of modern societies. According to this grounding, the idea of a critical self-reflection of the system's consequences for the other runs up against insurmountable hermeneutic or perceptual limits. In the third section (C), I used the example of the welfare-state to discuss this diagnosis and its grounding in its application to the normative perspective of equality. It became clear that there are consequences of the implementation of equality in the welfare-state—or, more precisely, impairments of the decisive conditions of the good life of individuals described in the neo-Aristotelian and neo-Nietzschean analyses—which cannot be adequately perceived by the reflection of equality itself in its democratically constituted enactment and implementation. This only constitutes, however, *one* concretization of the application of Luhmann's general diagnosis to the specific case of the idea of equality in the welfare-state. According to this concretization, there is a hermeneutic limit of self-reflection only with respect to *particular* environmental consequences. A second concretization concerns the concept, and not the object, of self-reflection as an adequate perception of its own environmental consequences. Under the conditions of a normative description of both the system (by means of the claim to equality) and its consequences (for the good life of individuals), an adequate perception of these consequences can only consist—as became clear in the neo-Marxist analysis of the concept of democracy—in their being *judged* as (potential counter-) reasons.

In this fourth section, I will attempt to outline the consequences which this application to equality has, especially in its two above-mentioned concretizations, for Luhmann's general skeptical diagnosis of a dilemma of rationality of modern society. In order to do this, I would like to recapitulate the problem which this dilemma poses. The "truly utopian program" of rationality—the requirements of which Luhmann describes as both necessary and unsatisfiable—consists in the self-reflection of a system or, more generally, in a perspective upon the consequences which this first system or perspective has for other systems or perspectives. Luhmann emphasizes that, under the conditions of modern differentiation, this self-reflection can no longer be understood according to the traditional model of reason. This is true in two different (and also differently strong) respects.[38]

Firstly, the skeptical diagnosis of a dilemma of rationality is directed against the idea of reason as a neutral third party. According to this idea, there is an external standpoint with respect to both perspectives (one of which has consequences for the other). From this standpoint, the relationship between the perspectives can be described, questioned, and determined. In opposition to this, Luhmann's diagnosis of a dilemma implies that the question of the relationship between the two perspectives can always only be posed from one perspective or the other. When we reflectively pose the question of the relationship between the two perspectives, we are always already and always still irrevocably situated in one of the two perspectives. The different perspectives can only enter into a relationship with one another in such a way that they are perceived by means of one another, that is, in such a way that they are taken *into one another* in the process of perception.

Secondly, the skeptical diagnosis of a dilemma of rationality is also directed against the idea of reason as a neutral continuum. According to this idea, there are always transitions and mediations between the two perspectives (one of which has consequences for the other) that guarantee an adequate translation and judgment. In opposition to this, Luhmann's diagnosis of a dilemma implies that the two perspectives can be fundamentally heterogeneous to one another. When we reflectively refer from one perspective to the other in order to assess the former's consequences upon the latter, we always already and always still orient ourselves toward one particular model of perception or one particular criterion of judgment. The self-reflective perception and judgment of the system's consequences for the other implies, at the same time, an evaluation and rectification of the other in accordance with the system's own criterion and model.

After this recapitulation of the objections to a traditional concept of reason which are contained in Luhmann's skeptical diagnosis of an irresoluble dilemma of rationality, I can now return to the question posed above. This question asks whether these objections must also simultaneously lead to the wholesale abandonment of the idea of the critical self-reflection of a social system or normative perspective upon its violent environmental consequences. The resigned conclusion which Luhmann draws from his diagnosis seems to imply an affirmative answer to this question: "The environment becomes relevant insofar as it appears on the screens of our own system. . . . The system is dependent upon a blind flight which operates in accordance with tested, internally controlled indicators."[39] What is attainable, then, is not an insight which replaces blindness, but instead an insight into blindness itself: "We certainly cannot see what we do not see, but we can perhaps at least see that we do not see what we do not see."[40] If these "limitations of all observations" are acknowledged, however, then new "relationships of interaction with a greater transparency" can be formed: "We certainly still do not know what happens in the black box; but we know how we can deal with it, how we can use it."[41] The only difference is that these interactions are no longer based upon the illusion of an adequate perception. By abandoning the impossible, the project of knowing the other as itself, the system achieves the possible, the controllable registering of the other from outside, that is, from the perspective in which this other appears on the system's "screens" as a potentially disturbing fact.

By drawing this conclusion, Luhmann formulates the direct countermodel to the concept of self-reflection which was presented above using the example of the neo-Marxist analysis of consequences. The neo-Marxist analysis understands the self-reflective perception of a system's consequences as their judgment from the standpoint which asks about the degree to which these consequences can be viewed as valid counter-reasons—in accordance with the criterion of equality. By contrast, the system-theoretical analysis understands the self-reflective perception of a system's consequences as their registering from the standpoint which asks about the degree to which these consequences can be viewed as disturbing events—in accordance with the criterion of the reproduction of a system. If we apply this alternative to the destructive consequences which the idea of equality of the welfare-state has for the conduct of life of individuals—which are emphasized by the neo-Aristotelian and neo-Nietzschean analyses—then it only allows for a choice between two equally unconvincing possibilities. The first possibility consists in understanding the perception of a system's consequences as a judgment concerning external reasons. In this case, however, the welfare-state can no longer consider the impairments which the establishment of equality can give rise to—in the communal practice and transgressive processuality of life—as well-grounded objections; for these do not constitute good reasons for the reflection of equality. The second possibility consists in understanding the perception of a system's consequences as a registering of disturbing facts. In this case, too, the welfare-state can no longer consider the resistance of individuals, which arises in the name of the communal practice or transgressive processuality of their lives, as a well-grounded objection—for on the screens of a system there appear no reasons whatsoever. In the face of the destructive consequences of equality for communal practice and transgressive processuality, the choice between the neo-Marxist and system-theoretical understandings of self-reflection is a choice between two forms of blindness. It is a choice between a judgment of heterogeneous reasons, which must necessarily turn out to be negative, and a registering of disturbing facts, which can only be enacted in accordance with the criterion of a system's imperative of self-maintenance.

This alternative is not complete, however. The system of the welfare-state can refer to its environmental consequences not only by evaluating counterreasons (according to its criteria), or by registering disturbing facts (by means of its instruments), but also by ascertaining the existence of good counterreasons as facts. The impairments of communal practice and transgressive processuality which are brought to light—as against the social implementation of equality—in the name of the good life of indi-

viduals can certainly not be validated as good counterreasons in the reflection of equality. Nevertheless, the reflection of equality is able to expand
itself by means of the knowledge that these objections to equality are well
grounded in a different normative perspective, one which is heterogeneous
with respect to equality itself. On the basis of the reflection of equality, we
cannot know whether the objections to equality fail to be well grounded—
nor can we know whether they are grounded in a heterogeneous manner;
we can know this, however, *in the process of* the reflection of equality. One
normative perspective, the perspective of equality, is in fact able to reflectively extend itself, then, by means of an adequate perception of the other normative perspective, the perspective of the good life of individuals in
their communal practice and transgressive processuality; and it is able to
extend itself in such a way that it refers to the *results* of this different and
heterogeneous external justification as facts. This knowledge—which the
reflection of equality can obtain concerning the well-groundedness and legitimacy of the objections which are directed against it—is not, then, the
result of current participation in a process of justification. Instead, it is a
knowledge which consists in the retrospective remembrance of both a heterogeneous practice of justification and the results which this practice gave
rise to in its own time and place.

This is more than what still seems possible from the perspective of
Luhmann's skepticism in the face of the diagnosed dilemma of rationality.
This diagnosis reduces eccentric self-reflection to the zero degree of a perception of disturbances which is conscious of its own blindness. In contrast, the remembrance of the conditions of the good life of individuals, by
means of which the reflection of equality extends itself, retains a reference
to external claims of *justification*: it relates to the deviations and resistances of individuals not only as strategically calculable events, but also as the
results of good reasons. At the same time, however, this is less than what
was promised by the traditional concept of reason, and less than what was
practiced by the neo-Marxist analysis of consequences in its model of democratization. Neither of these take into account the fact that eccentric
self-reflection is interrupted by insurmountable hermeneutic limits. For the
remembrance of the conditions of the good life of individuals—by means
of which the reflection of equality extends itself—is simultaneously governed by the law of an irreducible externality. This remembrance does not

relate to external justification as such, the force of which can only be judged from inside by means of participation. Instead, it relates to external justification as a result which is retrospectively ascertainable from outside. The self-reflection of the welfare-state has to extend itself, then, in order to satisfy the requirement that a system's eccentric self-reflection upon its own consequences be rational. It has to extend itself by means of a *remembrance* of the results which were obtained by completely different modes of justification—those oriented toward the maintenance of communal practice and transgressive processuality. The perception of the system's consequences for the other means here the remembrance of the other in the system.

Such a solution of the hermeneutic problem of the perception of consequences would also have consequences with respect to the practical problem of making a decision in the conflict between normative perspectives. The outlined elucidation of the type and locus of retrospective knowledge—which the reflection of equality is able to obtain with respect to the whole spectrum of its consequences for individuals—does not provide us with any criteria of decision. It provides us, however, with a suggested understanding of the act of decision. This act should be understood neither as a submission to the mere power of facts nor as an insight into the "unforced force" of the better argument; it should be understood, instead, as a recognition of the power of heterogeneous justifications. If the adequate perception of a conflicting heterogeneous perspective implies the formation of an ability to remember, then the respect for such a perspective implies, in the process of decision, the recognition of its indissoluble power. This recognition of the perspective of the other can only take place by means of the limitation of our own perspective. The practice that corresponds to the hermeneutics of remembrance is a politics of memory.

In opposition to the unsatisfactory alternative between the system-theoretical and neo-Marxist understandings of self-reflection as a perception of consequences, I have made a series of suggestions concerning a third possibility. I would like to conclude this series with one final suggestion that once again concerns Hegel's above-mentioned "image" of a "tragedy in ethical life." In an interpretation of the final scene of the *Oresteia*, Hegel uses this image to formulate a model of the reconciliation that follows the dissolution of the unity of ethical life. Hegel obtains his model of a tragic reconciliation or tragic reason by reading this final scene as a scene of remembrance. What is remembered is a claim whose reasons are heterogeneous, a claim that our own dominant perspective has to reject as unjustified but which, at the same time, has to be recognized in its invincible "power" and specific "necessity." A practice of reconciliation corresponds to this scene of remembrance; it is the only one that is still possible in a world of hermeneutic difference and normative conflict. One power can recognize another only by limiting itself, by "giving up and sacrificing part of itself."[42]

4

Liberalism in Conflict:
Between Justice and Freedom

A. Tragedy in Ethical Life

In his early essay "On the Scientific Ways of Treating Natural Law," Hegel describes the revolutionary transformation of the ethical-political order through the emergence of the modern principle of equal subjective freedom as a "tragedy in ethical life."[1] On a closer view, however, the discourse of a "tragedy in ethical life" does not apply to the instantaneous event of this revolution, but instead to its long-term consequences: after the emergence of the modern principle of subjective freedom, the ethical-political order *consists* in the enactment of the drama of a tragic bifurcation. For, from this point onward, this order remains determined by fundamental principles which are both opposed to one another and irreducible, and which therefore can only recognize one another in "struggle"—a struggle which (and this is the point of application for Hegel's metaphor of tragedy) can only be arbitrated in such a way that it always breaks out anew.

The diagnosis of modernity as a tragedy in ethical life can also be found in some of the authors commonly known as "communitarians." Modern society, as Charles Taylor claims, is "outside of Arcadia," and therefore "can be seen under different, mutually irreducible perspectives," which are in "great and increasing tension" with one another[2]—and which thus lead to a "conflict,"[3] concerning which we "have to recognize that we are rightly pulled in both directions."[4] In the same way, Michael Walzer speaks of the "inevitable conflicts of commitment and loyalty" which define the "complexity" of civil society.[5] It is true that these authors differ in the affirmativeness of their relation to the modern reality of such conflicts—Taylor, for instance, tends to emphasize their risks, whereas Walzer stresses the chances that they open up. The adherence to the "tragic" diagnosis, however—which claims that an adequate picture of modern societies cannot be obtained without a recognition of their deep, and even insurmountable, conflictuality—unites these authors in a common front against the liberal theory of modernity.

For at the center of the liberal theory of modernity we find antitragic confidence in the fact that the ethical-political order of modernity is founded upon a concept of justice which consists in nothing other than the equality of freedom, which is guaranteed and put at the disposal of individuals: "Right is the restriction of each individual's freedom so that it harmonizes with the freedom of everyone else (in so far as this is possible within the terms of a general law)."[6] What Rawls calls, with reference to Kant, the "thesis of priority,"[7] that is, the thesis of the always decisive priority of justice as the right of equal freedom, is closely related to this. The thesis of priority is directly opposed, then, to the "tragic" diagnosis of an indissoluble conflictuality. At the same time, however, the unconditionality of the liberal priority of justice has a double, indeed, unequally strong, meaning.

In its first meaning, the thesis of the priority of justice only applies to the political order. According to this meaning, justice always has, in cases of conflict, a *political* priority, that is, a priority in the normative order of society; values and goods, for instance, the greatest well-being of everybody, or the preservation of community and its religious and cultural traditions, are always secondary to this priority. In its second meaning, however, the thesis of priority does not only refer to the public order, but also to the private life-conduct of particular individuals. According to this meaning, in cases of conflict justice always has an *ethical* priority with regard to the decisions of individuals; values and goods, for instance, the well-being of an individual or his particular group, are always secondary to this priority.

Two versions of the tragic (counter)diagnosis correspond to this double meaning of the liberal thesis of the priority of the right of equal freedom: the republican and the romantic. The republican version of the tragic diagnosis argues against the thesis of priority in its political meaning; the romantic version, by contrast, argues against the thesis of priority in its ethical meaning. According to the republican version, the priority of justice cannot have an unrestricted political validity because political orders are based upon a freedom of collective self-government, from whose enactment claims can arise which fundamentally conflict with what is legally required. For political freedom requires, according to the republican thesis, a seamless patriotic identification with a political community that is based upon prepolitical "we identities."[8] According to the romantic version of the tragic diagnosis, by contrast, the priority of justice cannot have an unrestricted ethical validity because the private conduct of life is based upon a freedom of individual self-choice whose enactment can also give rise to claims that fundamentally conflict with what is legally required. For private freedom requires, according to the romantic thesis, the individual's seamless personal identification with himself in his specific particular determination.

There are, then, two different dimensions of freedom. The two versions of the tragic diagnosis claim that the maintenance and enactment of these two dimensions can conflict with the legally guaranteed equal freedom of everybody without their being secondary to it in principle. According to the republican version, this is the dimension of the political freedom of collective self-government; according to the romantic version, it is the dimension of the private freedom of individual self-choice. The republican version of the tragic diagnosis therefore describes the indissoluble conflict of modernity in political terms, as a conflict between the incommensurable basic principles of the public order. The romantic version, by contrast, describes this conflict in ethical terms, as a conflict between the incommensurable basic principles of private life-conduct. This second, "romantic" conflict would be misunderstood, however, if its *meaning* were limited to this private sphere only because it has its *place* in the life-conduct of particular individuals. For it is precisely justice, according to the romantic claim, which the freedom of accomplished life-conduct can enter into conflict with, the very justice that is, according to the liberal claim, the "first virtue" (Rawls) of the political. Whereas the republican version of the tragic diagnosis claims the existence of an indissoluble conflict *in* the political order, the romantic version claims the existence of an indissoluble conflict *with* the political order—and precisely when the liberal priority of justice is applied to this order.

On the basis of these elucidations of the different versions of the tragic diagnosis, we can now attempt a first schematic classification of the specific reading of this diagnosis proposed by communitarianism. The communitarianism of the above-mentioned authors understands itself (to a large extent) as an elaboration of the republican objection to the liberal priority of justice—an objection that is raised in the name of a community which, although it is already grounded prepolitically, still needs, at the same time, to be articulated politically. The liberal critique, however, has rejected this concept of a community for good reasons.[9] For the central claim of the republican objection, which argues that the political freedom of self-government necessarily consists in the patriotic identification with a community which is also necessarily particular, is untenable. This does not invalidate, however, the communitarian arguments in favor of the truth of the tragic diagnosis and its objection to the liberal picture of modern societies. These arguments merely need to be understood differently, that is, in the sense of the romantic, and not the republican, version. According to *this* reading, the communitarian theory of community does not apply to a *political* value that is alternative to justice; instead, it undertakes a description of the freedom of an accomplished life-conduct in its conflict with the unconditional priority of liberal justice. It is this reading of communitarianism—and hence the romantic version of the tragic diagnosis—which I would like to elucidate in what follows.

B. Plural Freedom

According to the proposal just outlined, communitarianism needs to be understood not as a conception of the political freedom of collective self-government which collides with the liberal priority of the right of equal freedom, but as a theory of the private freedom of individual life-conduct. This opens up the question, however, of whether communitarianism can even be understood as the description of something that collides with the liberal priority of the right of equal freedom. For if communitarianism is a description of *private* freedom, then it is a description of precisely what should be protected by the basic liberal right of the equal freedom of everybody. But how can a description of something that is protected by liberal justice simultaneously be a description of something with which it conflicts? Can communitarianism—and, indeed, the *romantic* version of the tragic diagnosis—even be understood as a *version* of this diagnosis?

In order to answer these questions, we need first of all to reflect upon the locus and type of the concept of freedom in the liberal theory of justice. "Revisionist" liberals,[10] for instance, Dworkin, Larmore, Rawls, and Rorty, want—in contrast to traditional liberals—to preserve the neutrality of liberal rights with respect to all the historical and cultural presuppositions contained in values such as autonomy and individuality. In contradistinction to this, I presuppose in what follows, without being able to sufficiently justify it here, that specifically liberal rights cannot be grounded solely on the basis of the concept of justice; these rights can only be justified when this concept is taken together with the idea of subjective freedom. This liberal idea of subjective freedom is an interpretation of the idea of a free choice of our own lives, but it does not coincide with it; rather than being trivial and universal, then, it is demanding, as well as culturally and historically situated. For in the idea of a free choice of our own lives, we need to differentiate between two levels.

The difference between these two levels consists in the way in which—and this means, in the first place, how "strongly"—they understand the claim to a free conduct of our own lives. I would like to call the first sense of freedom the freedom of a person, and the second sense the freedom of a subject. The freedom of a person is a freedom from the domination of *others*; whoever is free as a person is not subjected to the arbitrariness of others. The freedom of a subject, however, requires more than this: it is also a freedom from the domination of *we*; whoever is free as a subject is not subjected to the power of a community.

Personal freedom, as a freedom from the subjection to the arbitrariness of others, consists in the capacity to be a master of oneself and not a slave. To be personally free, then, an individual only needs to be the author of the decisions that concern his actions. According to this sense, even the members of an ethical community that tolerates no deviation from its ideas of virtue are free. The specifically liberal basic rights do not, however, exhaust themselves in this. These rights cannot be obtained from the concept of personal freedom; instead, they are based upon the concept of subjective freedom. According to the sense of subjective freedom, the free choice of our own lives does not only imply that we are not completely dominated by the arbitrariness of individual others; it also implies that we completely determine and form our lives ourselves. Whereas according to the idea of personal freedom, the free choice of our own lives only implies that *we ourselves*, and no other in particular, dominate these lives, according to the idea of subjective freedom it further implies that *I myself*, and no communal we, lead my life. It is true that even subjective freedom does not imply that we determine our lives as we would like to in *every* respect—for this would only be a concept of negative freedom, on the basis of which no rights can be grounded. Subjective freedom implies, however, that we determine our lives as we would like to in every *relevant* respect. What is regarded as relevant can undergo historical and cultural change and can be interpreted in a more or less inclusive way. Nevertheless, it is only when subjective freedom in this sense is a good (and when the corresponding practices are regarded as relevant) that such specifically liberal rights as the freedom of religion, opinion, press, association, and so on can be justified.[11]

We need to distinguish now, as against personal and subjective freedom, a third level of the concept of freedom, a level at which a plurality of different doctrines of freedom can be found. The first two levels of the concept of freedom suggest what is at stake in free choices; that is, they suggest the *role*—person or subject—*in which* we make decisions or choices. The doctrines of freedom that constitute the third level of the concept of freedom do not undertake a further concretization of the role in which we freely choose; instead, they further concretize the *mode* of this choice. They suggest conflicting interpretations of what an ability to actually, truly, and freely choose our own life requires, that is, of the necessary acts and presuppositions of this free choice. The third level of the concept of freedom is the level of conflicting perfectionist understandings of freedom.

We can distinguish between three doctrines of freedom that are accorded a central significance in the contemporary theory and practice of liberal societies. I will call these the bourgeois model of the rational plan, the communitarian model of communal practice, and the individualist model of experimental perfectibility. The bourgeois model of the rational planning of life characterizes the doctrine of freedom that traditionally—

from Locke to Kant to Rawls—was connected with the justification of liberalism. By contrast, both the communitarian and individualist models have their roots in the romantic critique of the bourgeois model of planning. I will thus combine them in what follows under the heading of the "romantic" doctrines of freedom.

The first of the three conflicting doctrines of freedom is the doctrine of the plan of life—a doctrine that John Rawls, in *A Theory of Justice*, formulated by means of an Aristotelian motif taken up by Royce. According to this model, a truly free choice of our own life consists in its planning in the light of rational reflection. We can only speak of an enactment of subjective freedom in the choice of our lives if this choice takes place in the light of rational considerations. Rawls does not characterize these considerations in terms of their procedure, the rational *planning* of life, but instead in terms of their result, the rational *plan* of life. According to Rawls, that which decisively determines the orientation of the rational construction of plans of life is the desire to minimize the danger of the contingent failure brought about by external circumstances.[12] This means that the chosen plan of life needs to be "rational" in the sense that all internal and external risks are adequately calculated within it. If this is so, then even in the case of failure a relationship of self-affirmation can be preserved—one that draws its power from the knowledge of the rationality of the failed plan of life. In order to determine the rationality of plans of life, Rawls enumerates three further structural features: plans of life are reasonable if they are harmonious (with respect to the multiplicity of needs), realistic (with respect to the expectation of circumstances), and continuous (with respect to their overseeable duration). What is of decisive importance for the bourgeois model of the rational plan of life is, then, the connection of free self-choice with the concept of a risk-calculating and contingency-minimizing reason. As a consequence, this model remains dependent upon the idea of a self-relation which Locke explicitly described according to the model of the relationship to property: if (self-) preservation is the aim of a plan of life, then (self-) possession is its precondition.

I have already mentioned that the two other doctrines of freedom have their origin in the romantic critique of the first doctrine of a plan.[13] This is true, first of all, of the communitarian model of communal practice represented by authors such as Alasdair MacIntyre, Michael Sandel, and

Charles Taylor. This model connects free self-choice with relationships of "membership," that is, with participation in accomplished intersubjective relationships. Accomplished intersubjective relationships are understood in such a way that they constitute a common practice that consists, in turn, in the enactment of a common order of values. According to the claim of the communitarian model of practice, without participating in communal practice we cannot truly and freely choose our own lives. For it is only communal practice which makes possible the "mode of self-understanding" which we require for the enactment of freedom.[14]

We can now distinguish between two varieties of the justification of this claim: a substantial one that is directed toward the content of choice, and a formal one which is directed toward its procedure. According to the substantial variety, free self-choice consists in the affirmative orientation toward pregiven values. For MacIntyre, for instance, to freely choose our own lives means to embark on a "search" which, in contradistinction to the illusions of "modern individualism," would remain hopeless and disoriented in the absence of the bindingness of "inherited" moral "starting points."[15] In the course of this quest for our own lives, the aim returns to the beginning; for the values of common practice constitute the irreducible content of the individual search. As against this, the formal version of the communitarian model of communal practice refers to the procedure of choice.[16] According to this model, free choice needs to enact *itself* as an intersubjective practice of consultation, correction, and help; for the "actual practice of the guiding control of our own lives" is possible only when we have obtained an authentic insight into an articulation of the needs and valuations which are central to them. And we actually obtain this insight and articulation only in the intersubjective processes which—even in the formal variety of the communitarian model—remain related to the communal practices and values which are, *as a whole*, unquestionable.

Finally, the third central doctrine of freedom is the individualist model of experimental perfectibility, a model that has been elaborated, with an ever-increasing radicalism, from Schlegel to Nietzsche. This model of experimental perfectibility connects a truly free self-choice with a processual liquefaction of everything pregiven and achieved in an endless process of ateleological transformation. Friedrich Schlegel, for instance, does not understand perfectibility as "the paralyzing idea of the unimprovable," as the idea of the teleological progression toward an aim, but instead as the "ineradicable human capacity of perfection," as the ability to always again overcome every achieved state of self-being.[17] In the absence of the capacity of perfectibility—as the power of overcoming—self-choice cannot succeed. If the enactment of self-choice is a central *definiens* of true freedom, then its formation is one of the latter's central preconditions. It is for this reason that authors such as Humboldt and Mill, who base their theory of liberal politics upon the model of perfectibility, above all emphasize two preconditions of a transgressively understood freedom: an objective one and a subjective one. The objective precondition consists in the "diversity of situations" and experiences which need to be at the disposal of a particular individual in order for his choice to count, in the emphatic sense, as individually free, as the "energetic activity" of his "originality."[18] The subjective precondition consists in the readiness and, even more, the ability to accept that "the worth of different modes of life should be proved practically,"[19] that is, in the readiness or ability to understand our own lives and hence constantly revise them as "experiments" and "trials."[20] Taken together, the objective and subjective preconditions describe a relationship of distance with respect to every achieved, and even freely chosen, state that is conceived as a central moment of freedom: "he who is nowhere an outsider, can nowhere be perfectly at home. One cannot travel and, at the same time, cultivate one's field."[21] And insofar as this relationship of distance contains an active moment, the individualist model of perfectibility is, from the very beginning, linked to an affirmation of that which Schlegel calls the "hereditary defect of all greatness, the ability to also destroy," and which Humboldt calls "dangerous restlessness."[22]

The three doctrines of freedom are distinguished by their views concerning the necessary preconditions of true freedom in the choice of our lives. According to the bourgeois model of planning, the choice of a truly free life needs to be enacted in the form of a rational weighing that is oriented toward contingency-avoiding preservation as the substantially determined norm of reason. According to the communitarian model of practice (primarily in its formal variety), the choice of a truly free life needs to be enacted in the form of participation in a communal practice—the order of values of which is, as a whole, pregiven. Finally, according to the individualist model of perfectibility, the choice of a truly free life needs to be enacted in the process of diverse experiments that already make reference to transformability and transgressivity. Models of perfectibility and planning—in their rejection of the traditionalist model of practice—give pride of place to the distance from pregiven practices and values. On the other hand, the model of perfectibility and the model of practice agree in their skepticism concerning the metaphorics of (self-) possession toward which the model of planning is oriented. Finally, the model of practice and the model of planning agree in their rejection of the "irresponsibility" which is implicit in the idea of experimental perfectibility.

We can summarize these similarities and differences by elucidating the metaphor that conceives the subject as the "author" of his own life. For all three doctrines of freedom employ this metaphor as a point of orientation—even if they give to it fundamentally different meanings. The most common use of this metaphor can be found in the model of the plan of life, for this use orients itself toward an understanding of authorship which became prominent in the bourgeois conception of literature and which today is a commonplace. What is decisive here is the power of disposing one's own life; this explains the connection of this understanding with the concept of autonomy, which Joseph Raz describes as "(part) authorship of one's life."[23] The authorship of an autonomous subject is "partial" because it does not imply a power of invention, but instead a power of ordering and ruling: "The autonomous person is a (part) author of his own life. The ideal of personal autonomy is the vision of people controlling, to some degree, their own destiny, fashioning it through successive decisions throughout their lives."[24] The rational plan of life, which is programmed toward realism, harmony, and continuity, makes possible and extends authorship as this power of control.

It is precisely this part-author given the power of disposal who is degraded by the communitarian model of practice to the level of a mere "*co*-author";[25] according to this model, we can lead our lives only together with others. It is for this reason that the communitarian model of practice displaces authorship from the individual to his communal practice with others. In MacIntyre, for instance, the subject once again becomes a traditional storyteller. In storytelling, however, "the key question for men is not about their own authorship."[26] The question of bourgeois authors, the question as to how they *want* to view themselves, once again turns back into the preceding and insurmountable question of the storytellers: "Of what story or stories do I find myself a part?" This question concerns the way in which these storytellers *have* to view themselves as a consequence of their always already being entangled in these stories. In their depersonalization, however—their lack of an author—these stories resemble mythological narratives; because they are entangled with an objective order of "characters" and "roles," they are not invented, but instead handed down through tradition. The claim that we are the subjects of our own stories reduces itself to the ability to tell an understandable story about ourselves by means of an orientation toward those stories which are incorporated in the existing practice.

Nothing could be clearer than the opposition between this communitarian idea of coauthorship and the idea which Mill has in mind when he says that "among the works of man which human life is rightly employed in perfecting and beautifying, the first in importance surely is man himself";[27] for the man who creates himself as his own work gives himself "his own mode," to the extremes of eccentricity: "Human beings are not like sheep; and even sheep are not undistinguishably alike."[28] The individualistic model of experimental perfectibility is also opposed, however, to the authorship of a subject who, according to the model of planning, rationally calculates the risks of his identity. For the model of perfectibility proclaims that particular individuals are the authors of their own lives, and thus radically individualized, precisely because they (partially) give up control over them. To be the authors of our lives does not imply that we subject these lives to our own laws, but, on the contrary, that we expose ourselves to the external "diversity" of situations and experiences. Whereas, in the model of practice, the metaphor of authorship is oriented toward the traditional storyteller and, in the model of planning, toward the bourgeois writer, the model of perfectibility reformulates a moment of the romantic concept of "prose": it conceives the author not as the origin of a language, but instead as the decentered scene of a dialogue between incommensurable languages.

C. Individual Perfection and Social Justice

The outline of the doctrines of freedom given in the previous section was bound up with the thesis that all three can be classified as pertaining to the third level of the concept of freedom, that is, to the level which can be understood as a necessarily plural concretization of the fundamental liberal idea of subjective freedom. When applied to the first conception, the conception of a plan of life, this classification implies—in contrast to the assumption of traditional liberalism—that it does not constitute *the* canonical interpretation of subjective freedom in liberal societies, but instead only one interpretation among others.

What appears to be more problematic than this, however, is the classification of the two "romantic" doctrines of freedom—the communitarian doctrine of communal practice and the individualist doctrine of experimental perfectibility—as pertaining to the third level of the concept of freedom. For what goes along with this classification is a correction of the common self-understanding of these doctrines or, more precisely, of the idea that they are opposed to liberalism. According to this understanding, both the communitarian and individualist understandings of freedom are opposed to liberalism precisely because they formulate an alternative to subjective freedom, not a variety of it. This assumption of a fundamental opposition between liberalism and romanticism is revised by means of a classification of the two romantic doctrines of freedom as pertaining to the third level of the concept of freedom. This classification proposes that we understand the motives of these romantic doctrines in such a way that they can be integrated into an expanded conception of liberalism that is detached from exclusive concentration upon the concept of a plan of life. The romantic doctrines of freedom do not formulate, then, a different model than that of liberalism, but instead models of "another liberalism,"[29] or "redescriptions which serve liberal purposes."[30]

According to this reading, the fundamental opposition between the two romantic doctrines of freedom, on the one hand, and liberalism, on the other, turns into a partial opposition between these doctrines and a particular traditional reading of liberalism—and hence into an opposition which is not directed against liberalism but instead is founded upon it. At the same time, however, the thesis of the opposition between liberalism and the romantic doctrines of freedom contains a kernel of truth that cannot be dissolved in this way without remainder. And this moment of truth in the opposition between liberalism and the romantic doctrines of freedom is what makes up, at the same time, the moment of truth in the tragic diagnosis formulated at the beginning. For the moment of truth of the thesis of opposition consists in the unavoidable risk of a conflict between (subjective) freedom and (liberal) justice.[31]

I have already pointed out that the thesis of such a conflict necessarily has to appear paradoxical, because liberal justice consists in nothing other than the protection of equal subjective freedom for everybody. The priority of right and justice with respect to all other political values follows precisely from the fact that "the whole concept of an external right is derived entirely from the concept of freedom in the mutual external relationships of human beings."[32] The locus and object of the conflict between justice and freedom becomes apparent, however, if we unfold the ambiguity of this thesis of priority. The priority of justice is not only a priority *in the name of* subjective freedom; it is, at the same time, a priority *to* subjective freedom. For it is in the name of the freedom of *everybody*, whose external coexistence it guarantees, that justice subordinates the freedom of *individuals* to particular restrictions: "The concept of justice is independent from and prior to the concept of goodness in the sense that its principles limit the conceptions of the good which are permissible."[33] The priority of justice over all other political values is valid because it serves subjective freedom; nevertheless, the priority of justice can also imply a limitation of subjective freedom.

It is true that liberalism has always been aware of this. The fundamental liberal distinction between public justice and private freedom is accompanied by the recognition of their irreducible and loss-inducing heterogeneity. At the same time, however, liberalism has undervalued the conflictual potential that is contained in this loss-inducing heterogeneity of justice and freedom. The conflict between justice and freedom arises from the fact that the question concerning the loss of freedom that can legitimately be demanded appears in different guises in these two perspectives—public and private, political and individual. In its political guise, and in both of the meanings distinguished above, the priority of justice possesses an absolute validity. Justice always possesses priority over other political values, and, as a basic political principle, it always possesses priority over (conflicting) individual values. This is how things appear when viewed from the perspective of social institutions. Nevertheless, if things are to appear in the same way for individuals—over whose free choice the political justice of social institutions claims priority in cases of conflict—

then the priority of justice would also have to be individually valid. In this case, the priority of liberal justice would not only be a priority for institutions, and for us as participants in these institutions, but also for us as individuals; it would be not only a politically valid priority, but an ethically valid one.

The question as to whether the limitations of freedom—which even liberal justice cannot avoid imposing upon individuals—are always acceptable losses or the source of undecidable conflicts can only be decided if we ask whether the political priority of liberal justice can be extended and turned into an ethical priority which is also valid for individuals. The question as to whether the thesis of priority has an ethical meaning, whether it is also valid for individuals, can only be decided, however, if we take into consideration what makes up the true freedom of individuals. It is for this reason that the three doctrines of freedom outlined above enter into conflict with one another over the ethical claim to the priority of justice. The two romantic doctrines are situated on one side, then, and the doctrine of the plan of life on the other. The concept of a plan of life describes the freedom of individuals in such a way that the limitations which claims to justice impose upon them in cases of conflict still do not appear, at the same time, as external (heteronomous) limitations of their true freedom (understood as autonomy). This is why the claim to priority of justice does not allow for the emergence of a structurally irresolvable conflict with individual freedom. The romantic doctrines of freedom, by contrast, insist (by means of different arguments) that the limitations that the just order imposes upon individuals can be unacceptable for structural reasons, that is, for reasons of the constitution of the (true) freedom of individuals. Even the romantic doctrines of freedom do not dispute, however, the possibility of a reduction in the extent and field of the limitations that are imposed by liberal justice and the conflicts to which they give rise. But from a romantic perspective, the efforts which aim at this reduction are subjected to a condition which renders impossible their complete accomplishment: the justificatory nexus between justice and freedom requires an infinite effort—one which tries to coordinate the individual pursuit of true freedom with a socially institutionalized justice. This nexus does not contain, however, the promise of a final resolution of the collisions and conflicts between these two moments.

D. Double Contingency

The romantic doctrines of freedom do not only claim, in general terms, that conflicts between freedom and justice are possible in principle; they also point out the features of individual freedom which are responsible for these conflicts. In this sense, they are opposed by the doctrine of the plan of life, which attempts to prove, in its exemplary Rawlsian elucidation, that the political priority of justice is always acceptable from the perspective of individuals. This proof is intended to support a far-reaching claim: the claim of justice to institute a social "pact of reconciliation." In order to obtain a tenable "pact of reconciliation,"[34] it does not suffice to reach agreement about principles of justice; individuals need to endorse the judgment "that the principles they acknowledge are to override these beliefs when there is a conflict."[35] Principles of social justice are only able to institute social reconciliation between *all* particular individuals if there is also a reconciliation between *every* individual and social justice—if, as Royce puts it in his elucidation of the concept of a plan of life, "one happy sort of union takes place between the inner and the outer, between my social world and myself."[36] This "happy union" is obtained by means of the "loyalty" (Royce) of individuals to the principles of justice; this loyalty secures, as Rawls puts it, that "each frames his plans in conformity with them. Plans that happen to be out of line must be revised."[37] This obligation to revise our own plans of life in the name of justice includes the possibility that "we may in the end suffer a very great loss or be ruined."[38] The concept of the plan of life is supposed to prove that the limitations and revisions which are required by the absolute priority of justice are nevertheless rational—more precisely, that they are rational *for* individuals in the enactment, and not the impairment, of their true freedom.

In attempting to prove this, Rawls introduces three different arguments which can be ordered according to their diminishing range and strength, and their increasing plausibility. To each of these three arguments, which are introduced by the concept of a plan of life, there corresponds a counterargument derived from the romantic doctrines of freedom.

In the first argument, Rawls undertakes a doubly Aristotelian reformulation of the Kantian thesis according to which the just action of a person is the "most adequate possible expression of his nature as a free and

equal rational being."[39] Just action consists in "maintaining . . . public ar-
rangements";[40] and that by means of which we "best express" our "nature"
is simultaneously that by means of which we "achieve the widest regulative excellences of which each is capable."[41] By means of this double reinterpretation, the Kantian starting point, which imposes the obligation of
justice even at the cost of "ruin," leads to an Aristotelian result, in which
the individually good and the socially just are harmonized to the point of
their indiscernability: "It follows that the collective activity of justice is the
preeminent form of human flourishing."[42] According to this reinterpretation, there *can* be no conflict between the individually and freely chosen
conceptions of the good and the requirements of political justice—for activity in the name of political justice is the highest good toward which particular individuals unavoidably orient themselves in their truly and freely
chosen plans of life.

The first argument of the concept of a plan of life summarizes the
ethical priority of justice by claiming that justice possesses the "highest value" in every life, and that the activity that is oriented toward social justice
is, for human beings, the "best way to express their nature." The romantic
doctrines of freedom, by contrast, point to both the historical and the individual plurality of conceptions of the good—a plurality which renders
claims such as the above invalid from the outset: the concept of the true
freedom of individuals does not imply that, in the practice of their freedom, these individuals always strive toward justice as the highest good.

This originally romantic objection was not only appropriated by
Rawls in his later work. The concept of a plan of life (in *A Theory of Justice*)
already attempts to give a second and different justification of the individual validity of the priority of justice, a justification which is based upon
the structural, and not the substantial, determinations of plans of life. In
this second justification, the idea of reason that obtains in a planned, that
is, truly free, relationship to our own lives possesses a central significance.
For the very rationality of plans of life ought already to imply that they are
subjected to the conditions of justice: this rationality subordinates plans of
life to the "higher-order desire to follow, in ways consistent with his sense
of right and justice, the principles of rational choice."[43] Here, justice is no
longer the highest good *in* every plan of life, but instead that which "corresponds" to every chosen good: the concept of a life-planning reason im-

plies "the desire to adopt a particular point of view, that of justice itself."[44] Rawls elucidates this orientation of rational life-planning toward the criteria of justice in a double manner, that is, in a manner which corresponds to the thoroughgoing ambivalence of his concept of reason. On the one hand, reason itself is already understood, with reference to Kant, as an impartial and just consideration of every participant.[45] At the same time, however, Rawls also understands reason as a prudence that weighs risks— something which, for reasons of self-preservation, motivates individuals to calculate the limitations brought about by justice in the same way as they calculate every other external fact.

These two elucidations of the priority of justice—both of which try to ground this priority in the concept of reason—are, however, less than convincing: the first because it understands its point of departure, the concept of reason, in terms which are too demanding, that is, as a procedure which is already neutral in itself; the second because it interprets its result, the priority of justice, in terms which are not demanding enough, that is, as a mere prudential measure. At the same time, both of these elucidations are unable to do justice to a fact that is emphasized by the romantic doctrines of freedom: the fact of the ineluctable *incommensurability* between the leading standpoints of rational practical deliberation. In the practice of individual freedom, then, the concept of reason does not imply that justice is always the strongest reason.

This shows that even Rawls's second attempt to justify the priority of justice in the framework and upon the basis of individual freedom—upon the basis of a formal, and no longer substantial, determination of the highest good of planning reason—fails to attain its aim. For Rawls, however, what follows from this failure is not the abandonment of the thesis of priority and its political and ethical justification by means of the concept of a plan of life, but instead a transformation of the *meaning* of the expectable justification of the thesis of priority. This insight leads Rawls to a third and more promising argument, more promising precisely because it involves a recognizably weaker claim: the claim that the *reasons* for the priority of justice for individuals are always "decisive" is transformed into the claim that the consequences which follow for individuals from the priority of justice are always acceptable.[46] It is for this reason that the theory of a plan of life plays a completely different role in the third argument than it does in the first two. In this argument, it forms a basis for deriving the fundamental concepts of the priority of justice, and is then transformed into the role of a model of a truly free self-relation which makes the demands of justice with respect to individual freedom appear acceptable according to the logic of freedom itself, and which thus makes these demands appear satisfiable.

Rawls considers the individual acceptableness of the requirements of justice as guaranteed by a quality of the truly free self-relation to which the concept of a plan of life gives pride of place: the quality of (self-) responsibility. Responsibility primarily refers not to a state but to an ability; we *are* responsible for our plans of life insofar as we are *able* to assume responsibility for them. The fact that we are able to assume responsibility for our plans of life in turn presupposes that we are able to dispose over them, to shape, adjust, and transform them.[47] The idea of autonomy or self-determination implied by the concept of a plan of life has, therefore, a double reference: it refers not only to the (fictitious) instantaneous act of the devising of plans of life, but also to the continuous relationship to them. Self-determination is not a punctual ability, but instead a permanent one: it is the ability to continuously transform and adjust plans of life.

This reference to the ability of self-guiding and self-control, implied by the concept of a plan of life, no longer suffices to guarantee a "reconciliation" between the claims of social justice and those of individual freedom. This reference cannot justify the strong claim of the necessary orientation of life-planning individuals toward justice—as a value that is decisive in cases of conflict. For this would require the success of one of the two previous arguments which attempted to present justice as the highest good or strongest reason. By contrast, the weaker justification is provided by the concept of a plan of life in Rawls's third argument in favor of the thesis of priority: it refers to a concept of true freedom which involves a self-relation of responsible self-control—a concept which makes the requirements to which justice subjects particular individuals seem fundamentally satisfiable. According to the concept of a plan of life, the requirements of justice can only collide with certain freely chosen *plans*, but never with the freedom of self-responsible *planning* itself. For, according to this doctrine of freedom, the ability to (re)shape our plans of life in the light of our reasonable considerations—including those that concern the weight of the requirements of justice—is of central importance for the accomplishment of a truly free self-choice. According to this third argument, the justification of the priority of justice provided by the concept of a plan of life no longer refers to the reason of decision, but instead to the ability of disposal as a determination of true freedom.

The romantic doctrines of freedom dispute the fundamental acceptableness of the priority of justice even with respect to this third argument: as against the thesis that the self-relation of true freedom consists in the permanent ability to revise and adapt our own plans of life on the basis of rational considerations, the romantic doctrines of freedom point toward a feature of truly free self-relations which can be characterized as their "double contingency." For it is precisely with respect to the truly free self-relation that the romantic doctrines of freedom bring to the fore, in a double manner, a dimension of unavailability. Whereas, for the concept of a plan of life, unavailability only appears as a limit of freedom, for the romantic doctrines of freedom, it appears as an element of freedom. For, as against the autonomous authorship of guiding control, both communitarian coauthorship and individual self-experiment understand true freedom as an enactment of processes which are not at the disposal of a subject and hence contingent.

The first moment of contingency is described by the communitarian doctrine of freedom in the image of the coauthorship of subject and communal practice. For this doctrine implies the (partial) unavailability of that which subjects are thanks to their participation in particular communal practices. According to the communitarian doctrine of freedom, subjects are truly free only as members of inescapably particular groups. That which subjects have become by means of their membership characterizes, then, the determining qualities that are beyond their control without being a limit of their (true) freedom. The concept of a character, however, exceeds this. It includes all the qualities of human beings which, prior to the influence of their autonomous authorship, irrevocably determine them; according to Michael Sandel's formulation, character is constituted by those aims and qualities which we do not possess, but instead simply *are*—or which, indeed, possess *us*.[48] Even if such subject-constituting qualities are always supposed to be traces of relationships of membership, what is decisive for the understanding of the phenomenon of character, however, is not the origin and content of commitments, but instead their kind and force. The character of a human being is constituted by qualities, and therefore by aims, which are so inextricably caught up and entangled with the basic features of his identity that the requirement of their trans-formability would be absurd—because it could not even be conceived for *this particular* human being. This means that the true freedom of these in-dividuals cannot imply that they should acquire the disposal over these de-terminations. By means of their character, and hence innocently, persons are determined by conditions which are beyond their control.

If the concept of character describes the first moment of double con-tingency, then the concept of experiment describes its second moment. For the individualist doctrine of freedom also reformulates a moment of self-relational unavailability by using an image of the linguistic experi-ments carried out by a decentered author—experiments which cross one another to form the scene of a dialogue. In this way, this doctrine brings to light a second limit of the ideal of free self-possession that the concept of a plan of life introduces in order to secure the priority of justice. For inso-far as individuals experimentally relate to themselves and their lives, they also gradually expose themselves to the uncontrollable dynamics of these experiments.[49]

The dimension of unavailability that renders itself apparent in the decentered experiments of individuals is fundamentally different from the unavailability of their character traits. In their experimental self-relation, individuals always again transgress each achieved form of their self-being; this capacity of distancing assimilates the self-experiment to the image of a free, autonomous self-possession. At the same time, however, the experi-ments of individuals acquire their own uncontrollable dynamics. In their experimental self-relation, individuals break, on the one hand, with every determination—even with the determination of their own character; on the other hand, however, they do not reacquire their power of self-posses-sion in these experiments, but instead expose themselves to the logic, and especially the chances, of the process of their own experiments. It is for this reason that the experimental decenterings of individuals—like the de-terminations of their character—also place limits upon the sphere of their planning and reasoning decisions. When taken together, these two phe-nomena make up the central romantic idea that the affirmation of con-tingency—in its two guises of the contingency of being determined and the contingency of experiment—is an integral moment of an idea of true freedom. When taken together, these two phenomena also formulate the counterthesis to the thesis of a plan of life that claims that the self-transformations required by justice are fundamentally acceptable from the perspectives of individuals themselves. The individual perfection obtained by the acquirement of true freedom contains, according to the romantic idea, a certain measure of (affirmed) contingency—something which makes the fundamental priority of social justice appear unacceptable to individuals.

E. After the End of Sincerity

From the outset I have been distinguishing between two versions, a republican one and a romantic one, of the "tragic" diagnosis of an insurmountable conflictuality in the liberal order. The efforts of liberal theorists are generally directed toward the refutation of the objection that is connected with the first, the republican version. For this objection has a greater weight, claiming the validity of those political values which can oppose, and therefore also limit, the liberal legal order. In opposition to this, liberal theory shows that the liberal legal order is not situated at the same level as these values: liberal justice is a normative determination of the relationship between (opposing) values, and is therefore reflective with respect to them; for this reason it cannot be directly opposed to them.

Although I find this liberal metacritique of the republican objection convincing, it involves a misleading self-understanding. This self-understanding becomes apparent in the thesis that the level of political justice and the level of conflicting private values are linked only by a relationship of reflexivity which allows for their clear, and more importantly, strict, delimitation. This thesis is both true and false. It is true when the issue at stake is the *justification* of public justice, a justification that does not depend on any of the conflicting private values and doctrines of freedom—not even upon the doctrine of a plan of life. The positive effect produced by this strict delimitation of political justice and the private conduct of life consists, therefore, in the detachment of liberal rights and liberal politics from the perfectionist doctrine of freedom. For it is only on this condition that liberal societies can hope to survive unimpaired the crisis of the concept of a plan of life—a crisis which Lionel Trilling described, with the romantic critique of a plan of life in mind, as the end of sincerity and authenticity.[50] Liberal societies can hope to find by means of a strict delimitation between public and private, even after the end of sincerity, a satisfactory justification of the liberal legal order. Nevertheless, the hope to survive *unchanged* the crisis of the doctrine of a plan of life and to regain the former stability of liberal societies—a hope which is perhaps more characteristic of liberal theories than liberal societies—is unrealistic. After the end of sincerity, liberal societies can no longer unproblematically secure their public order upon the basis of private life-projects; and the mere delimitation of the two spheres cannot replace this security. This also shows what is false in the idea of a strict delimitation between public justice and private freedom. This delimitation cannot be strict because public justice is not only reflective *with respect to* conflicting private values; it is also a value *among*, and hence in conflict *with*, other private values. The fact that plural doctrines of freedom are not necessary for the justification of liberal justice renders the choice of them fundamentally private, although not without consequences for public justice: even as private, these doctrines can be opposed to liberal justice. At the beginning of this chapter, I characterized the thesis of this opposition as the "romantic" version of the tragic diagnosis. This version does not relate to the fundamental principle of the political itself, but instead only to its acceptance and stability: the romantic objection concerns the question of whether the politically unconditional validity of equal freedom reaches as far as, and hence is secured in, the level of the private conduct of life. Using the two romantic doctrines of freedom—the individualist and the communitarian—I have tried to show why this question can be given a negative answer not only from an empirical, but also from a normative, perspective.

If liberalism gives up its traditional form, and hence its foundation in the model of a plan of life, it does not become, however, free of conflict. For if liberalism is able to solve one conflict, the conflict concerning the basic values of the political order, it unavoidably exposes itself to another, the conflict concerning the private acceptance of this order. The solution of the old conflict and the creation of the new one are closely interrelated. This gives a description of what constitutes, under the conditions of liberal modernity, a universal fact—the fact that, as Rawls puts it in a citation from Isaiah Berlin, "there is no social world without loss."[51]

PART III

FORMS OF SOVEREIGNTY

The Permanence of Revolution

A. A "Monstruous Tragicomic Scene": Burke

Perspicacious contemporaries were already able to recognize in the events of 1789 precisely that future which some less perspicacious observers of our own time, that is, the time after 1989, believe (or perhaps only hope) belongs irrevocably to the past. The present of this revolution—"the most astonishing that has hitherto happened in the world"[1]—is, as these perspicacious observers perceived, its future. The revolution has no present; it is always already beyond its own present and beyond its own form. The revolution defines itself as its own future, it defines the future as (the future of the) revolution. It is for this reason that, in each present moment, the revolution is still to come. The spirit of revolution is the "spirit of innovation,"[2] "the spirit of change that is gone abroad."[3] The revolution is a beginning which, because it wants to be an absolute beginning, can come to no end. The revolutionaries act in such a way—and this is the reproach which Burke addresses to them—as if they "had never been moulded into civil society and had everything to begin anew";[4] they undertake nothing less than a "decomposition of the whole civil and political mass for the purpose of originating a new civil order out of the first elements of society."[5] Those who want to return to the beginnings in this way always have to go further. The permanence of revolution—which Trotsky declares, 150 years later, as its law—is, as was clear from the first moment for an observer like Burke, inscribed into it from its very beginning. Revolution is *defined* by the fact that it always has to go further. The revolution—which commences in order to "try to bring our fate under control, try to make the lot of every member of society independent of accidental circumstances, happy or unhappy"—entangles itself in the fate of having to proceed ever further without end; according to the judgment of Burke, this is truly "a monstruous tragicomic scene."[6]

With this aesthetic judgment on the revolution—"a monstruous tragicomic scene"—Burke did not only express his feelings of regret, contempt, and horror; he also indirectly pointed out where we are to find the reason for the revolution's need to always go further. The scene of revolution is "monstruous" and "tragicomic" because, from its own point of view, "the most opposite passions necessarily succeed and sometimes mix with each other in the mind."[7] The scene of revolution is "monstruous" and "tragicomic" because it is traversed by oppositions which, as a result of their remaining undissolved and unrecognized, condemn it to permanence. According to Burke, these oppositions already apply to the fundamental principle of revolution, which he locates in the idea of the equal rights of all human beings and understands as the claim that human beings are "strictly equal and . . . entitled to equal rights in their own government."[8] This idea of equality is, as Burke puts it, "abstract," as is first of all apparent in its sources: human rights are metaphysical and not political;[9] they are an "abstract rule," "taught *a priori*," independently of "times and circumstances."[10] The abstractness of human rights becomes apparent, secondly, in its consequences: because human rights are metaphysical and not political, they cannot be realized. "Government is not made in virtue of natural rights, which may and do exist in total independence of it, and exist in much greater clearness and in much greater degree of abstract perfection; but their abstract perfection is their practical defect."[11] This practical defect of perfection consists in being unrealizable, and in the fact that its realization thus requires an infinite effort and sacrifice. This is the self-contradiction which is contained in the fundamental principle of revolution, the principle of the equality of natural rights; and this self-contradiction condemns revolution to a permanent and endless continuation. By means of the idea of equality, the revolution imposes upon itself an obligation which no political action or institution will ever be able to satisfy.

Edmund Burke wrote his *Reflections on the Revolution in France* in

1789–90, in the form of a letter to a "gentleman in Paris" who had asked him about his views concerning the revolutionary events. As the subtitle of the *Reflections* makes clear,[12] Burke was also concerned with the "proceedings in certain societies in London relative to that event," in the course of which prorevolutionary declarations had been made. Burke's dramatic evocation of the monstrous and tragicomic features of revolution might have been able to cast doubt on the sympathies felt for the French Revolution by these supporters—and it might have been able to remind them of the merits of their own English Revolution of 1688. Whatever the success of Burke's essay with English readers, however, his critique was able to produce little influence on the part of French revolutionaries. For the features of the French Revolution which alternately horrify and amuse Burke are point-by-point identical with those which inspire and inflame the radical party which is simultaneously forming in Paris. For Burke, the picture of the revolution as a process of continual and precipitate revolutionizing— as a process which is driven by and expresses the inner contradictions of the fundamental principle of the revolution—is horrifying; for radicals like Babeuf, however, this picture represents the ideal toward which revolutionary politics should be directed. The conservative observers and opponents of revolution (such as Burke) are distinguished from its radical participants and precipitators (such as Babeuf) not by the content of *what* they see in the revolution, but instead by the way in which they evaluate it. The two groups are united—over and above their short-term failure and their long-term success—by the fact that they do not interpret revolution as a one-off act by means of which a new order is erected; they interpret it, instead, as a continual process which is always again driven beyond itself as a result of the internal contradictoriness of its principle. The two groups become enemies, however, because of the way in which they judge this process. If we follow Burke's metaphorics, we can understand this struggle between conservatives and radicals, which concerns the evaluation of the revolution, as a struggle between two critics confronted by a dramatic scene: the world-historical drama of the revolution. Whereas Burke perceives the revolutionary dynamic as monstrous and tragicomic, this dynamic produces on the radicals the opposite impression of the sublime. The radical discourse opposes Burke's denunciation of the revolutionary scene with an aesthetic affirmation, and it formulates this affirmation in a sublime judgment.

This conflict between aesthetic judgments is, at the same time, a conflict between political evaluations. The question as to whether the scene of revolution is, on the one hand, monstrous and tragicomic or, on the other hand, sublime concerns the revolution's legitimacy and its principle of equality. In what follows, I will discuss this question by inquiring into the procedure, reasons, and prospects which are appealed to by the radical party in its attempt to affirmatively rewrite Burke's negative judgment. We will see that the radical discourse of the adherents of the revolution is internally divided: the radical theorists of revolution are united by the fact that, when confronted with the "abstract" equality of rights, they do not, like Burke, diminish the stakes, but instead increase them by orienting themselves toward the perfection of equality. The radical theorists do not conceive the continuation of the revolution as monstrous, then, but instead as legitimate—and precisely because it is motivated by the sublimity of the normative demand for equality (B). What divides the radical theorists of the revolution is the way in which they understand this requirement of the perfection of equality. They elucidate their reasons for this requirement in opposing ways—one party conceives these reasons in utopian terms, the other conceives them subversively (C); as a consequence, they also have opposing understandings of the limits which the revolutionary perfection of equality runs up against (D). Before we can outline these differentiations of the radical discourse of revolution, however, we first of all need to correctly understand Burke's negative judgment.

The aesthetic judgment of the French Revolution as a "monstrous tragicomic scene" is not a single judgment; when viewed correctly, it can be seen instead as containing two judgments—and, what is more, two tensely differing aesthetic characterizations of the revolutionary event. These two aesthetic characterizations point toward two different aspects of Burke's thesis of the fundamental self-contradiction of the revolution—a self-contradiction which entangles the revolution in an interminable process and condemns it to permanence. The revolutionary process appears to Burke as *monstrous* because he discovers in it a logic of self-transgression. A body is monstrous if it is out of proportion with respect to its purpose; if, according to Kant's definition of the monstrous, "by its magnitude it nullifies the purpose that constitutes its concept."[13] If we think in romantic terms here, like Burke, then such a monstrous deformation of a body appears to be the result of an attempt to impose upon it an external purpose.[14] This is precisely what takes place in the revolution: the revolutionary principle of equality is a purpose which is alien to every political embodiment; it is a purpose which must always again overcome each of its political embodiments, and which can only represent itself *in* the political body in the form of its growth into a terrible and deformed magnitude and power.

The impression of the *tragicomic* character of the revolution is, by contrast, completely different. This impression does not arise because the revolutionary principle transgresses and distorts each of its embodiments; it arises, on the contrary, because the revolutionary principle undermines itself in each of its embodiments. Accordingly, it is the revolution itself which brings about what it struggles against—and what struggles against it. The revolutionary principle of equality is tragicomic because every step of its realization can bring about nothing other than a (new and different) inequality. The principle of equality is tragicomic because every attempt to translate it into political regulations ends up—and this is what Burke points out to the French National Assembly—with "the utter subversion of your equalizing principle,"[15] that is, with the recourse to "a principle totally different from the equality of men, and utterly irreconcilable to it"[16]—a principle of new hierarchical discrimination.[17] In a process which is both tragic and comic, the revolution obstructs its own success. Because this obstruction remains hidden to it, the revolution always continues to search for this success—and, as a consequence, always continues to fail. Whereas the revolution has monstrous consequences in the infinite *progressivity* of its self-transcending claim, it is tragicomic in the interminable *circularity* of its attempts and failures.

In these two aesthetic predicates, the monstrous and the tragicomic, Burke thus advances two different readings of the futile permanence of the revolution: according to the first reading, there is an infinite continuation of its self-transcending; according to the second reading, there is an endless circular movement of its self-undermining. How does the judgment of the sublime—by means of which the radical discourse replies to the conservative critique of the revolution—relate to this?

B. "Perfect Equality": Babeuf

In his "Manifesto of Equals" and his self-defense in the trial of 1797, François-Noel Babeuf, who assumed the name Gracchus, formulated the sublime reading of the revolutionary process with great decisiveness (something which he certainly did not lack), and in a manner which greatly influenced radical discourse. At the center of Babeuf's manifesto stands the conviction that the French Revolution is "only the forerunner of another, even greater, that shall finally put an end to the era of revolutions. The people have swept away the kings and priests who have been leagued against them. Next they will sweep away the modern upstarts, the tyrants and tricksters who have usurped the ancient seats of power."[18]

The task of the present is to bring about this future revolution: "The hour for decisive action has now struck," to "offer" the "world" a "fascinating play,"[19] to decisively lead the revolution beyond its present state. For Babeuf, as for Burke, this dynamic of the revolution follows from its own principle—a principle which is opposed to political reality. Nevertheless, Babeuf reads this opposition in a different way than Burke: not from the perspective of political reality, and as a sign of the illusoriness of the revolutionary principle, but from the perspective of the revolutionary principle, and as a sign of the fact that the revolution is concerned with something "far better and far more just" than that which it has attained—or even dared to demand—so far.[20] This is the core of that sublime interpretation of the revolutionary process which radicals oppose to the conservative critique: the process of revolutionary self-overcoming is not, for radicals, an end in itself; this process becomes necessary, rather, in the name of the infinite claim which is raised by radicals in their appeal to the normatively correct principle of equality, that is, in their appeal to the correct understanding of this normative principle.

Babeuf also sees this normative principle in the idea of equality; the revolution has committed itself to this idea with its declaration of the rights of man. Babeuf understands revolution, in the horizon of the theory of natural law, as the political act by means of which society attempts to reproduce that equality of human beings which it lost when it departed from the state of nature.[21] What is decisive for the radical discourse, however, is the way in which it interprets the declaration of the rights of man, which is only a first and incomplete step in the realization of the program of the social (re)production of the natural equality of all human beings. With this interpretation, radical discourse decisively departs from those theories which we can retrospectively call "liberal." For authors such as Locke, Voltaire, Jaucourt, and Kant, the equality which can be socially reproduced by means of laws is limited from the very beginning for structural reasons. When Jaucourt, the author of the *Encyclopédie*'s article on equality, claims that men become "equal again by means of laws," he hastily reassures his readers that this can in no way be understood in such a way that he "fanatically approves of that illusion of absolute equality which can hardly bring about a community in a state."[22] In his *Dictionnaire philosophique*, Voltaire similarly claims that equality "is, at the same time, the most natural and the most chimerical thing": it is natural if it is understood as the equality of human beings "in the depth of their hearts"; it is chimerical if we try to derive from it the equality of offices, property, and social and economic position, that is, if the fact of "natural" equality is taken as the basis of a demand for "absolute" or "perfect" equality in the state of society.[23]

Locke had already provided the decisive argument for this liberal conviction of the necessary limitation of equality—an argument which is again taken up by Kant—when, in a later paragraph of the *Second Treatise*, he rejected those radical demands which had been derived from the natural equality established in the first paragraphs: "Though I have said above, Chap. II, *That all Men by Nature are equal*, I cannot be supposed to understand all sorts of Equality."[24] The inequality which exists because of age or virtue, excellence or income, because of birth, alliances, or good deeds, nature, gratitude or respect—"all this consists with the *Equality*, which all Men are in, in respect of Jurisdiction or Dominion one over another, which was the *Equality* I there spoke of, as proper to the Business in hand, being that *equal Right* that every Man hath, *to his Natural Freedom*, without being subjected to the Will or Authority of any other Man."[25] This is the argument of liberals in favor of an internally limited equality: a limitation of equality is made necessary not primarily because of the circumstances and difficulties of its realization, but instead because the idea of equality is already limited from the very beginning—and because it cannot even be meaningfully comprehended except as limited. According to this liberal position, social equality can only be the equality of the right to natural or negative freedom; the idea of equality is limited in this way in accordance with its very concept.

The radical position is directed against this liberal thesis, according to which the equality required by the declaration of the rights of man is limited, in its very concept, to the one and only right to the equal freedom of the will.[26] For Babeuf, the "political equality of right," that is, the equality of all citizens before the law and in legislation, is merely "abstract" or "conditioned."[27] For on its reverse side, inequalities of all kinds and degrees unfold: the "brute force and instinct" of human beings "establish between one man and another a wide de facto inequality, notwithstanding the formal equality of rights."[28] The liberal theorists had also in no way disputed this. In opposition to them, however, Babeuf sees a contradiction in this simultaneity of legal equality and actual inequality. At the basis of this view, there lies a different interpretation of the idea of equality. The equality which is limited to the legal sphere is "unreal," a "legal fiction, beautiful, but baseless,"[29] according to its own criterion. In order "to have any other object than the achievement in life itself of the rights of man,"[30] that is, in order to actually be able to achieve what it requires, we therefore need to go beyond it: "What else do we need other than equality before the law? We need not only this equality as it is written down in the Declaration of the Rights of Man and of the Citizen; we need it in life, in our very midst, in our homes."[31] Equality remains unreal as long as it is realized merely as political-legal equality; in order to realize equality, we need to exceed its political-legal form.

This surpassing of every given and limited form of equality is what constitutes the decisive difference between the liberal and radical understandings of it. The principle of equal rights can certainly be understood—as is shown by Rawls's, Dworkin's, and Sen's development of liberalism into its social or political form—in a more comprehensive sense than in Locke or Kant; an equal right does not only have to be an equal right to negative freedom. In the social or political liberalism which extends equality, however, this equality is still limited to the "central social arrangement" in its distinction from the "remoter peripheries" of society—where inequality needs to be accepted.[32] From the perspective of the radicals, by contrast, the principle of legal equality is subjected to a dynamic which cannot be limited in advance by any distinction between dimensions. This dynamic follows from the fact that every legal arrangement of equality, however narrow or broad its limits, needs to be understood as the result of the realization of a demand which, according to *its* meaning and validity, is absolute or infinite. For the radicals, the demand of equality is not, as Locke (*and* Sen) maintain, a demand which is determined and limited from the beginning by rights. The demand of equality is motivated by an unlimited demand—a demand, as Babeuf puts it, for something which is "greater or more sublime" than such determination and limitation.

The radical discourse contains two elucidations of this claim concerning the ("sublime") infinity of the idea of equality which are fundamentally different, and even opposing, not only in their justifications, but also in their consequences. The first of these elucidations derives its thesis solely from the *concept* of equality. According to this elucidation, the idea of equality itself already aims at the ideal of a "perfect" equality. This is the conviction which serves as a basis for Babeuf's critique of the abstractness and unreality of legal-political equality—the conviction that all definite and hence limited demands for equality are motivated by "the memory of a Golden Age when there reigned among men that true and perfect equality."[33] Behind every demand for equality there stands, then, a utopia of equality. In its first version, the radical discourse elucidates the sublime infinity of the demand for equality by means of its utopian content.

It is difficult to see how Babeuf might want to justify this claim, although he was not particularly concerned with justifications. He had as evidence the revolutionary events which were taking place before his eyes—events which referred, in their symbolic self-interpretations, to a utopia of equality which exceeds the content of its political-legal rulings. The role of this utopia of equality was played here by ancient democratic republics. The appeal to these republics in the political, celebratory, and artistic rhetoric of the revolution was decisively influenced by a determination of democracy which, in Montesquieu's exemplary formulation, defined the "love of democracy" as the "love of equality."[34] In ancient democracy, Montesquieu continues, "real equality" was "the very soul of a democracy,"[35] for this democracy was subjected to the "principle of equality"[36]—the principle that "every individual ought here to enjoy the same happiness and the same advantages."[37] It is in the name of *this* ideal of perfect equality, an ideal bound up with ancient democracy, that the French Revolution's declaration of the equal rights of all human beings takes place. This is the evidence which Babeuf appeals to: in the absence of the ideal of an "actual" or "perfect" equality—an ideal which Locke delimits the equality of the right to natural or negative freedom *against*—this equality of right could not even have been politically established. In the revolutionary struggle, nobody risks his life for the equality of right alone. This struggle could only have taken place, at least in Paris—and this is the conviction of both Babeuf and Burke—because it was a struggle in the name of, or, more precisely, under the guise of something different: a utopian state of equality which far exceeds what is struggled for.[38]

Whatever the more general plausibility of the link which Babeuf establishes between the revolutionary demand for equality and a utopia of equality, the political consequences of this utopian reading become strikingly apparent precisely in the French example. For the ancient democracy which functions here as a utopia of equality can only guarantee the same to everybody insofar as it presupposes that everybody already wants the same. "The love of equality, in a democracy, limits ambition to the sole desire, the sole happiness of rendering to one's country greater services than other citizens."[39] Democratic equality, in the ancient sense, is an equality of entitlements only because it is an equality of virtue, or of the striving for virtue, which is in "service to the fatherland." Every citizen of Babeuf's "republic of equals" must also want the same, that is, the public good; otherwise he is "ambitious" or even "selfish."[40] When Babeuf threateningly adds that such a citizen "probably will not at first like" the way in which the "republic of equals" deals with him, this already suggests the consequences of the revolutionary utopia when equality of virtue and love for the fatherland can no longer be presupposed, as they are in ancient democracies. As Hume already suspected of the idea of perfect equality, the revolutionary state must "degenerate into tyranny" in order to hunt out inequalities by means of "rigorous inquisition," and in order to be able to fight these inequalities in their roots.[41] According to the reading proposed above, however, this result is precisely what Burke's judgment of the monstrous character of the revolution is directed toward: the revolution displays a "monstruous" scene because, in the name of the principle of revolutionary equality, it allows political control to swell to a "terrible" magnitude and power. This applies most precisely to Babeuf. For if the infinity of the demand for equality is understood, as in Babeuf, in a utopian manner—as the demand for a state of perfect equality which is modeled according to the ancient republican ideal—then, under modern conditions, it will lead to precisely that monstrous expansion of the state which so terrified Burke during the revolution. In its first utopian version, then, the radical discourse is unable to successfully refute Burke's objection.

C. The "Categorical Imperative" of Upheaval: Marx

The first utopian version of the radical discourse needs to be distinguished, however, from a second. This second version can be extrapolated from the famous formulation by means of which the young Marx grasped the impetus of revolution: "The criticism of religion ends with the doctrine that *for man the supreme being is man*, and thus with the *categorical imperative to overthrow all conditions* in which man is a debased, enslaved, neglected and contemptible being—conditions that are best described in the exclamation of a Frenchman on the occasion of a proposed tax on dogs: Poor dogs! They want to treat you like human beings!"[42]

Like Babeuf, Marx traces the political-legal revolution, which follows from the critique of religion, back to an imperative which impels it and, at the same time, leads beyond it. We once again find here the "sublime" interpretation of the process of revolution in the discourse of radicals—an interpretation which is directed against both conservatives and liberals. Marx's formulation, however, defines the imperative of revolution in a completely different way than Babeuf. Babeuf understood this imperative, in a utopian manner, as "the first rule of nature"—according to which we have to produce a state of perfect equality. In Marx's formulation, by contrast, the imperative of revolution aims "*to overthrow all conditions* in which man is a debased, enslaved, neglected and contemptible being." Marx does not interpret the imperative of revolution in a utopian manner, but instead subversively. This Marxian imperative of subversion also *leads*—in the same way as Babeuf's utopian imperative—to the demand that we overcome the existing order of merely political-legal equality, which is conceived as "abstract," in favor of an order of "real" equality. Nevertheless, whereas Babeuf believed that the demand for (more) equality which motivates the revolutionary process is grounded in the desirability of its *aim* of egalitarian relationships, Marx's formulation traces the revolutionary demand of equality back to a preceding and, what is more, negatively oriented impulse: the impulse which is directed *against* all relationships of debasement and contempt. This is the decisive difference between the two versions of radical discourse. For Babeuf, the revolutionary demand for (more) equality is original—it has its origin in the intrinsic value of a state of perfect equality. From the perspective of Marx's formulation, by contrast, the demand for equality which keeps the revolutionary process in motion is methodologically *secondary*: it is a response to the prior imperative of subversion—according to which we should overthrow all relationships of debasement and contempt. Revolution demands equality because it expects it to overcome debasement and contempt. Revolution leads to the demand for the perfection of equality, but it *begins* with the objection to debasement and contempt.

From the beginning, however, and by means of two untenable preliminary decisions, Marx prevented this fundamental reinterpretation of revolution—from utopia to subversion—from extending into far-reaching consequences. The first decision is expressed in the latent objectivism of Marx's formulation—according to which the imperative of revolution is directed against "all conditions in which man *is* a debased, enslaved, neglected and contemptible being." The existence and means of the debasement, enslavement, neglect, and contempt of human beings are, for Marx, objectively ascertainable—this is a question of (correct) theory. The second decision by means of which Marx denies himself the benefit of his formulation consists in a class-theoretical narrowing of the definition of "*all conditions* in which man is a debased, enslaved, neglected and contemptible being." "All" relationships of debasement, enslavement, neglect, and contempt are concentrated, for Marx, in the work and life conditions of a single class, the proletariat. When taken together, these two decisions produce the effect that Marx fails to properly understand that very same objection to debasement and contempt which, according to his own reinterpretation, constitutes the presupposition and beginning of the revolutionary process. Debasement, neglect, enslavement, and contempt cannot, firstly, be comprehended objectively; instead, these phenomena are affectively experienced *by individuals*. It is for this reason, secondly, that a single experience of debasement, neglect, enslavement, and contempt cannot replace or represent all other such experiences; what counts is the experience of *each individual*.

If we take these two objections seriously, then we can see that Marx's reinterpretation of revolution opens itself up to a reading which is able to liberate radical discourse from the utopian premises which it rests upon in Babeuf. According to Marx's reinterpretation, revolution is not motivated by utopian demands for equality, but instead by the objection to debasement, neglect, enslavement, and contempt. In the light of the two objections stated above, this claim needs to be understood in such a way that the origin of revolution is seen to be constituted by individual experiences of debasement, neglect, enslavement, and contempt—which are the experiences of each individual. In its beginning, revolution is nothing more than the reorientation of the political toward such experiences of debasement and contempt. Revolution is the place or, better, the time in which everybody's experiences of debasement, neglect, enslavement, and contempt are expressed and brought to light. It is for this reason that revolution cannot be defined by its future, that is, by the state of equality which it attempts to produce; instead, it can only be defined by its present, a present which attempts to break with the past. Revolution has to be defined by the practice which it itself enacts. This is not a practice which demands that everybody should receive the same; instead, it is a practice which realizes, here and now, the state in which everybody gives voice—once again or for the first time—to their experiences of debasement, neglect, enslavement, and contempt.

Because this revolutionary practice consists in a bringing to light of the experiences of everybody, we can also characterize it as "democratic." Of equal importance, however, is the fact that this revolutionary practice is hermeneutic; revolution needs to interpret before it can transform.[43] Revolution is an act of interpretation: it is an interpretation which derives a demand for a different state of society from the experiences of debasement, neglect, enslavement, and contempt which it gives voice to. By means of this derivation, revolution redescribes the subversive impulses which are directed against individual debasement, neglect, enslavement, and contempt as political demands. We can speak of "derivation" and "redescription" here because the interpreted experiences and the resulting demand for equality are linked to one another in a relationship of indissoluble asymmetry. Experiences of debasement, neglect, enslavement, and contempt originate in the feeling that an individual has been injured in a dimension which is essential for the accomplishment of his life. This feeling is already bound up with both a motive and a reason for a counterreaction: the fact that somebody *feels* himself to be injured motivates his counterreaction; and the fact that somebody feels himself to be *injured* justifies this counterreaction. If somebody feels himself to be injured in a dimension which is essential for his life, he already has a good reason for an individual counterreaction.

This does not already suffice, however, as a good reason for a political revolution. In the same way that revolution begins by giving voice to the experiences of each individual, without being able to consist solely in this, these feelings of injury can only become revolutionary demands to the extent that they can be interpreted politically (in a particular way). In this political reinterpretation of individual feelings of injury, revolution necessarily *distances* itself from that with which it begins. In the process of interpretation which is enacted by revolution, a difference opens up between the starting point and the result. Revolutionary demands emerge by means of an interpretation of individual feelings of injury; at the same time, however, these feelings are reshaped, and put in their proper place as injuries which can be explained socially, on the basis of relationships of inequality, and fought against politically, by means of the establishment of relationships of equality. Revolutionary demands are the result of a reinterpretation which derives from an individual perspective of felt injury and, at the same time, departs from it.

The early Marx, as we saw above, already distorted the interpretative character of the revolutionary process as a result of the objectivism of his theory of classes. This is why he could not adequately express the double relationship of justification *and* difference between individual feelings of injury and political-revolutionary demands of equality. This relationship left traces, however, in Marx's formulation of the categorical imperative of revolution. For this formulation is traversed by ambivalences which can only be elucidated if they are traced back to the difference between the two perspectives which are linked to one another in the revolutionary act of interpretation: political demands for revolution and individual experiences of injury.

The first of these ambivalences becomes apparent in the fact that not all of the feelings of injury which are mentioned by Marx—feelings of debasement, enslavement, neglect, and contempt—can be equally translated into revolutionary demands. What individuals equally experience as injury is presented to the revolution under two completely different aspects. From a political perspective, these feelings of injury differ with respect to their causes—and hence also with respect to the extent to which they can be contested. Neglect, for instance, is a condition the cause of which remains indeterminate; it can be the result of fate or accident. The expressions "debasement," "enslavement," and "contempt," by contrast, refer—at one and the same time—to an affectively disclosed state *and* to an action which has brought this state about. By means of these expressions, then, we interpret the injury of an individual as the result of an action. Whereas, from an individual perspective, we equally feel, and hence also equally react against, the injuries of debasement, enslavement, neglect, *and* contempt, revolutionary or, more generally, political action can only be directed against those injuries which—like debasement, enslavement, and neglect, and *unlike* contempt—can be understood as the result of an action. Indeed, the cause of such politically interpretable individual injury has to allow for its own further limitation. Marx's formulation points in this direction when it demands that we overthrow "*all conditions* in which man is a debased, enslaved, neglected and contemptible being." Individually experienced injuries can become revolutionary demands only if, firstly, they are not brought about by fate or accident (as is the case with feelings of neglect), and if, secondly, they can be understood as debasements, enslavements, and forms of contempt which are brought about by transformable social relationships.

Individual feelings of injury are first of all indeterminate, then, with respect to their causes; what is decisive for individuals is the fact *that* they feel injured. Revolution, by contrast, interprets these feelings by determining them to be caused by social relationships which can be transformed by means of revolutionary action. As Marx's own examples make clear, this interpretation and determination is, at the same time, a process of cutting down and narrowing: what we individually experience as an injury can be brought about not only by social relationships, but also by individual actions—and even by accident and fate. There is a fundamental asymmetry between individual feelings of injury and revolutionary demands: even if a revolution gives voice to all feelings of injury, it can only take some of them seriously.

The ambivalence between an individual and political perspective is clear, however, not only in this first aspect of Marx's formulation—in the question concerning the causes of injury—but also in its second aspect, which concerns the constitution of injury. The expressions used by Marx—"debasement," "enslavement," "neglect," and "contempt"—characterize the injuries which are done to individuals under completely different aspects: in feelings of debasement and contempt, we are concerned with the value which is accorded to an individual (which can furthermore relate to achievement or status); in feelings of enslavement, we are concerned with freedom and self-determination; in feelings of neglect, we are concerned with the need for security and closeness. This shows why Marx enumerates precisely *these* feelings of injury: they obviously concern the impairment of fundamental needs or claims whose satisfaction or fulfillment can be demanded by revolution. Because Marx misrecognizes the interpretative character of revolution, however, he fails to show that, when this vocabulary of feelings is used for political aims, it already presupposes, at a fundamental level, interpretations which go beyond individual feelings of injury, that is, interpretations which redescribe and delimit these feelings in such a way that they lead to political demands for revolutionary "upheaval." This reinterpretation needs to assume, firstly, that feelings of injury can be rendered transparent with respect to presupposed and disappointed expectations. Secondly, it needs to assume that these impaired expectations are shared by everybody. Thirdly and finally, the political recourse to individual feelings of injury implies that we are concerned here not only with claims which are impaired by certain social relationships, but also with claims which can be satisfied by means of the establishment of different social relationships. None of these assumptions is self-evident; each of them selects and isolates an ever narrower circle of the phenomena of individual feelings of injury. What is omitted by the first assumption can be characterized as the dimension of "attunement" in feelings of injury—a dimension which does not exhaust itself in their semantic content of unsatisfied expectation. The second assumption reduces feelings of injury by omitting the dimension of the individual—a dimension which is inherent in all affectively disclosed expectations. Finally, the third interpretative premise reduces our affective expectations by eliminating their moment of irredeemability, a moment which accompanies every expectation and compels it to outlive every possible satisfaction. This renders apparent the second aspect in which a revolution which raises demands for more equality needs to undertake a reinterpretation of its starting point—of individual feelings of injury. Revolution interprets these feelings as something which they are not in themselves, that is, from the perspective of individuals: it interprets them not only as objections *to* existing social relationships, the first aspect of the causes of injury, but also as political demands *for* different social relationships, the second aspect of the constitution of injury.

The revolutionary act of interpretation—this is how we can summarize the process described above—makes out of individually experienced injuries a political problem of social relationships. This reinterpretation works, if it does work, like a translation: individually experienced debasement, enslavement, neglect, and contempt come to appear as so many forms of oppression to which we are subjected as social persons, that is, by means of the social relationships in which we live; and they come to appear as claims which can be satisfied by different social relationships. All political demands, and especially demands for (more) equality, originate from such processes of the interpretation and translation of individual experiences of injury. This is the objection which the subversive discourse makes to both the liberal and utopian concepts of equality—an objection which concerns the *status* of the demand for (more) equality. According to both the liberal and utopian conceptions, this demand is grounded in itself. According to the subversive conception, by contrast, the demand for (more) equality is one of the political demands into which individual experiences of injury can be translated.

What is decisive here is the fact that this translation of individual injury into a political problem of social oppression cannot succeed completely; it cannot imply a replacement. This means that individual experiences of injury always possess a broader scope than that which is demanded by revolution. For we can also experience as injurious many situations which are not brought about socially, and which certainly cannot be made good on politically.[44] Nevertheless, individual experiences of injury remain the ground for revolutionary demands: these demands emerge from these feelings by means of processes of political (re)interpretation. This is true not only in a motivational sense, but also in a normative one: individual feelings of injury motivate revolutionary demands; at the same time, however, they also grant them a claim to normativity. Revolutionary demands are raised in the name of the struggle against individually experienced injuries. This characterizes the meaning of revolutionary demands, a meaning which their interpretatively obtained content always and necessarily falls behind.

D. The Tragicomedy of Revolution: Excurses on Danton and Figaro

From the perspective of the above-drawn consequences of Marx's formulation of the categorical imperative of upheaval, the subversive version of radical discourse appears as a conception of the ineradicable difference between the normative motivation of revolution, which stems from individual experiences of injury, and the normative content of its demands, in which these injuries are traced back to politically transformable social relationships. In these consequences, the subversive version of radical discourse contradicts Babeuf's utopian version. Both of these versions agree that the revolutionary process always has further to go. This appeared to Burke as a monstrous self-transcending of the revolution in the direction of an aimless and self-destructive magnitude. As against this, I have described the radical discourse, in both of its versions, as a "sublime" reading of the revolution: this discourse explains—and hence justifies—the permanence of the revolutionary process on the basis of the normative content of its fundamental impetus. For the normative content of revolution does not exhaust itself in an understanding of equality which is limited to negative freedoms—this is the wholly convincing objection which radical discourse, once again in both of its versions, raises against liberalism. The *opposition* between the utopian and subversive version of radical discourse opens up, however, with regard to the question concerning the understanding of this fundamental impetus of the process of revolution and its irredeemable surplus.

This opposition can be determined, firstly, with respect to its content: Babeuf's utopian version understands the impetus of revolution as the *striving toward* perfect equality; Marx's subversive version, by contrast, understands this impetus as a *struggle against* debasement, enslavement, neglect, and contempt. The utopian version understands the impetus of revolution positively, the subversive version understands it negatively. In both versions, the impetus of revolution is understood in such a way that it drives the revolutionary process ever further. The two versions understand the ground of this conviction, however, in completely different terms. In Babeuf's utopian version, the surplus of the impetus of revolution is understood quantitatively: revolution is motivated by the desire for an equality which is greater than that which it can demand and implement at any particular time. Qualitatively, however, these two moments do not differ at all: revolution desires equality, and revolution establishes equality; in a final utopian state, the two moments should coincide. The utopian version expresses a position of identity. In the subversive version of radical discourse, by contrast—which I have taken from Marx's formulation of the "categorical imperative" of revolution—the surplus of the impetus of revolution over revolutionary measures is understood qualitatively. This is why I called this version a position of difference. This means that the revolutionary demand for equality—according to the subversive version of radical discourse—is not an aim in itself, but instead a means for the realization of a prior and irredeemable motivation.[45] The demand for equality is raised in an objection to individually experienced injuries. The egalitarian relationships which are demanded by revolution remain related to these injuries in accordance with their normative meaning. It is for this reason that these relationships cannot be measured according to the simple criterion of their ability to achieve "more" equality. This would be an empty criterion because there is always *still* more equality. Revolutionary demands and measures are directed, rather, toward the overcoming, *by means* of more equality, of the very same experiences of debasement, enslavement, neglect, and contempt which first motivate them.

This opposition between the fundamental normative understandings of the two forms of radical discourse has decisive political consequences. As we saw above, Babeuf's utopian version is unable to convincingly refute Burke's objection that revolution has to degenerate into a monstrous magnitude. This immediately follows from the fact that Babeuf is only able to see a quantitative difference between the impetus of revolution and its demands and measures—and from the fact that he sees these two moments as qualitatively identical. This is why the impetus of revolution only exerts its influence in one direction—toward an ever broader expansion of equality. In contrast to Babeuf's identitarian conception, Marx's categorical imperative of revolution grounds the demand for equality in something other, upon which this demand remains dependent. This other—the objection to individually experienced injury—drives the revolutionary demand for equality at the same time as it limits it. The "categorical imperative" of the overcoming of individually experienced injury is both the ground and the *corrective* of the revolutionary demand for equality.[46]

This also allows the subversive version of radical discourse to convincingly confront Burke's second aesthetic judgment upon the scene of revolution—according to which this scene is not only monstrous, but also tragicomic. At what does this judgment of the tragicomic aim? According to a superficial determination, the tragic and the comic differ with respect to their outcome: an outcome is tragic if it is bad, if we lament or fear it; it is comic if it is good, if we laugh about or enjoy it. The tragic and the comic also possess a common structure, however: they are—and both the Sophoclean character of Oedipus and the Aristophanean character of Socrates show this in an exemplary manner—both forms of self-undermining. This is why I claimed at the outset that Burke's judgment of the tragicomic summarizes his diagnosis, according to which there occurs, in the process of revolution, an "utter subversion of its own principle of equality." The revolution is both tragic and comic in its own self-contradiction. This is also obviously the reason for Burke's conviction that his "mixed feeling" of the tragicomic justifies a negative political judgment. The revolution falls prey to Burke's critique not because it cannot be definitively described as either tragic *or* comic, that is, because it mixes up these two determinations; instead, it falls prey to his critique because it has a structure which is untenable in both cases—the structure of a self-contradiction which cannot be resolved, but instead only avoided.

The utopian version of radical discourse recognizes the self-contradiction of revolution which Burke diagnoses only in the aesthetic variant of bourgeois tragic drama: it is only because of betrayal or weakness that the revolution can undermine its "sublime" principle in the very attempt to realize it. The contradictions which the revolution entangles itself in appear to utopian radicals in a double aspect: they pose a constant threat and thus require an unrelenting vigilance; but, at the same time, they are fundamentally avoidable and do not put into question the project of revolution. According to the subversive version of radical discourse, this comforting certainty, by means of which the utopian radicals underplay that self-undermining of the revolution observed by Burke, is misleading. This follows from the difference which this version locates at the center of revolution: the difference between the individual experience of debasement, enslavement, neglect, and contempt and the political demand for (more) equality. This tension does not only imply that the demand for equality can be justifiably driven ever further; it brings about the inverse movement, which Burke describes as the self-undermining of the revolution. In the subversive version of radical discourse, the self-undermining of the revolution is no longer accidental; it is, rather, a necessary moment.

Furthermore, the subversive version of radical discourse admits the necessity with which the revolution undermines itself in two different forms. In the first form, the self-undermining of the revolution is something that *happens* to it, for the revolution also brings about a social order of equality which not only cannot overcome all insults and debasements, but instead is the cause of new ones. To every social order, there correspond experiences of injury and debasement which not only cannot be done away with by this order, but which are instead produced by it. This also applies—as to every order—to the new order of equality which the revolution sets up. It is *only* to the revolution, however, that this appears as a fatal logic of self-undermining. For only the revolution is impelled by the drive to "subvert" *all* relationships of injury and debasement. Nonrevolutionary political conceptions—like, in the end, Rawls's political liberalism—can classify the new injuries and debasements which they bring about as the unfortunate side effects of a good thing.[47] For a politics which understands itself as revolutionary in the sense defined above, however, these injuries and debasements constitute a tragedy.[48] This is the view of Georg Büchner's Danton, for whom the revolution, because it gives a hearing to the complaints of everybody, is compelled to hear the cries of those who he killed in the name of the revolution. Danton's "enemy," which hounds him to death, is his "memory"—which he counterposes to Robespierre's "conscience." Danton does not oppose the revolution, however: he understands it differently, not as the subversion of a certainly known normative principle, but instead as the reorientation toward the injuries of everybody. Danton takes this revolutionary reorientation to the extreme: to the point where it turns against revolution and revolutionaries, including himself.

If, in this first form, the self-undermining of the revolution is its fate, then, in a second form, it is its own act: the self-undermining of the revolution does not only happen to it; the revolution *wants* and, indeed has to want, to undermine itself. That is, what appeared to Burke as self-contradictory—sometimes tragic, sometimes comic, but in every case self-contradictory—the fact that the revolution takes recourse to "a principle totally different from the equality of men, and utterly irreconcilable to it," belongs, according to the subversive version of radical discourse, to a conclusive self-understanding of the revolution. This is what informs the view and action of Ödön von Horvarth's Figaro—even if only as a stage-character—when, by releasing its enemies, he seals the fate of the very same revolution in which he has participated. This is not, as Count Almaviva at first suspects, the "end" of the revolution; it is, as the simple words of Figaro make clear, its victory: "only now has the revolution triumphed, because it is no longer necessary to lock in the dungeon men who cannot help being its enemies." This also follows from the fundamental tension that, according to the subversive version of radical discourse, the revolution enacts and indeed is made of. If the revolutionary demand of equality is only raised in objection to individually experienced insult and injury; and if, however, at the same time, the revolutionary order of equality leads to new—different and hopefully fewer—insults and injuries, then the self-undermining and self-withdrawal of the revolutionary aim of equality, in the name of individually experienced insult and injury, belong to the arsenal of the revolution's political measures.

The first form of self-undermining, the one that fatefully happens to the revolution, is tragic; the second form, the one that the revolution itself enacts, is comic. For subversive radicals, as for Burke, the self-undermining of the revolution consists of both forms; it is sometimes tragic, sometimes comic, and sometimes both at the same time—that is, tragicomic. The fact that the revolution undermines, whether unintentionally or intentionally, its own pursuit of equality is not, however, an argument against it, but instead an argument for it. It is only this which provides a full description of the subversive version of radical discourse. For what is demonstrated here is the fact that only the subversive version of radical discourse can fully do justice to Burke's critical diagnosis of the revolution. Burke criticizes the revolution because of the permanence of its process—which he saw as grounded in its principle of equality. Liberals reject this claim by understanding the revolution as a unique act of the establishment of an egalitarian basic order. The price for this is the limitation of the idea of equality in respects which are determined in advance. As against this, the utopian radicals accept the progress of the revolution—indeed, they demand this as a consequence of the surplus content of the idea of equality. This affirmation of the revolutionary process and its accelerating progress also remains attached, however, to the idea of its possible end: in a utopian state of realized equality. Only the subversive version of radical discourse is able to think the permanence of the revolutionary process with Burke and, at the same time, to justify its normative content against him. And it is able to do this precisely because it considers the permanence of the revolutionary process in both of the aspects identified by Burke.

At the beginning of this chapter, I distinguished these two aspects as those of the infinite progressivity and endless circularity of the revolutionary process. It is on the basis of his observation of these two aspects that Burke grounds his negative aesthetic judgments of the revolution as monstrous and tragicomic. The subversive version of radical discourse rejects these judgments by normatively justifying the double temporal logic of the revolutionary process, that is, its progressivity and circularity. This logic follows from the normatively correct understanding of the revolutionary principle of equality. According to this understanding, the revolutionary process continues infinitely because the principle of equality has to be continually examined and transformed in the light of individual experiences of injury; this is the subversive reinterpretation of Burke's demonstration of the progressivity of the revolutionary process. At the same time, the revolutionary process always withdraws itself because the principle of equality must also be refracted and restricted by the differently directed demand of the avoidance of individual injury; this is the subversive reinterpretation of Burke's demonstration of the circularity of the revolutionary process. The subversive version of the radical discourse of revolution does not only elucidate, however, the normative meaning of the two aspects of the permanence of the revolutionary process described by Burke; it also, and at the same time, elucidates the internal connection between these aspects. For both the infinite progressivity and the endless circularity of the revolutionary process follow from the same: the new understanding of the revolutionary principle of equality, which is neither restricted in a liberal fashion nor finalized in a utopian one. This basic principle defines the subversive version of radical discourse by means of its difference with respect to individual experiences of injury, and therefore defines it as internally divided. It is for this reason that the subversive version of radical discourse can think the infinite progress of the revolutionary process without delivering it over to terror; and it is for this reason that it can think the always again necessary self-withdrawal of the revolutionary process without surrendering it to absurdity.

Mercy and Law: Carl Schmitt's Concept of Sovereignty

A. Neutrality and Sovereignty

Carl Schmitt diagnosed the "age" of liberalism, which he thought had come to an end, in terms of a "neutralization."[1] This diagnosis of neutralization is connected with Schmitt's more general—and, since Hans Blumenberg's critique, highly controversial—description of modernity as the result of a process of secularization. More concretely, however, a central aspect of the neutralization diagnosed by Schmitt is constituted by that far-reaching transformation in the concept of the political which he sees as being bound up with the establishment of liberal, parliamentary democracies. "Neutralization" implies here that the sphere of the political has lost its "independence." Carl Schmitt explains this loss of independence as the result of an ascent of the "rationalistic concept of law" in the theory and practice of liberal democracies: the political is neutralized when (or because) it is subordinated to a rationalistic concept of law. And, when the rationalistic concept of law is observed more closely, it can certainly be seen to be accompanied by a double neutralization of the political: the law appears neutral in its ground and in its consequences. It appears neutral in its *ground*, firstly, because when the law—and here that means, above all, the "basic" law—is understood rationalistically it is not seen to emerge on the basis of an independent political foundation; the law is not made, but instead discovered as that which everybody already wanted. The law appears neutral in its *consequences*, secondly, because when it is understood rationalistically it is not seen to realize itself by means of an independent process of application; the law is realized not by means of an interpretation or correction, but instead by means of an immanent determination of its cases, as that which they already mean in themselves. The law legislates and interprets itself; this is the double neutralization of political, that is, of publicly binding, decisive action that is practiced by the rationalistic concept of law.

If Schmitt conceives such neutralization as the decisive characteristic of the liberal form of the political, then his opposition to this is epitomized by the idea of the recovery of political sovereignty. The sovereignty of the political implies here (at the very least) that the political is not determined by means of a rationalistically understood concept of law. This requirement relates to both aspects of neutralization. It applies, firstly, to the formulation and passing of laws—which has to be understood, according to Schmitt, as a process of sovereign decision. It is this aspect of the idea of sovereignty which, for the most part, stands at the fore in contemporary discussions concerning the independence of the political. The fact that it has to be understood as a process of sovereign decision applies above all, however, for Schmitt, to the interpretation and application of laws. Schmitt is pursuing here, first of all, a political aim: he is concerned with the justification of the dictatorship of a "highest authority which is legally able to dissolve the law."[2] This is the sovereignty of the *executive*, a sovereignty which Schmitt gives the right to "suspend" the law—at least temporarily and in particular situations. Schmitt's writings from the 1920s, and the numerous critiques of them which have been advanced since then, turn around the question of the necessity and possibility of such an executive sovereignty. It is easy to overlook here the fact that Schmitt did not originally ground his basic idea—the idea that a sovereign decision is required not only for the establishment of laws, but also for their application—by means of an analysis of executive decisions. Instead, he grounded this idea by means of an analysis of juridical decisions. If we observe the actual and "contemporary" practice of legal decisions—and this is already Schmitt's thesis in *Law and Judgment*—then the application of laws proves to be an underivable and "independent problem."[3] Application is underivably "independent" with respect to the very laws it applies; the application of laws is always also concerned with something *other* than laws and their application. And, at the same time, the application of laws is the confrontation of laws with their other; Schmitt calls this other the "concrete individuality, the social actuality of life."[4] For this reason—because application confronts the perspective of law with the *other* perspective of "life"—application is always also accompanied by the possibility of a "dissolution" or "suspension" of the law.[5] And it is this possibility that turns the application of law into a sovereign decision.

In what follows, I want to show how Carl Schmitt's concept of sovereign decision presents itself when it is observed from this perspective, that is, from the perspective of his analysis of the "contemporary" practice of the application of law. I therefore consider Carl Schmitt's concept of sovereign decision in a form which is systematically restricted with respect to its far-reaching political implications (and heavy burdens). I am only interested here in a first characteristic of the work of Carl Schmitt; I am not interested in the conclusions he draws—in my view, unjustifiably—from this characteristic. By means of this approach, however, the objective ground of Schmitt's concept of sovereignty emerges more clearly. This ground consists in the critique of a political order which considers itself neutral, in the sense that it considers itself to be relieved of the confrontation with, and implementation with respect to, its other, in the sense that its relationship to its other does not appear to it as an "independent problem." As against this, Schmitt calls "sovereign" an attitude which enacts and endures the confrontation of law with the "concrete individuality of life." I want to show in what follows that Schmitt is right to defend such a sovereign attitude against liberal neutralizations. He is wrong, however—that is, he sacrifices the potential of his concept of sovereignty—when he orients his elucidation toward the model of dictatorship. This orientation is not, however, accidental: it is grounded in a fundamental conceptual deficiency, in the absence of an appropriate concept of justice.

B. Application and Exception

The thesis that the application of laws is more than the mere application of laws is not new; it is as old as the concept of law itself. Beyond that, in recent language-theoretical discussions concerning the relationship between rule and action, norm and practice, this thesis has been repeatedly put forward without inferring from the independence of application the sovereignty of the decision, which, according to Schmitt, in applying the rule simultaneously "dissolves" or "suspends" it. Schmitt himself repeatedly turned this "innocent" understanding of the independence of application, as one could call it, against rationalism, "for which everything concrete is only a case of the application of a general law."[6] Interpreted "rationalistically," the application of law appears to be a mere subsumption, the "technical functionalism" of a self-propelling "machine."[7] "Every concrete juridical decision," however, as Schmitt objects, "contains a moment of contentful indifference, because the juridical conclusion is not derivable from its premises without remainder."[8] The application of law never attains a "calculable determinacy." The reason for this is certainly "that a concrete fact has to be judged concretely, even if the only standard given for this judgment is a legal principle in its general universality. There is, then, every time, a transformation."[9] No norm "interprets and administers, protects or looks after itself," for no norm already *contains* the cases of its application.[10] The application of a norm in a concrete situation therefore "adds something," because every norm—in the name of its generality, and hence necessarily—is indeterminate with respect to its cases.[11] There follows from this, in a double sense, an indeterminacy of the norm's meaning: an indeterminacy of its semantics and of its relevance. There is an indeterminacy of semantics because an act of interpretation is required in order for us to be able to use the linguistic expression of a norm as a description of the existing facts. And there is an indeterminacy of relevance because an act of weighing is required in order for us to be able to evaluate the specific weight of a norm in the judgment of a case. This is a first way, then, in which we can speak of the "independence" of application with respect to the law: the application of the general to the singular cannot be solely derived from the general; for the general only acquires its meaning in its application *to* the singular.

This independence of application, which is also described by Schmitt, cannot, however, be the one which is implied by his concept of sovereignty. For, in the sense elucidated so far, independence simply means that the application of a law is, at the same time, its transformation: every new application transforms the law, to the extent that (as Wittgenstein says) it "continues" those prior applications which constitute the meaning of the law. The continuation of prior applications does not imply their undifferentiated repetition, but instead a transformation—sometimes greater and sometimes smaller—indeed, a transformation of the individual application and hence of the whole law which is interpreted by means of its applications.[12] In contradistinction to this transformative moment, Schmitt calls the application of a law "sovereign" if or because it *suspends* the law. The transformation of laws is not, however, the same thing as their suspension. (These two things *would* only be the same if the rationalistic understanding of the application of law, which Schmitt rightly criticizes, were correct.) This is also the reason why Schmitt does not ground the moment of sovereignty in the application of law upon the fact that all situations are irreducibly concrete, and hence upon the fact that all applications of the law are transformative. Instead, he grounds this moment upon the fact that some of these situations are "situations of exception": "The definition of sovereignty which is customary today—and which goes back to Bodin—arose from the knowledge of the fact that, in consideration of the concrete situation, it always again becomes necessary to make exceptions from the generally valid law; and he is sovereign who decides on the exception."[13] The application of law has to be sovereign because in every individual case and situation we have to decide not only how, but also *whether* a law can be applied—we have to decide whether law can be realized at all. In Schmitt's sense, an exception is not an exception from the application of a particular law in favor of another, but instead an exception of the law itself. With a view to this possibility of exception, every realization of law must also decide upon the existence of a state of exception. It is this decision, and this decision alone, which Schmitt calls "sovereign."

The explanation of the sovereign decision's relationship to the exception already refers, before every further determination, to two of its most important aspects: its cognitive content and its reflective status. In Schmitt's elucidation of sovereignty, it has certainly become customary to emphasize, under the heading of "decisionism" which Schmitt himself has provided, the moment of an equally definitive and underivable decision. Schmitt's thesis—that the realization of law requires sovereign decision— then takes the form of an observation according to which both juridical and political discussion cannot go on endlessly, but instead requires a decision that cannot be derived with "calculable determinacy." According to this conception, he who possesses the "highest power" of decision is sovereign. If, on the other hand, the first sentence of *Political Theology* describes as sovereign he "who decides upon the state of exception," "it is this case which makes the question of the subject of sovereignty, that is, the question of sovereignty in general, relevant."[14] If sovereign decision can be determined and justified only on the basis of its relation to the state of exception,[15] then the fundamental aspect of Schmitt's concept of sovereign decision is not the fact that it is a decision which is made in the last instance or with the highest power. What is fundamental, rather, is *that which* sovereignty decides *upon*: it decides on nothing at all, but instead upon the existence of the state of emergency. Although Schmitt insists that the situation of exception cannot be "described according to the state of affairs" and that the claim of its actuality cannot "be justified without remainder," we can refer to this as the diagnostical or *cognitive* dimension of the concept of sovereign decision. The decision upon the state of exception is certainly a "decision in the eminent sense"; this is its decisionistic moment. At the same time, however, it is also a decision concerning the question whether a situation is or is not a state of exception. The sovereign decision ascertains and determines the type of a situation.

As against a merely decisionistic understanding, the cognitive content of sovereign decision is the first aspect which follows from the constitutive relationship of decision to the exception. The second aspect is that of the specific reflexivity of sovereign decision; this second aspect also conflicts with a one-sided decisionistic understanding which externally opposes the sovereign decision to the application of laws. The sovereign decision is not reflective here in the sense that it weighs up different possibilities. Following Kierkegaard, Schmitt criticizes such a reflective stance as the aesthetic attitude of the avoidance and, indeed, prevention of choice and decision. For when it is understood aesthetically, reflection consists in a "deliberation" which seizes an intention "with a hundred arms," plays out the "manifoldness" of all its facets and aspects in "imaginary constructions in thought," only in order, in the end, not to have "advanced a step further."[16] As against this, then, the sovereign decision is not reflective because it plays out the alternatives to the customary application of laws, but instead because it directs itself toward the "presupposition" of this application: toward that which it blindly and unthinkingly presupposes. This presupposition of the application of laws or norms is the presupposition of the absence of exception, of the "normality" of a situation. And "actual normality" is certainly "not merely an 'external presupposition' [of the norm] which the jurist can ignore; it belongs, rather, to its immanent validity. . . . A normal situation has to be created, and he is sovereign who definitely decides whether this normal state reigns."[17] Because it ascertains the exceptionality or normality of a situation, the sovereign decision stands in a relationship of reflexivity with respect to the customary application of norms. The right of sovereign decision to suspend the customary application of norms is not characterized by the fact that it results from a final authority, but instead by the fact that it follows from such a reflective attitude. The sovereign decision suspends the application of norms and laws by reflecting upon it. A decision is sovereign, then, when it interrupts this customary application with the question concerning the type of the situation and hence its own presupposition. The sovereign attitude ends with a definitive decision—this is the decisionistic moment. It begins, however, diagnostically and reflectively, with a radical question concerning the normality which is assumed. A realization of law is sovereign when it puts itself in question, when it puts this question to itself.

C. The Presupposition of Homogeneity

A decision is sovereign when—in a particular situation, and with a view to the application of laws—it poses the question of exceptionality or normality. Schmitt talks of the "absolute form" of a state of exception "if the situation in which legal precepts can be valid first has to be created."[18] For in order for us to be able to validly apply legal precepts, the situation must fulfill certain presuppositions. "Every general norm requires a normal currency of life-conditions to which it ought be applied according to the case and which is subjected to its normative regulation. The norm needs a homogeneous medium."[19] The state of exception, by contrast, is a state of disintegrated normality—something which implies, according to Schmitt, a broken "homogeneity." This is why the reflective diagnostics of the sovereign decision is directed toward the "homogeneity" of the "medium" in which norms or laws come to be applied: the leading question of this diagnostics is the question of whether homogeneity exists or not. For the existence of homogeneity is, as regards the application of norms or laws, the presupposition of "normality."

This connection between the application of laws and the presupposition of homogeneity can be elucidated on two different levels. On the first level, the concept of homogeneity refers to the transformative logic of the application of laws described above. We are concerned here with the application of the same laws to different cases and, to this extent, with a claim or production of equality; insofar as a law can be applied to different cases, these cases *are* equal from the perspective of this law. The talk of a "homogeneity" of cases as a "presupposition" of the application of laws refers to the fact that our concept of the validity of the application of laws is not exhausted by means of such a concept of equality as the merely abstract applicability of the same laws. The applicability of a law is already taken for granted if a situation *can* be described as the case of a law on the basis of individual features. "Homogeneity," however, aims at a similarity of cases which exceeds the mere applicability of a law. The "homogeneity" of the (different) cases does not only make the application of the (same) laws possible, it also renders it "appropriate" in a substantial sense:[20] it is a commonality of cases which is "concrete" to the extent that it exists in the light of the weighted or, more precisely, appropriate application of a law, that is, an application which considers the case in all of its aspects. If such a homogeneity does not exist, then it is inappropriate to apply the law, despite its applicability. An exception has to be made to the application of the law; its application must be disregarded.

Once again, however, Carl Schmitt's concept of homogeneity aims at something different from, and more specific than, this claim to appropriateness. This is demonstrated by his understanding of *non*homogeneity, of heterogeneity in the state of "exception," "emergency," or "conflict."[21] Such a disintegration of homogeneity, of the homogeneity which is the presupposition for the application of laws, sets in a situation of irreconcilable conflict—a situation exemplified for Schmitt by the religious civil wars of the seventeenth century or by the ideologically charged and paramilitarily enacted class struggles of the 1920s. In contrast to these conflicts, the homogeneity which constitutes the normality of a situation characterizes political "unity." This is no longer homogeneity in the (just described first) sense of an objective similarity of different cases—which, in the light of all aspects, allows the application of the same law to appear appropriate. Schmitt understands homogeneity, rather, in a (second) sense: as a political agreement which binds together both sides, the addressees and the authors, of the application of laws.

It is in Schmitt's theory of democracy, formulated in polemical opposition to liberal parlamentarianism, and under the explicit inclusion of dictatorship, that this political agreement is most clearly described as the "substantial homogeneity of the whole people."[22] Political agreement here is traced back to the existence of common features in a restricted group. On the other hand, however—and up to the point of his transformation from a thinker of sovereign decision into a thinker of "concrete order" in 1933–34—Schmitt repeatedly criticized the attempt to trace political unity back to a prepolitical—ethnic, cultural, social, religious, or even moral—commonality.[23] Such a tracing back constitutes, for Schmitt, an apolitical substantialism, a common feature of all varieties of political romanticism.[24] This critique of political romanticism corresponds to Schmitt's definition of the political by means of the distinction between friend and enemy—a definition which does not determine political homogeneity positively and substantially, but instead negatively and formally. Accordingly, a political unity is homogeneous when it is not afflicted by the "most intensive opposition" between friend and enemy. This does not mean that in the politically homogeneous unity there is no dissent, no conflict of interests and opinions. It does mean, however, that this conflict is "relativized," that it does not assume the "most extreme degree of intensity" which is bound up with the genuinely "political" determination of the other as an enemy. For, in this latter case, the other is determined as someone who "is existentially something other and alien, in such a way that, in the extreme case, conflicts with him are possible which can be decided neither by means of a codification made in advance nor by means of the verdict of a 'disinterested' and hence 'neutral' third party."[25] In contrast to such a state of hostility and conflict, political homogeneity reigns when conflicts unfold within the framework and limits of commonly shared convictions. Political homogeneity, understood negatively and formally, is nothing more than the absence of "existential" hostility.[26]

Such homogeneity, suggests the thesis of Carl Schmitt just cited, is the presupposition of normality of the customary application of norms or laws. The application of a norm presupposes normality because it can only succeed when no hostility reigns. The application of norms is only possible where these norms and the procedures and instances of their application are fundamentally accepted. The "enemy," by contrast, is someone who does not accept the application of norms—and this always means someone who does not accept the particular application of particular norms. And the enemy is certainly someone who does not accept these norms "existentially": someone whose existence is at stake in the question of the acceptance of norms and their application; and hence someone who is ready to *put* his existence on the line in resistance against these norms and their application. Norms require the normal situation for their application because they presuppose that they do not conform to such an existential hostility.

This presupposition of normality is rendered customary in the typical application of norms and laws; in the sovereign attitude, by contrast, it is explicitly called into question. Sovereignty begins with the question concerning normality or exceptionality. From the perspective of this question, normality or homogeneity thus appear as "improbable" (Luhmann), or as a "problem" (Nietzsche). The sovereign attitude views normality not as something which is always already secured, but, on the contrary, as something which is endangered. For "the possibility and risk of an inequality" is inextirpable from every conceivable form of political homogeneity.[27] This is the more precise version of the objection which Schmitt directs against the liberal "striving for a neutral sphere." Liberalism understands the political order as "a neutral field in which conflict comes to an end,"[28] indeed, in which conflict and hostility are excluded. Schmitt objects to this by claiming that in "the field held to be neutral," there "immediately" unfolds "with new intensity the opposition between human beings and between interests."[29] There is no form of political unity or homogeneity—not even the supposedly neutral liberal form—which can, in principle, do away with the opposition between friend and enemy. The question concerning normality poses itself, therefore, in every situation in which the law is to be applied: as a question of whether the "medium" of the application of laws is "homogeneous" enough to prevent any hostility to the norms and laws which are applied. The necessity of the sovereign attitude is grounded in the possibility of a disintegration of political homogeneity, that is, in the possibility of a situation of exception, of existential hostility.

D. Dictatorship and Mercy

We can speak of an "exception" in a twofold manner: an exception can exist (in a situation) and an exception can be made (from a law). These two meanings stand in a relationship of grounding: it is because a situation of exception exists that an exception from the application of the law must be made. The situation of exception requires a law of emergency or exception. Sovereignty is defined by the ascertainment of the (possible) existence of a situation of exception, and hence by the ascertainment of the (possible) necessity of the making of an exception. The sovereign has the right to a decision which suspends the validity of the norms of law or, more precisely, which suspends the application of laws in a particular situation. So far, I have described sovereignty against a too narrow, decisionistic understanding as an attitude of the reflective questioning of the customary presuppositions of normality. This objection to decisionism does not mean that there could be a sovereignty without decision. Sovereign decision is only adequately understood, however, when it is viewed in connection with sovereign questioning or reflection. The sovereign "measures" are grounded in a law of emergency, which is itself derived from a situation of emergency. Sovereignty is not arbitrariness.

Schmitt described the sovereign action of exception according to the model of dictatorship; the legitimation of dictatorship is the political aim of Schmitt's doctrine of sovereignty. And it is certainly true that—with regard to both aspects of the exception, the aspect of its ascertainment and the aspect of its making—Schmitt's analysis of sovereignty is preformed by his political preference for dictatorship. To ascertain an exception, that is, to describe a situation as a situation of exception, means to diagnose a dissolution of that homogeneity which forms the presupposition of normality of the application of laws. In order to ground his preference for dictatorship, Schmitt gives a specific interpretation to this disintegration of homogeneity: he understands it solely as a problem of order. "The achievement of a normal state consists, above all, in the bringing about, *within* the state and its territories, of a complete pacification, it consists in the production of 'peace, security, and order' which creates the *normal* situation."[30] Exception and emergency consist in disorder and "chaos."[31] Schmitt is thinking here of civil wars and conflicts which transpose the essentially political, and "most intensive," opposition between friend and enemy into the political unity—and which, as a consequence, dissolve the normality which allows for the application of legal norms. The disintegration of presupposed homogeneity implies here the refusal of assent and subjugation to the binding norms, procedures, and instances of decision—the refusal of assent and subjugation to "state" order (in the comprehensive sense). In such a situation, Schmitt claims, dictatorial measures are required to restore and secure this order: "In the state of exception, the state suspends the law by virtue of a right to self-preservation, as one says. The two elements of the concept of a 'legal order' confront one another here and prove their conceptual independence." The motto of dictatorship is order against law, but in the name of the law. If the order which allows for the law dissolves in the situation of emergency or exception, then the "guarantee-function" of the state must temporarily become independent with respect to the "idea of law": the dictator must suspend the validity of law in order to guarantee its presupposition.

Along with this model of dictatorship, however, and in contrast to its identification with the idea of sovereignty, Schmitt has repeatedly referred, in his history of ideas, to the "other case of a concrete exception" which determines the "modern thought of sovereignty," that is, to the case of mercy.[32] Mercy, however—and this is what I want to show in what follows—is not only a further case of sovereign action; above all, it certainly cannot be understood according to the same model as dictatorship. It is for this reason that Schmitt's repeated references to mercy, surreptitiously and in the absence of any explicit reflection, dissolve his own identification of sovereignty and dictatorship, and point toward a nondictatorial form of the sovereign suspension of law. The case of mercy referred to by Schmitt can be understood, among other cases, as the paradigm of a politics of sovereignty which is entirely opposed to dictatorship.

Mercy is, like dictatorship, a way to suspend the law by making an exception from its application. Dictatorship and mercy enact this suspension, however, in opposing directions: the exception from the application of law which is made by dictatorial measures means to deny somebody a right in the name of order; the exception in mercy, by contrast, means to abstain from the application of a law in the name of somebody. Mercy—as Radbruch claims, taking over an expression from Seneca's definition of clemency (*clementia*)—is "moderation" (*moderatio*) in the application of law.[33] Seneca's complete definition runs as follows: "Clemency is restraint that waives something from deserved and owed punishment." The narrow sense of mercy is the waiving of or abstention from punishment.[34] To this extent, mercy first of all aims at the consequences of a judgment, without calling into question the fact that the judgment is (in the above-quoted sense) "appropriate": the application of the law was appropriate and the punishment is therefore "deserved and owed" (*merita ac debita*). The "dialectic of mercy"—of which Otto Kirchheimer has spoken—consists, however, in the fact that the "restraint" in punishment does not fail to affect the correctness of the judgment from which it results.[35] This is what distinguishes (individual) mercy from (collective) amnesty: because it is concerned with "peace, security, and order," amnesty follows from political calculations. Amnesty is, then, a form of sovereign action which can be understood according to the paradigm of dictatorship—as an intervention in the name of order. Because the waiving of punishment in amnesty has its sole ground in a weighing of the *external* consequences of the application of a law, it remains without consequences for the judgment whose enforcement it refuses. The "restraint" of mercy in the carrying out of punishment, by contrast, is grounded in a reservation with respect to the application of the law itself. According to Radbruch, mercy acquires its justification and, indeed, its necessity as a result of its opposition to the "cold gloominess of the legal world"; according to Kirchheimer, mercy should "correct the imperfection of the legal system as such."[36]

In order to understand the extent to which the case of mercy can be seen—against dictatorship—as another paradigm of sovereign politics, we need to distinguish between two different conceptions of it: a first one which identifies mercy with the model of dictatorial sovereignty, and a second one which opposes it to this model. These two conceptions of mercy are grounded in two different determinations of the "imperfection of the legal system"—through the correction of which mercy acquires its justification. The first conception understands this as an imperfection of *form*; this is the theory of mercy which Nietzsche develops in the second, legal-theoretical essay of *On the Genealogy of Morals*. Nietzsche arrives at this theory as the result of a theory of punishment which—because it is "Roman," that is, genuinely legal—is intended to be antimoral. From this perspective, punishment is an action by means of which a creditor's "*making suffer*" of a debtor is allowed. If the basic impetus of punishment is here the "great festival pleasure" in "cruelty,"[37] then its basic law is that of the "balancing out," the "equivalence between injury and pain."[38] In this way, punishment presupposes the instance of, as Nietzsche puts it, a "sovereign" third party: in order for there to be punishment, there needs to be an "institution of *law*" in which the "imperative declaration" of a "supreme power" which can "impose measure and bounds upon the excesses of the reactive pathos and . . . compel it to come to terms."[39] The order of equivalence of punishment is the result of a "creation and imposition of forms" by means of which political "artists" produce the "ruling structure" as their own "work."[40] Punishment realizes the pleasure that is taken in the inflicting of suffering upon the other, but in the framework and under the conditions of a sovereignly "imposed" form of equivalence.

Nietzsche also understands mercy from the perspective of this political concept of form—this understanding of the legal order and the state as the result of a sovereign design:

It is not unthinkable that a society might attain such a *consciousness of power* that it could allow itself the noblest luxury possible to it—letting those who harm it go *unpunished*. . . . The justice which began with, "everything is dischargeable, everything must be discharged," ends by winking and letting those incapable of discharging their debt go free: it ends, as does every good thing on earth, by *overcoming itself*. This self-overcoming of justice: one knows the beautiful name it has given itself—*mercy*; it goes without saying that mercy remains the privilege of the most powerful man, or better, his—beyond the law.[41]

Mercy is the prerogative of the "sovereign" and "highest" power—it is the means by which this power "overcomes" the order of equivalence which binds together crime and punishment. And the "most powerful" enact this overcoming as "artists," for aesthetic reasons: "They do not know what guilt, responsibility, or consideration are, these born organizers; they exemplify that terrible artists' egoism that has the look of bronze and knows itself justified to all eternity in its 'work,' like a mother in her child."[42] Mercy is a mode of the politico-aesthetic perfection of form in which the order of merely legal equivalence is interrupted and exceeded by the expressive act of the sovereign power of a political artist.

In this first conception of mercy—as a "luxurious" mode of the political expression of power by means of which the "imperfection" (Kirchheimer) of the *form* of law is corrected—the question of the hierarchical relationship between the subject who exercises mercy and the one who receives it stands in the foreground.[43] Mercy is defined here as a "prerogative of the most powerful" (Nietzsche). This is how it becomes an object of Enlightenment polemics. For these polemics, the law of mercy is "of all the rights of the sovereign . . . the slipperiest one for him to exercise; for it must be exercised in such a way as to show the splendor of his majesty although he is thereby doing injustice in the highest degree."[44] By means of this understanding, however, the Enlightenment polemics conceal a layer of mercy's meaning—one that finds expression in a second conception. In this second conception, mercy is not understood as a correction of the form of law, but instead as a correction of its justice. Mercy is no longer, here, a groundlessly generous clemency which operates beyond the law, but instead a justified and acquitting suspension of the law: a correction of its imperfection in the name of justice. If, in the first conception of mercy, the question *who?* stands in the foreground—the question regarding the author of mercy—then, in this second conception, the question *for whom?* comes to the fore—the question regarding the addressees of mercy and their situation. In the second conception, mercy is grounded in something "immanent to human beings"; it is necessary because it is intended to redress that emergency in which the addressee finds himself as the result of the adherence to or application of a law.[45]

It is here, in this second conception of an acquittal grounded in its addressee, that mercy corresponds to Carl Schmitt's concept of sovereignty: mercy makes an exception because a situation of exception or emergency exists. The emergency or exception, however—in the name of which mercy makes an exception—is not the one which Schmitt describes, in his exclusive orientation toward dictatorship, as a disintegration of order. The emergency which mercy attempts to rectify is not chaos, but instead injustice. Mercy distinguishes itself from the measures of dictatorship, then, by means of another experience of the situation of exception. The fundamental characteristic of every situation of exception is the disintegration of that homogeneity which forms the presupposition of normality for the application of laws. This disintegration of homogeneity into "existential" enmity or "hostility" is externally described by dictatorship as a dissolution of order, a refusal of subjugation to the norms, procedures, and instances of publicly binding decision. The experience from inside is distinguished from this by the fact that it conceives the adherence to—and hence also the application of—the norms of law as something that can imply an "existential" threat to persons. More precisely, this experience is distinguished by the fact that it understands that even the appropriate adherence to or application of the law *cannot* "existentially" do justice to its addressees, in the "concrete individuality, the social actuality of life." Whereas Schmitt, as a result of his political preference for dictatorship, only sees in the state of exception a loss of stability and order, mercy describes the fragmentation of homogeneity in terms of a loss of justice. At the same time, this pinpoints what I referred to at the beginning of this chapter as the fundamental conceptual deficiency of Schmitt's analysis of sovereignty—a deficiency which finds expression in his political preference for dictatorship and which emerges in comparison with the other sovereign act of mercy. This deficiency consists in the fact that Schmitt was in no way able to conceive the exception—and political normality or homogeneity—as a problem of justice; instead, he conceived it exclusively as a problem of stable order. Just as sovereign perfection stands at the center of Nietzsche's theory of mercy, the sovereign preservation of form or order stands at the center of Schmitt's theory of dictatorship. As against this, the second conception understands mercy as a correction of the imperfect justice of the system of law, one which serves to do justice to the existential enmity between the addressee of mercy and the law.

E. Mercy and Equity

The (second) conception outlined in the last section grounds mercy in the situation of the subject to whom it is granted: the act of mercy does not acquire its meaning by expressing the sovereign power of a political artist, but by doing justice to its addressee in his heterogeneous situation. This thesis stands in explicit opposition to a theory of mercy which sees, in every claim to give it a ground, a betrayal of its "real meaning."[46] According to Grewe, mercy is a "product of the dispensatory force of the head of state,"[47] which, in its decisions—as a "*princeps* standing above the law"—is not bound up with any justifications whatsoever. Politically, this theory of mercy is concerned with the restoration and preservation of the "connection between power and mercy"; more generally, it is concerned with the justification of a state executive (as the instance granting mercy) which is free from every legal "codification."[48] The path to this political aim consists, however, in a false conceptual conclusion, which is to a large extent characterized (despite all differences in point of departure) by the juridical definition of mercy: because the sovereign meaning of mercy is constituted by the fact that it is not subject to a legal claim, and because no legal reason can be given for it, the conclusion is drawn that it should not be related to any claim and reason at all. As we read over and over in Grewe, Radbruch, Kaufmann, and others, this constitutes the "metaphysical," "mystical," or "transcendent" essence of mercy. Juridical reflection attempts to understand mercy according to the following alternative: "either mercy is to be understood as a groundless gift of forgiving goodness or as a legal favor which stands in need of a cause."[49] To oppose the "juridification" (Kaufmann) and "codification" (Grewe) of mercy, indeed, to conceive mercy as a gift or offering, does not imply, however, that it has no ground in the situation of its addressees. Mercy is justified *without* being codifiable and juridified. This is demonstrated by its difference from legally integrated equity—a difference which Grewe has rightly emphasized: "equity and mercy are, however, totally different things."[50] For this difference does not consist in the fact that equity is justified and mercy groundless; it consists, rather, in the way in which *each of them* is justified.

Mercy and equity are frequently identified with one another, and the expressions "mercy" and "equity" are often used as substitutes for one another. As against this, I want to suggest that equity (as a translation of *epieikeia*) be understood as the virtue or, more generally, as the attitude of the appropriate application of law; and, by contrast, that mercy be understood as a form of the sovereign reflection and suspension of the application of law. At a first glance, nevertheless, equity and mercy seem to be concerned with the same phenomenon: the experience—most comprehensively articulated by Jacques Derrida—that by means of the application of norms and laws, persons can be seen to be subjected to a universality which does not protect and make possible their particularity, but instead deprives them of it.[51] As against the universality of law, equity and mercy bring to light the "particular in its particular situation" (Derrida). And they certainly do this in the name of justice: "To address oneself to the other in the language of the other is, it seems, the condition of all possible justice, but apparently, in all rigor, it is not only impossible . . . but even excluded by justice as law (*droit*), inasmuch as justice as right seems to imply an element of universality, the appeal to a third party who suspends the unilaterality or singularity of the idioms."[52] The "imperfection" of the law is its universality; both mercy and equity correct this imperfect universality of the law in the name of the particularity of its addressees and their situation—in the name of a justice which is directed toward particularity.

This generalizing description conceals, however (and this even explains the insufficiency of Derrida's elucidation), the fact that equity and mercy attempt to correct two different aspects of legal universality. Equity reacts to problems of application which arise from the *formal generality* of every formulation of law; mercy, by contrast, in the sense just defined, reacts to distortions which arise from the *egalitarian content* of the modern, liberal concept of law. Equity and mercy attempt to resolve two entirely different problems of the application of law.

Aristotle defines equity as that mode of application of law which is capable of doing justice to the difference—a difference that we have just described following Derrida but that was already emphasized by Plato—between the generality of law and the particularity of cases, and that is capable of doing this, however, without giving up the power of law in favor of a "wise and good" ruler who places "the power of art higher . . . than the laws" and decrees it to be "better than the old laws."[53] The fact that "law is always a general statement, yet there are cases which it is not possible to cover in a general statement" also certainly belongs, for Aristotle, to the customary experience of law: "while it is necessary to speak in general terms, it is not possible to do so correctly."[54] This does not require, however, that the application of the law be replaced by a personal "art" (of government); instead, it requires a "correction" of the law by means of a better or—in the sense already elucidated above—"more appropriate" application. This is the definition of equity: equity corrects the blindness which is grounded in the generality of the law by attempting to do justice to the particular case. It does this, however, by once again applying a—better adapted—law: an application of law is "equitable" when it operates "by deciding as the lawgiver would himself decide if he were present on the occasion, and would have enacted if he had been cognizant of the case in question."[55] Equity—the consideration of a case which the law treats inappropriately as a result of its generality—does not stand opposed to the application of general laws. The consideration of the particular, the "never simple" case takes place in equity with a view to *another* general law.

In contrast to this, mercy does not judge in the name of another law, but instead in the name of the other of the law—for the emergency which it wants to set right is a consequence of the law's egalitarian content and not of its formal generality. Mercy directs itself toward the "existential" threat or violence which the equal treatment of everybody can imply for the "particular in a particular situation." For such equality of consideration can only, in principle, be directed toward abstractly described chances or scopes of freedom. In normal situations, there is a "homogeneity" between these abstractly described scopes of action, which are equally granted to everybody, and the concrete enactments of life, which everybody is entitled to. This defines the "normality" which is unreflectively presupposed in the customary application of law. If that which is deemed necessary for the individual cannot be realized within the scopes of action which are open to everybody, however, this normality can fragment, and an "existential" heterogeneity, an enmity or even hostility, can arise between that which is equally permitted and that which is individually necessary.[56] This is the situation (of exception) to which mercy reacts. Equity undertakes the correction of a universal law, in order that its normative content, which the legislator has "in mind," can appropriately come to light in a particular case. Mercy, by contrast, rests upon the diagnosis that even an appropriate application, which brings to light the egalitarian content of a law, must remain existentially alien to its addressees in this particular case. Mercy is concerned, as Ivan Nagel has claimed with a view to the *Prince of Homburg*, with the "incommensurability of the individual" *as regards* the legal idea of equality.[57]

Equity and mercy consequently receive their determination on two entirely different fronts. The theory of equity is directed against a concept of law which reduces it to abstractly general laws and their application (in such a way that a consideration of concrete cases can only follow from supralegal decisions). The theory of mercy, by contrast, is directed against a

concept of law which, as a consequence of its "neutrality" or, more precisely, its equality, demands "unconditional priority" and "obedience."[58] For,
as against egalitarian law, mercy appeals to a "law of emergency"—which
even an "appropriate" or "equitable" application of law cannot satisfy. Mercy is an objection to the "rationalistic concept of law" (Schmitt) in *this*
sense: it does not accept the law's claim to priority as unconditional, but
instead confronts it with the other perspective of the "concrete individuality, the social actuality of life."

With regard to dictatorship and mercy—a case of sovereign decision
described by Schmitt himself, and a case of it introduced here as against
him—we can see, in an extreme form and an acute manner, why political decision cannot be a mere, or even merely appropriate, application of
egalitarian law. With regard to dictatorship and mercy, the reason becomes
apparent for both the critique of liberal neutralization mentioned earlier
and the apology for the independence of the political which is directed
against it. For both this critique and this apology have their ground in the
insight into the presupposition of normality, a presupposed normal situation, made by every application of law. With regard to dictatorship and
mercy, we can see that this is the case in two different respects. In both respects, "normality" means homogeneity: the absence of existential enmity or hostility. The emergence of an existential hostility to the application
of law can be described, however, in two different ways: from outside as
a problem of order (for the political community), from inside as a problem of justice (with respect to the particular individual). The *way* in which
existential hostility is described in the individual case is not solely determined by this case. We can see in this case either a problem of the securing
of order or a problem of the affording of justice, and the view which we
take will depend upon the state—the state of *strength*—in which a political community finds itself.

The presupposition of normality, as the presupposition of homogeneity, of the customary application of law cannot only fragment, however,
in the two different ways which are demonstrated, in an extreme and acute
fashion, by dictatorship and mercy. This presupposition can also—above
all, and even more fundamentally—be *made* in two different ways: implicitly and unquestioningly or explicitly and as a problem. To unquestioningly presuppose normality means to assume that political homogeneity, the
absence of existential hostility, is, in principle, unendangered and always

guaranteed. There is, however, no such form of political homogeneity. Viewed more precisely, then, to unquestioningly presuppose the existence of normality means to unquestioningly rely upon the success of those processes of normalization which eliminate existential enmity and hostility. The sovereign attitude described by Schmitt—which I have attempted to outline here and, in some respects, to extend—is directed against this unquestioning presupposition: the sovereign attitude does not put its trust in processes of normalization, processes whose means frequently awaken little trust; instead, it always again asks whether normality exists—and, if it does not exist, it always again asks how its fragmentation can be described and dealt with. Sovereignty implies a consciousness of the continual difference between that which is legally permitted and that which is existentially required. And it implies a political action which is conscious of this difference—and which, as a consequence, exceeds the formulation and application of laws.

Notes

PREFACE

1. Edmund Burke, *Reflections on the Revolution in France*, ed. J. G. A. Pocock (Indianapolis, Ind.: Hackett, 1987), p. 54; my emphasis. For a more detailed discussion of Burke's diagnosis see Chapter 5, "The Permanence of Revolution."

2. Ibid., p. 160.

3. Ibid.

4. Ibid.

5. John Rawls, "Justice as Fairness: Political Not Metaphysical," in *Collected Papers*, ed. Samuel Freeman (Cambridge, Mass.: Harvard University Press, 1999), pp. 388–414. On Rawls, see Chapter 4, "Liberalism in Conflict: Between Justice and Freedom."

6. Ibid., p. 404, note.

7. Christoph Menke, *Tragödie im Sittlichen: Gerechtigkeit und Freiheit nach Hegel* (Frankfurt am Main: Suhrkamp, 1996).

CHAPTER 1: THE SELF-REFLECTION OF EQUALITY

1. On different occasions, I have tested out the theses of this chapter in presentations. For comments and criticism, I thank the participants of the discussions. Bert van den Brink, Lutz Ellrich, Alexander García Düttmann, Andrea Kern, and Martin Saar read and helpfully commented upon the penultimate version.

2. This is what above all characterizes the Anglo-Saxon debate concerning the modern concept of equality, the debate for and against "egalitarianism"; both sides only understand equality, for the main part, as equal distribution.

3. See Chapter 6, "Mercy and Law: Carl Schmitt's Concept of Sovereignty."

4. In the history of the idea of equality, modern consciousness therefore represents a decisive step of *delimitation*. The Christian articulation of the idea of equality restricts it, for instance, to the "spiritual." Indeed, equality determines here the communication between believers in the congregation. The relationships which arise from their different social statuses remain unaffected, however. In modern theorists (Locke and Voltaire), this logic continues in another manner.

These authors also put the demand of equality in force in a central sphere (one which they define in different ways: as that of faith, nature, or humanity), but, at the same time, they restrict it to this sphere: equality does not apply on a global or social scale (see Chapter 5, "The Permanence of Revolution"). In modernity, this restriction is sublated: equal treatment becomes the basic demand in the sense that it provides the condition for every further normative entitlement.

5. I understand "dialectical" here—in the sense of the "descriptive anticipations" of Hegel's *Encyclopaedia Logic*—as "negatively rational," as that which "sublates itself by virtue of its own nature, and passes over, of itself, into its opposite." G. W. F. Hegel, *The Encyclopaedia Logic: Part 1 of the Encyclopaedia of the Philosophical Sciences with the Zusätze* (1830), trans. T. F. Geraets, W. A. Suchting, and H. S. Harris (Indianapolis, Ind.: Hackett, 1991), § 79 and § 81. Another word for this is "tragic." See Christoph Menke, *Tragödie im Sittlichen: Gerechtigkeit und Freiheit nach Hegel* (Frankfurt am Main: Suhrkamp, 1996), chap. 1.

6. Niklas Luhmann, *Paradigm Lost: Über die ethische Reflexion der Moral* (Frankfurt am Main: Suhrkamp, 1990); for a more detailed discussion of Luhmann's concept of reflection see Chapter 3, "Equality and Coercion: a Hermeneutic Limit of Modern Self-Reflection."

7. And with the very same step modern ethics conceals the circularity of its procedure, believing that it can extract from the concept of justification per se that which, in truth, only follows from its own specific concept of normative justification, and hence from a concept of justification which already contains in itself the idea of equality, the consideration of everybody. I return to this once again below, in Section C.

8. Luhmann, *Paradigm Lost*, p. 13.

9. Friedrich Schiller, *On the Aesthetic Education of Man: In a Series of Letters*, ed. and trans. Elizabeth M. Wilkinson and L. A. Willoughby (Oxford: Clarendon Press, 1989), p. 19.

10. Ibid. Edmund Burke also reacted to the experience of the revolution by formulating an ethical questioning of equality; see Chapter 5. So did Alexis de Tocqueville; see Christoph Menke, "Despotie, Individualismus, Vereinheitlichung: Tocqueville über Freiheit und Gleichheit," in *Die Gegenwart der Gerechtigkeit. Diskurse zwischen Recht, praktischer Philosophie und Politik*, ed. Christoph Demmerling and Thomas Rentsch (Berlin: Akademie, 1995), pp. 142–54.

11. Schiller, *Aesthetic Education*, p. 19.

12. Immanuel Kant, *Logic*, trans. Robert S. Hartman and Wolfang Schwarz (Indianapolis: Bobbs-Merrill, 1974), 1, § 6, note.

13. An "operation of reflection" is the general title under which Kant places, in the *Critique of Judgment*, the analysis of the process of the formation of universality. The second "maxim" of such reflection is that of a "*broadened way of thinking.*" A "man" has a "*broadened way of thinking* if he overrides the private subjec-

tive conditions of his judgment, into which so many others are locked, as it were, and reflects on his own judgment from a *universal standpoint* (which he can determine only by transferring himself to the standpoint of others)." Immanuel Kant, *Critique of Judgment*, trans. Werner S. Pluhar (Indianapolis, Ind.: Hackett, 1987), § 40. The addition which Kant places in brackets is here decisive; Kant no longer understands the "universal standpoint" as given, but instead as the result of a process. We can call this process "discursive" to the extent that it consists in "running through" a multitude of different determinations. See Albrecht Wellmer, "Ethics and Dialogue: Elements of Moral Judgment in Kant and Discourse Ethics," in *The Persistence of Modernity: Essays on Aesthetics, Ethics and Postmodernism*, trans. David Midgley (Cambridge: Polity Press, 1991), pp. 113–231.

14. These formulations rely upon Dworkin's distinction between two modes of equal treatment: "to treat all those in charge *as equals*, that is, as entitled to equal concern and respect," and "to treat all those in charge *equally* in the distribution of some resource of opportunity." Ronald Dworkin, "Liberalism," in *A Matter of Principle*, by Ronald Dworkin (Cambridge, Mass.: Harvard University Press, 1985), p. 190.

15. In contemporary ethical discussion, this has been most clearly emphasized by feminist and poststructuralist positions. See Annette C. Baier, *Moral Prejudices: Essays on Ethics* (Cambridge, Mass.: Harvard University Press, 1994), chaps. 1–5; Seyla Benhabib, *Situating the Self: Gender, Community, and Postmodernism in Contemporary Ethics* (New York: Routledge, 1992), chaps. 5–8; and Stephen K. White, *Political Theory and Postmodernism* (Cambridge: Cambridge University Press, 1991).

16. This appears, however, to be a basic assumption of Derrida's deconstructive theory of justice. See Chapter 2, Section B.

17. The conflict concerning the correct concept of individuality stands at the center of Stanley Cavell's conception of an agonistic perfectionism. See Stanley Cavell, *Conditions Handsome and Unhandsome: The Constitution of Emersonian Perfectionism* (Chicago: University of Chicago Press, 1990), chaps. 1 and 3; and his *In Quest of the Ordinary: Lines of Skepticism and Romanticism* (Chicago: University of Chicago Press, 1988).

18. See Alain Badiou, *Saint Paul, the Foundation of Universalism*, trans. Ray Brassier (Stanford, Calif.: Stanford University Press, 2003).

19. See Martha C. Nussbaum, "Aristotelian Social Democracy," in *Liberalism and the Good*, ed. R. Bruce Douglass, Gerald Mara, and Henry Richardson (New York: Routledge, 1990), pp. 203–52. For a more differentiated discussion of the question of the universal determination of the good or successful life see Martin Seel, *Versuch über die Form des Glücks* (Frankfurt am Main: Suhrkamp, 1995).

20. See Judith N. Shklar, *The Faces of Injustice* (New Haven, Conn.: Yale University Press, 1990), pp. 83–126. For a more detailed discussion of this concept of

violence, see the two chapters in Part II; on the process of complaint and its interpretation sketched in what follows, see Chapter 5.

21. See above, note 7. I incorporate here Albrecht Wellmer's compelling criticism of the most developed contemporary attempt at a strong, discourse-theoreti-
cal justification of the principle of equality, the so-called "ultimate or fundamental
justification." See Wellmer, "Ethics and Dialogue"; and similarly Ernst Tugend-
hat, *Vorlesungen über Ethik* (Frankfurt am Main: Suhrkamp, 1996), pp. 65–78.

22. For a more detailed discussion of this connection between individual complaint and social equality, see Chapter 5, Section C.

23. In contemporary ethics, this has been most consistently emphasized by
Emmanuel Lévinas. The relationship to the other with which he is concerned is
not an I-Thou relationship (as in friendship), and its "conversation is not a pa-
thetic confrontation of two beings absenting themselves from the things and from
the others. Discourse is not love." Emmanuel Lévinas, *Totality and Infinity: An Essay on Exteriority*, trans. Alphonso Lingis (Pittsburgh: Duquesne University Press,
1979), p. 76. In what follows, the distinction between different roles and forms of
doing justice to individuals means that the normative orientation toward the other individual cannot be restricted to relationships of personal and affective bonding. See, however, Axel Honneth, *The Struggle for Recognition: The Moral Gram-
mar of Social Conflicts*, trans. Joel Anderson (Cambridge: Polity Press, 1995), pp.
95–130.

24. For more detail, see the discussion of Adorno's concept of solidarity in
Chapter, 2, Section B.

25. Following Michael Walzer, Alexander García Düttmann has described the
form of this universal doing justice to individuals as "reiterative universalism." See
his *Between Cultures: Tensions in the Struggle for Recognition*, trans. Ken Woodgate
(London: Verso, 2000).

26. The following considerations outline the consequences which arise for the
undertaking of an ethical questioning of equality from its structural elucidation—
an elucidation given in Section B. In Chapter 2, I will pursue this further by comparing three different versions of such a questioning of equality: genealogy, deconstruction, and critical theory. I will also go into the individual steps of the program
which is only outlined here in a general manner.

27. This is intended to emphasize the fact that there are forms of the external questioning of equality which are not subject to the dialectic described at the
beginning, and further elucidated in what follows. This dialectic only applies to
an *ethical* questioning of equality. A functionalistic sociology and psychology, by
contrast, can inquire about the costs of the orientation of equality from a strictly
external perspective. Examples of such a form of the questioning of equality can
be found in Luhmann and Nietzsche.

28. This is most obvious in the field of law; see, emphatically, Robert M. Cov-

er, "Violence and the Word," in *Narrative, Violence, and the Law: The Essays of Robert Cover*, ed. Martha Minow, Michael Ryan, and Austin Sarat (Ann Arbor: University of Michigan Press, 1992), pp. 203 ff. It applies just as much, however, to the field of morality, and can also be seen here in the role of sanction and punishment.

29. See Bernard Williams, "Persons, Character, and Morality," in *Moral Luck: Philosophical Papers, 1973–1980*, by Bernard Williams (Cambridge: Cambridge University Press, 1981), pp. 1–19; and Harry Frankfurt, "Equality and Respect," *Social Research* 64, no. 1 (Spring 1997): 3–15. For a more detailed analysis of the conflict between equality and individuality, see Chapters 3 and 4.

30. If such a restriction of equality is to be possible, then the collapse of its "strong" justification has to be presupposed. The "strong" justification seemed to secure for equality a fundamental priority. The critique of the strong program of justification also dissolves this principle of priority. The conflict between the two normative attitudes is not only empirically open, because we can never know how strong the challenge by that which according to reason is weaker will be. It is also *normatively* open, because neither of the two attitudes can be justified in a fundamentally better fashion, that is, both can only be justified in an equally good (or weak) fashion. See Seel, *Versuch über die Form des Glücks*, pp. 13–48 and 321–63.

31. For a more detailed discussion, see Chapter 2, Section B.

32. This is, once again, the thesis of the (negative) dialectic of equality put forward at the beginning. It simultaneously describes both my agreement with and critique of Axel Honneth's arguments concerning the relationship between justice and the affective attitudes of love, friendship, and community; see Axel Honneth, "Das Andere der Gerechtigkeit: Habermas und die ethische Herausforderung der Postmoderne," in *Deutsche Zeitschrift für Philosophie* 42 (1994): 195–220. My agreement with Honneth consists in the fact that we both grant the attitude of doing justice to individuals an essential function in the enactment of the attitude of the equal consideration of everybody. Honneth assumes, however, that this circumstance—the fact that the attitude of doing justice to individuals has a function *internal* to equality—excludes the possibility that it can be directed *against* equality. This only occurs in relationships of love, friendship, and community. In this argument, Honneth identifies the two aspects which I have previously distinguished: affective motivation and normative content. In its normative content, the attitude of doing justice to individuals always stands in tension with equality. Sometimes, however, and frequently because of relationships of love, friendship, and community, we are moved to intensify this latent tension into an open conflict with equality, and even into a decision against equality. Honneth claims that "the assumption of such a form of responsibility [in my way of speaking, of the responsibility of doing justice to individuals (C.M.)] cannot be expected of all human beings in the same way in which it is to be morally expected that they

respect the dignity of every other." Honneth, "Das Andere der Gerechtigkeit," p. 219. That which cannot be expected of everybody, however, is only the *practical weighting* which the lover, friend, or companion carries out when he is confronted, in his equal treatment, by the suffering of others. We can "expect" of everybody, on the other hand, the perception of the suffering of others, for this is a prerequisite of proper equal treatment itself.

33. On the question concerning the correct attitude with respect to the conflicts between equality and individuality, see the two chapters in Part III, "Forms of Sovereignty."

CHAPTER 2: GENEALOGY, DECONSTRUCTION, CRITIQUE

1. Because the idea of equality is the basic concept of modernity in both the moral and legal sense, I here consider the questioning of equality in critique, genealogy, and deconstruction without taking into account the difference between law and morality. In all three positions, the relationship between morality and law is represented differently. The comparison of Nietzsche and Derrida shows this most clearly: whereas Nietzsche brings the law to bear *against* egalitarian morality, for Derrida the law is the paradigm which *also* demonstrates the fundamental problem of egalitarian morality. Adorno, in turn, understands their relationship in a traditionally Kantian manner: law represents the moral idea of equality in a restricted sense.

2. Friedrich Nietzsche, *On the Genealogy of Morals*, trans. Walter Kaufmann (New York: Random House, 1967), pp. 21–22.

3. Friedrich Nietzsche, *The Gay Science: With a Prelude in Rhymes and an Appendix of Songs*, trans. Walter Kaufmann (New York: Vintage, 1974), § 107, p. 164.

4. Ibid., p. 21.

5. Friedrich Nietzsche, *Beyond Good and Evil* in *Basic Writings of Nietzsche*, trans. Walter Kaufmann (New York: Modern Library Giants, 1968), pp. 221–22.

6. Ibid.

7. This is the basic thesis of Spinoza's critique of morality; see *The Ethics*, trans. Samuel Shirley (Indianapolis, Ind.: Hackett, 1982), pt. 1, appendix. On Nietzsche and Spinoza see Yirmiyahu Yovel, *Spinoza and Other Heretics*, vol. 2, *The Adventures of Immanence* (Princeton, N.J.: Princeton University Press, 1989), pp. 132–35.

8. Nietzsche, *On the Genealogy of Morals*, p. 20.

9. Ibid., p. 153.

10. This is not intended to dispute Bernard Williams's emphasis of the fact that Nietzsche's moral psychology claims to be "more realistic" than that of its competitors; see Bernard Williams, "Nietzsche's Minimalist Moral Psychology," in *Making Sense of Humanity and Other Philosophical Papers, 1982–1993*, by Bernard Williams (Cambridge: Cambridge University Press, 1995), pp. 65–76. This certainly cannot be the reason, however, for Nietzsche's overcoming of morality—to

be "realistic" or "unrealistic" is, for Nietzsche, itself in turn a question of will, and hence of value. See Jean-Luc Nancy, "'Unsere Redlichkeit!' (Über Wahrheit im moralischen Sinn Bei Nietzsche)," in Nietzsche aus Frankreich, ed. Werner Hamacher (Frankfurt am Main: Ullstein, 1986), pp. 169 ff.

11. Nietzsche, *On the Genealogy of Morals*, p. 55.

12. Nietzsche, *Beyond Good and Evil*, p. 289.

13. Nietzsche, *The Gay Science*, § 345, p. 284.

14. Ibid., § 344, p. 282.

15. Nietzsche, *On the Genealogy of Morals*, p. 52. On what follows, see Michel Foucault, "Nietzsche, Genealogy, History," in *The Foucault Reader: An Introduction to Foucault's Thought*, ed. Paul Rabinow (New York: Random House, 1984), pp. 76–100. However, Foucault here understands the nonobjectivity of genealogical knowledge merely as (epistemic) perspectivity. It is only with Foucault's new interpretation of the genealogical undertaking that the "personal" in genealogy becomes recognizable as (ethical) normativity. See Foucault, *The History of Sexuality*, vol. 2, *The Use of Pleasure* (New York: Vintage Books, 1985). All translations of quotations are by translators of the current volume unless otherwise stated.

16. Nietzsche, *On the Genealogy of Morals*, p. 52.

17. Friedrich Nietzsche, *Human, All Too Human*, trans. Marion Faber (Lincoln: University of Nebraska Press, 1989), § 95, p. 66.

18. Friedrich Nietzsche, *Nachgelassene Fragmente, Winter 1870–71—Herbst 1872, 8 (115), Kritische Studienausgabe*, vol. 7, ed. Giorgio Colli and Mazzino Montinari (Berlin: de Gruyter, 1967), p. 266.

19. See H. Fink-Eitel, "Nietzsches Moralistik," *Deutsche Zeitschrift für Philosophie* 41 (1993): 865 ff. On what follows, see the perfectionist reading of Nietzsche in Daniel W. Conway, *Nietzsche and the Political* (London: Routledge, 1997). This goes back to Stanley Cavell, "Aversive Thinking: Emersonian Representations in Heidegger and Nietzsche," in *Conditions Handsome and Unhandsome: The Constitution of Emersonian Perfectionism*, by Stanley Cavell (Chicago: University of Chicago Press, 1990), pp. 33–63.

20. Nietzsche, *Beyond Good and Evil*, p. 327.

21. Theodor W. Adorno, *Minima Moralia: Reflections from Damaged Life*, trans. E. F. N. Jephcott (London: Verso, 1978), p. 15.

22. Ibid., pp. 90–91.

23. Ibid., p. 39.

24. Ibid., p. 27. Adorno sees in this the signature of the present; the model of rightness of bourgeois culture has been dissolved, but, in the process of this dissolution, no new and better model has been formed. For this dissolution was a dissolution into a purely functional rationality.

25. Ibid., p. 26.

26. Theodor W. Adorno, *Negative Dialectics*, trans. E. B. Ashton (London: Routledge, 1973), p. 283.

27. Ibid., p. 236.

28. Ibid., p. 260.

29. Ibid., p. 271.

30. Nietzsche, *On the Genealogy of Morals*, p. 87.

31. On Nietzsche, see Judith Butler, *The Psychic Life of Power: Theories in Subjection* (Stanford, Calif.: Stanford University Press, 1997), pp. 63–82. On Adorno, see Klaus Günther, "Dialektik der Aufklärung in der Idee der Freiheit: Zur Kritik des Freiheitsbegriffs bei Adorno," *Zeitschrift für philosophische Forschung* 39 (1985): 229–60.

32. Nietzsche, *On the Genealogy of Morals*, p. 59; see also pp. 31–33 and 84–85.

33. Ibid., p. 44.

34. Nietzsche, *Beyond Good and Evil*, p. 329.

35. Adorno, *Minima Moralia*, p. 156.

36. Adorno, *Negative Dialectics*, p. 256.

37. At least this is how their opposition is presented from Adorno's point of view; see *Minima Moralia*, no. 60 ("A word for morality"), and no. 100 ("Sur l'eau"). On Adorno's critique of Nietzsche, see Gerhard Schweppenhäuser, *Ethik nach Auschwitz: Adornos negative Moralphilosophie* (Hamburg: Argument, 1993), pp. 166 ff.

38. Nietzsche, *On the Genealogy of Morals*, p. 46.

39. Ibid., p. 45.

40. Ibid.

41. Adorno, *Negative Dialectics*, p. 256.

42. Ibid., p. 229.

43. Ibid., p. 228.

44. This is the argument which Bernard Williams has reconstructed in "Nietzsche's Minimalist Moral Psychology" (see above, note 10): egalitarian morality implies a (descriptively) false philosophical psychology—here, a false conception of the subject of action; and, as a (normative) consequence, this false conception runs up against the basic conditions of an individually accomplished life. On the relation between "subject" and "force," see Christoph Menke, "Ästhetische Subjektivität: Zu einem Grundbegriff moderner Ästhetik," in *Konzepte der Moderne*, ed. Gerhart von Graevenitz (Stuttgart: Metzler, 1999), pp. 593 ff.

45. Jacques Derrida, "Force of Law: The 'Mystical Foundation of Authority,'" in *Deconstruction and the Possibility of Justice*, ed. Drucilla Cornell, Michel Rosenfeld, and David Gray Carlson (New York: Routledge, 1992), pp. 3–67, p. 18. In contrast to Nietzsche and Adorno, Derrida above all considers the norms of equality of *law*. I ignore this difference here; on the reasons for this, see above, note 1.

46. Ibid.

47. Ibid., p. 13. The reference is the same for all the quotes which follow in this paragraph.

48. Ibid., pp. 16–17.

49. Ibid., p. 17.

50. Ibid., pp. 21–29.

51. Alexander García Düttmann, "Die Dehnbarkeit der Begriffe: Über Dekonstruktion, Kritik und Politik," in *Postmoderne und Politik*, ed. Jutta Georg-Lauer (Tübingen: Diskord, 1992), pp. 57–77. With this discussion of deconstruction and critique, I once again take up a question which I have dealt with in a first approach; see Christoph Menke, "'Absolute Interrogation': Metaphysikkritik und Sinnsubversion bei Jacques Derrida," *Philosophisches Jahrbuch* 97 (1990): 351–66.

52. Alexander García Düttmann has formulated this in the thesis that there cannot be, for conceptual reasons, "relationships of accomplished, undistorted recognition" (Axel Honneth); see his *Zwischen den Kulturen: Spannungen im Kampf um Anerkennung* (Frankfurt am Main: Suhrkamp, 1997), p. 154. In Derrida, we read the following: "there is never a moment that we can say *in the present* that a decision *is* just . . . or that someone is a just man—even less, '*I am* just'"; Derrida, "Force of Law," p. 23.

53. Jacques Derrida, "Violence and Metaphysics: An Essay on the Thought of Emmanuel Lévinas," in *Writing and Difference*, trans. Alan Bass (London: Routledge, 1978), pp. 79–153, p. 117. On the relationship between Derrida and Lévinas, see Simon Critchley, *The Ethics of Deconstruction* (Oxford: Blackwell, 1992).

54. Emmanuel Lévinas, *Totality and Infinity: An Essay on Exteriority*, trans. Alphonso Lingis (Pittsburgh: Duquesne University Press, 1979), pp. 65–66.

55. Derrida, "Violence and Metaphysics," p. 129.

56. See "Force of Law," pp. 17–22.

57. Ibid., p. 17.

58. García Düttmann, *Zwischen den Kulturen*, pp. 122.

59. Ibid., pp. 103 ff.

60. Nietzsche, *Beyond Good and Evil*, pp. 328–29.

61. Ibid., p. 306.

62. Nietzsche, *Morgenröte* (Berlin: de Gruyter, 1999), § 4, p. 16.

63. Nietzsche, *The Gay Science*, § 380, p. 342.

64. Adorno, *Negative Dialectics*, pp. 146–47.

65. Ibid., p. 146.

66. See ibid., p. 236.

67. Ibid., p. 147.

68. Ibid.

69. What is at issue here is the program of an immanent critique which should, at the same time, be a critique from outside: "paradoxically enough, to criticize it [identity] immanently means to criticize it from outside as well." Adorno, *Negative Dialectics*, p. 145.

70. Nietzsche, *Beyond Good and Evil*, p. 234.

71. Nietzsche, *On the Genealogy of Morals*, p. 145.

72. Adorno and Horkheimer, *Dialectic of Enlightenment*, trans. John Cumming (New York: Herder and Herder, 1972), p. 85.

73. This is the thesis, taken over from Schopenhauer, of Horkheimer's chapter on morality in *Dialectic of Enlightenment*: the Enlightenment's attempt to ground morality purely in reason destroys morality, for—as the "black writers of the bourgeoisie" have shown—"formalistic reason" is not "more closely allied to morality than to immorality"; ibid., pp. 117–18. Furthermore, because the Enlightenment wants to ground morality in reason alone, it reproduces the rationalistic hostility toward all affects and feelings, including moral ones—and therefore destroys the only foundation which morality can have; see ibid., pp. 89–92. Nietzsche does not only attest to this thesis, he already formulates it himself: he claims that Kant's attempt at grounding has "not lured us modern philosophers onto a more solid and less deceptive ground"; Nietzsche, *Morgenröte*, § 3, p. 13. For Kant's attempt to rationally ground the "moral kingdom" only expresses the pessimistic recognition of "the thorough *immorality* of nature and history"; Nietzsche, ibid., p. 14.

74. Nietzsche, *On the Genealogy of Morals*, p. 36.

75. Ibid., p. 49.

76. Ibid., pp. 36–37.

77. Ibid., p. 40.

78. Ibid., p. 38.

79. Ibid., p. 39.

80. Nietzsche, *Morgenröte*, § 76, p. 73

81. Ibid.

82. Nietzsche, *On the Genealogy of Morals*, pp. 162–63.

83. Ibid. p. 39.

84. Nietzsche, *Morgenröte*, § 516, p. 299.

85. Nietzsche, *On the Genealogy of Morals*, pp. 36–37.

86. Adorno, *Negative Dialectics*, p. 286.

87. Ibid., pp. 285–86.

88. Ibid., p. 299.

89. Adorno burdens this (plausible) consideration of the affective-impulsive ground of moral action with the perspective of the "phantasm of reconciling nature and the mind." Adorno, *Negative Dialectics*, p. 229; see Christoph Menke, "Kritische Theorie und tragische Erkenntnis," *Zeitschrift für kritische Theorie* 5 (1997): 60–63. With this idea of reconciliation, Adorno conceals the following problem: an action certainly can be morally good only if it arises from an impulse (because in the absence of an impulse it would not have a reason at all); but not every action which arises from an impulse or spontaneous stirring is already, as a consequence, good. Adorno inherits here a problem from Rousseau's moral philosophy, from which he probably took his concept of a moral "impulse" which

"precedes the use of any reflection"; see Jean-Jacques Rousseau, *A Discourse on Inequality*, trans. Maurice Cranston (Harmondsworth, Middlesex, U.K.: Penguin, 1984).

90. Adorno, *Negative Dialectics*, p. 277.

91. Max Scheler understood this as the Greek characteristic of Nietzsche's concept of love, and counterposed to it a Christian one; see Max Scheler, "Das Ressentiment im Aufbau der Moralen," in *Vom Umsturz der Werte* (Bern: Francke, 1955), pp. 70 ff. See Hans Joas, *The Genesis of Values*, trans. Gregory Moore (Chicago: University of Chicago Press, 2000). Adorno's feeling of solidarity fits awkwardly with this distinction. For although solidarity is related to the suffering other, it is not, like Christian love, "cowering" (Scheler).

92. Adorno, *Negative Dialectics*, p. 203.

93. Adorno's concept of a nonjudgmental, mimetic relationship to the other can be compared with Lévinas's concept of a nondetermining relationship to the other, which underlies his conception of religion. On the general relationship between Adorno and Lévinas, see Hent de Vries, *Theologie im pianissimo und zwischen Rationalität und Dekonstruktion: Die Aktualität der Denkfiguren Adornos und Lévinas* (Kampen: Kok, 1989).

94. Adorno, *Negative Dialectics*, pp. 285–86.

95. Nietzsche's objection to morality—according to which, in a formulation following from Emerson, it would produce a type of human being unsuitable as a "representative of humanity," as a result of its surpassing the latter's measure of perfection—rests upon an objective theory of value. Nietzsche here attempts to detach the critique of the consequences of morality from the individual experience or suffering of them; for the reference to these consequences would again, as Adorno makes clear, itself be moral. In Nietzsche, however, it remains unclear how such an objective measure of perfection is to be attained.

96. Adorno and Horkheimer, *Dialectic of Enlightenment*, pp. 102–3. On Horkheimer's ethics of sympathy, see Herbert Schnädelbach, "Max Horkheimer und die Moralphilosophie des Deutschen Idealismus," in *Max Horkheimer heute: Werk und Wirkung*, ed. Alfred Schmidt and Norbert Altwicker (Frankfurt am Main: Fischer, 1986), pp. 52ff.

97. Derrida, "Force of Law," p. 23.

98. See Lévinas's discussion of the problem of the third party as a figure for "all the Others" who interrupt the relation to this one incomparable or particular other; *Totality and Infinity*, pp. 212–14 and, above all, *Otherwise Than Being; or, Beyond Essence*, trans. Alphonso Lingis (The Hague: Nijhoff, 1981), chap. 5.3

99. This is the important difference—one which Derrida only hints at—from the concept of violence that is employed, to a large extent, in Critical Legal Studies. See Derrida "Force of Law," pp. 8–9; and, as an example, Stanley Fish, "Force," in *Doing What Comes Naturally: Change, Rhetoric, and the Practice of Theory in Lit-*

erary Legal Studies, by Stanley Fish (Durham, N.C.: Duke University Press, 1989), pp. 503–24. See also Anselm Haverkamp, "Kritik der Gewalt und die Möglichkeit von Gerechtigkeit," in *Gewalt und Gerechtigkeit: Derrida—Benjamin*, ed. Anselm Haverkamp (Frankfurt am Main: Suhrkamp, 1991), pp. 7–50.

100. This "symmetrical" formula for the relationship between the impulse of solidarity and the moral law does not contradict the genealogical asymmetry emphasized by Adorno (and Lévinas)—the fact that the impulse of solidarity is the origin of the moral law. Both things are true at the same time. For the fact that the moral law stems from the impulse of solidarity means two things: that the impulse of solidarity is the foundation even of the moral law, *and* that this impulse of solidarity is normatively deficient and consequently needs to produce the moral law.

101. Derrida, "Violence and Metaphysics," p. 313, note 21. On what follows, see Christoph Menke, "Für eine Politik der Dekonstruktion: Jacques Derrida über Recht und Gerechtigkeit," in *Gewalt und Gerechtigkeit*, ed. Haverkamp, pp. 279–87.

102. Derrida, "Force of Law," pp. 25–27 and 29–30.

ANNEX TO CHAPTER 2: ABILITY AND FAITH

1. Cf. Christoph Menke, "Zwischen Literatur und Dialektik," in *Was ist ein "philosophisches" Problem?* ed. Joachim Schulte and Uwe Justus Wenzel (Frankfurt am Main: Fischer, 2001), pp. 114–33.

2. The practical ability that makes accomplishment possible can, in addition, be understood in a transcendent or immanent sense. It is understood in a transcendent sense when it is understood as the capacity of imitation, remembrance, reiteration, or participation of or in an idea of accomplishment or the good that (logically) exists *prior to* every human practice and first makes possible its accomplishment. A philosophy of immanence, by contrast, attempts to explain the ability that allows practice to be accomplished only with reference to human practice itself.

3. Jacques Derrida, "Signature Event Context," in *Margins of Philosophy*, trans. Alan Bass (Chicago: University of Chicago Press, 1982), p. 328.

4. Cf. Jacques Derrida, *Of Grammatology*, trans. Gayatri Chakravorty Spivak (Baltimore: Johns Hopkins University Press, 1974).

5. Cf. Samuel C. Wheeler, III, *Deconstruction as Analytic Philosophy* (Stanford, Calif.: Stanford University Press, 2000), pp. 15 ff., 180 ff.

6. Jacques Derrida, "Force of Law: The 'Mystical Foundation of Authority,'" in *Deconstruction and the Possibility of Justice*, ed. Drucilla Cornell, Michel Rosenfeld, and David Gray Carlson (New York: Routledge, 1992). In what follows, I quote from this edition.

7. Derrida thus says that "our common axiom is that to be just or unjust and to exercise justice, I must be free and responsible for my actions, my behavior, my thought, my decisions" (22).

8. The question concerning this distinction links Derrida's text with Benja-

min's "Critique of Violence," which he analyzes in a further treatise (now the second part of "Force of Law"). It also distinguishes both Derrida and Benjamin from Carl Schmitt, who does not make this distinction.

9. I supplement and correct here the lines of interpretation of "Force of Law" outlined above, Chapter 2.

10. "Paradoxically, it is because of this overflowing of the performative, because of this always excessive haste of interpretation getting ahead of itself, because of this structural agency and precipitation of justice that the latter has no horizon of expectation (regulative or messianic). But for this very reason, it *may* have an *avenir,* a 'to-come,' which I rigorously distinguish from the future that can always reproduce the present. Justice remains, is yet, to come, *à venir,* it has an, it is *à-venir,* the very dimension of events irreducibly to come. It will always have it, this *à-venir,* and always has" (27).

11. Letter to author, from Alexander García Düttmann, explaining his translation of *présomption* as "Glaube" (faith).

12. For an analogous argument about the deconstructive logic of knowledge, cf. Alexander García Düttmann, "Dichtung und Wahrheit der Dekonstruktion," and Andrea Kern, "Wissen vom Standpunkte eines Menschen,'" both in *Philosophie der Dekonstruktion: Zum Verhältnis von Normativität und Praxis,* ed. Andrea Kern and Christoph Menke (Frankfurt am Main: Suhrkamp, 2002), pp. 72–79, 216–39.

13. For a more detailed discussion see L. Ellrich, "Zu einer pragmatischen Theorie der Rechtsgeltung bei Montaigne und Pascal," *Archiv für Rechts- und Sozialphilosophie* 74 (1988): 51–72.

14. Jacques Derrida, *Aporias,* trans. Thomas Dutoit (Stanford, Calif.: Stanford University Press, 1993).

15. The sentence that is often criticized as arrogant—"deconstruction is justice"—can also be understood in this sense. It should point to the aspect of the deconstructive insight into the aporias of making possible that itself makes accomplishment possible.

16. H. L. A. Hart, *The Concept of Law* (Oxford: Oxford University Press, 1994), pp. 20 ff.

17. On this motive in deconstruction cf. Hent de Vries, *Philosophy and the Turn to Religion* (Cambridge, Mass., 2000), passim; above all with reference to Jacques Derrida, "Faith and Knowledge," trans. Sam Weber, in *Religion,* ed. Jacques Derrida and Gianni Vattimo (Stanford, Calif.: Stanford University Press, 1998), pp. 1–78.

CHAPTER 3: EQUALITY AND COERCION

1. G. W. F. Hegel, "On the Scientific Ways of Treating Natural Law, on Its Place in Practical Philosophy, and Its Relation to the Positive Sciences of Right (1802–1803)," in *Political Writings,* ed. Lawrence Dickey and H. B. Nisbet, trans. H. B.

Nisbet (Cambridge: Cambridge University Press, 1999), pp. 102–80, p. 122.

2. Ibid., p. 132.

3. Ibid., p. 122; trans. modified.

4. Ibid., p. 119.

5. See G. W. F. Hegel, *The Difference Between Fichte's and Schelling's System of Philosophy*, trans. H. S. Harris and Walter Cerf (Albany: State University of New York Press, 1977).

6. See Christoph Menke, "Der 'Wendungspunkt' des Erkennens: Zu Begriff, Recht und Reichweite der Dialektik in Hegels Logic," in *Vernunftkritik nach Hegel: Analytisch-kritische Interpretationen zur Dialektik*, ed. Christoph Demmerling and Friedrich Kambartel (Frankfurt am Main: Suhrkamp, 1992), pp. 9 ff.

7. Niklas Luhmann, "Der Wohlfahrtsstaat zwischen Evolution und Rationalität," in *Soziologische Aufklärung*, vol. 4, *Beiträge zur funktionalen Differenzierung der Gesellschaft* (Opladen: Westdeutscher Verlag, 1987), pp. 114 ff. This is also the reference for the formulations which follow in this paragraph.

8. Ibid. In the formulation of this dilemma, Luhmann rightly appeals to deconstructive theories; see Niklas Luhmann, "Europäische Rationalität," in *Beobachtungen der Moderne*, by Niklas Luhmann (Opladen: Westdeutscher Verlag, 1992), pp. 60 ff. On the critique of the concept of reason, see ibid., pp. 76 ff., and the program of the "sociological Enlightenment" as the "clarification" of the "Enlightenment of reason"; Niklas Luhmann, "Soziologische Aufklärung," in *Soziologische Aufklärung*, vol. 1, *Aufsätze zur Theorie sozialer Systeme* (Opladen: Westdeutscher Verlag, 1970), pp. 67 ff.

9. "As system-rationality rationality is system-relative." Luhmann, "Soziologische Aufklärung," p. 79.

10. Luhmann, "Der Wohlfahrtsstaat zwischen Evolution und Rationalität," p. 114.

11. Ibid., p. 115.

12. Niklas Luhmann, *Soziale Systeme* (Frankfurt am Main: Suhrkamp, 1984), pp. 645 ff., p. 638.

13. See Niklas Luhmann, *Zweckbegriff und Systemrationalität* (Frankfurt am Main: Suhrkamp, 1973), pp. 166 ff.

14. Luhmann, *Soziale Systeme*, p. 645.

15. Ibid., p. 600.

16. Ibid., p. 619; generally, pp. 617–31. I have left out here an intermediate level—that of "reflexivity" (p. 601, pp. 610 ff.).

17. Ibid., p. 640.

18. Ibid., p. 642.

19. Luhmann, "Der Wohlfahrtsstaat zwischen Evolution und Rationalität," p. 114.

20. See Luhmann, *Soziale Systeme*, pp. 643–45.

21. Ibid., p. 645.

22. Niklas Luhmann, *Politische Theorie im Wohlfahrtsstaat* (Munich: Olzog, 1981), p. 91. See also Luhmann's methodical undermining of the normative content of moral, legal, or political equality; Niklas Luhmann, "Subjektive Rechte: Zum Umbau des Rechtsbewußtseins für die moderne Gesellschaft," in *Gesellschaftsstruktur und Semantik*, vol. 2, by Niklas Luhmann (Frankfurt am Main: Suhrkamp, 1981), p. 45; and his *Paradigm Lost: Über die ethische Reflexion der Moral* (Frankfurt am Main: Suhrkamp, 1990).

23. Luhmann, *Politische Theorie im Wohlfahrtsstaat*, p. 86.

24. Ibid., p. 132.

25. Ibid., p. 128.

26. Ibid., p. 156.

27. Ibid., p. 29.

28. Ibid., p. 122.

29. Ibid. As against this, see the determination of individuality—one which refuses all normative standpoints—as the continuity of consciousness and, hence, as mere self-preservation, in Luhmann, *Soziale Systeme*, pp. 346 ff.

30. Luhmann, *Politische Theorie im Wohlfahrtsstaat*, p. 128.

31. Jürgen Habermas, "The New Obscurity: The Crisis of the Welfare State and the Exhaustion of Utopian Energies," in *The New Conservatism: Cultural Criticism and the Historians' Debate*, ed. and trans. Shierry Weber Nicholsen (Cambridge: Polity Press, 1989), pp. 48–70, p. 58.

32. Ibid., pp. 58, 66. For a more detailed discussion, see Habermas, *The Theory of Communicative Action*, vol. 2, *The Critique of Functionalist Reason* (Cambridge: Polity Press, 1987), pp. 367–73. See also Nancy Fraser, "Women, Welfare, and the Politics of Need Interpretation," in *Unruly Practices: Power, Discourse, and Gender in Contemporary Social Theory*, by Nancy Fraser (Cambridge: Polity Press, 1989), pp. 144–60.

33. Charles Taylor, "The Nature and Scope of Distributive Justice," in *Philosophy and the Human Sciences: Philosophical Papers*, by Charles Taylor, vol. 2 (Cambridge: Cambridge University Press, 1985), pp. 289–317, p. 302.

34. Michel Foucault, *Discipline and Punish: The Birth of the Prison* (Harmondsworth, Middlesex, U.K.: Penguin, 1977), pp. 221–22.

35. Taylor, "The Nature and Scope of Distributive Justice," pp. 312–17; Foucault, *Discipline and Punish*. For a more detailed discussion of the implicit models of the good and the possibility of their impairment by means of equality, see Chapter 4, "Liberalism in Conflict: Between Justice and Freedom."

36. On the terminology, see Jürgen Habermas, *Between Facts and Norms: Contributions to a Discourse Theory of Law and Democracy*, trans. William Rehg (Cambridge: Polity Press, 1996), pp. 122–23.

37. On the concept of practical heterogeneity, see Christoph Menke, "Die Ver-

nunft im Widerstreit: Zum richtigen Umgang mit praktischen Konflikten," in *Zur Verteidigung der Vernunft gegen ihre Liebhaber und Verächter*, ed. Christoph Menke and Martin Seel (Frankfurt am Main: Suhrkamp, 1993), pp. 197–218.

38. On what follows, see Luhmann, "Europäische Rationalität," pp. 76 and 53. Jacques Derrida points in a similar direction in "Force of Law."

39. Luhmann, *Politische Theorie im Wohlfahrtsstaat*, p. 61.

40. Luhmann, "Europäische Rationalität," p. 84. See also Niklas Luhmann and Peter Fuchs, *Reden und Schweigen* (Frankfurt am Main: Suhrkamp, 1989), pp. 178 ff. For a more detailed discussion of the background theoretical assumptions, see Lutz Ellrich, "Semantik und Paradoxie," in *Germanistik und Komparatistik: DFG-Symposion 1993*, ed. Hendrik Birus (Stuttgart: Metzler, 1995), pp. 378 ff.

41. Luhmann, *Politische Theorie im Wohlfahrtsstaat*, p. 51.

42. G. W. F. Hegel, "On the Scientific Ways of Treating Natural Law," p. 151.

CHAPTER 4: LIBERALISM IN CONFLICT

1. G. W. F. Hegel, "On the Scientific Ways of Treating Natural Law, on Its Place in Practical Philosophy, and Its Relation to the Positive Sciences of Right (1802–1803)," in *Political Writings*, ed. Lawrence Dickey and H. B. Nisbet, trans. H. B. Nisbet (Cambridge: Cambridge University Press, 1999), p. 151, trans. modified. See also Christoph Menke, "On the Concept of Recognition: Hegel's Early Theory of Social Differentiation," *Praxis International* 12, no. 1 (April 1992): 70–82.

2. Charles Taylor, "The Nature and Scope of Distributive Justice," in *Philosophy and the Human Sciences: Philosophical Papers*, by Charles Taylor, vol. 2 (Cambridge: Cambridge University Press, 1985), pp. 211–29, pp. 314, 312–13, 315.

3. Charles Taylor, "Atomism," in *Philosophy and the Human Sciences*, vol. 2, p. 198.

4. Charles Taylor, *Sources of the Self: The Making of the Modern Identity* (Cambridge, Mass.: Harvard University Press, 1989), pp. 495–521.

5. Michael Walzer, "The Idea of Civil Society," *Dissent* (Spring 1991): 298.

6. Immanuel Kant, "On the Common Saying 'This May Be True in Theory, but It Does Not Apply in Practice,'" in *Political Writings*, ed. Hans Reiss, trans. H. B. Nisbet (Cambridge: Cambridge University Press, 1970), pp. 61–92, p. 73.

7. See John Rawls, *A Theory of Justice* (Cambridge, Mass.: Belknap Press of Harvard University Press, 1971), pp. 3–53; as well as John Rawls, "The Priority of Right and Ideas of the Good," in *Collected Papers*, ed. Samuel Freeman (Cambridge, Mass.: Harvard University Press, 1999), pp. 449–72.

8. Charles Taylor, "Cross-Purposes: The Liberal-Communitarian Debate," in *Philosophical Arguments* (Cambridge, Mass.: Harvard University Press, 1995), pp. 181–203.

9. See Ronald Dworkin, "Liberal Community," *California Law Review* 77 (1989): 479 ff.; and Rawls, "The Priority of Right and Ideas of the Good," pp. 465–70. Bert van den Brink has undertaken a defense of the republican version of the tragic diagnosis; see his *The Tragedy of Liberalism* (Albany: State University of New York Press, 2000).

10. This is the description given in Joseph Raz, *The Morality of Freedom* (Oxford: Oxford University Press, 1986), p. 6.

11. The argument advanced in this section can also be formulated as follows: "personal" freedom describes the minimal meaning of freedom—something which is *common* to the ancients and the moderns; "subjective" freedom, by contrast, implies the freedom of the moderns in Constant's sense; see Benjamin Constant, "The Freedom of the Ancients Compared with That of the Moderns," in *Political Writings*, trans. Biancamaria Fontana (Cambridge: Cambridge University Press, 1998), pp. 307–28.

12. Rawls, *A Theory of Justice*, pp. 416–24; on what follows see pp. 407–16. See also Josiah Royce, *The Philosophy of Loyalty* (New York: Macmillan, 1971), pp. 81 ff.; and Aristotle, *Nicomachean Ethics*, trans. H. Rackham (Cambridge, Mass.: Harvard University Press, 1934), 6.1.13.

13. On the two forms of the romantic critique, see Charles Larmore, *Patterns of Moral Complexity* (Cambridge: Cambridge University Press, 1987), pp. 91 ff.; and Arthur O. Lovejoy, *The Great Chain of Being* (New York: Harper and Row, 1960), pp. 288–314. See also Hauke Brunkhorst, "Romantik, Rationalität und Rorty," in *Der entzauberte Intellektuelle: Über die neue Beliebigkeit des Denkens*, by Hauke Brunhorst (Hamburg: Junius, 1990), pp. 189 ff.

14. Michael J. Sandel, *Liberalism and the Limits of Justice* (Cambridge: Cambridge University Press, 1982), p. 150.

15. Alasdair MacIntyre, *After Virtue* (London: Duckworth, 1981), pp. 220–22.

16. See Charles Taylor, "What's Wrong with Negative Liberty," in *Philosophy and the Human Sciences*, pp. 211–29; and *Sources of the Self*.

17. Friedrich Schlegel, *Georg Forster*, in *Kritische Schriften* (Munich: Hanser, 1971), pp. 342 and 333.

18. Wilhelm von Humboldt, "Ideen zu einem Versuch, die Gränzen der Wirksamkeit des Staats zu bestimmen," in *Werke*, vol. 1 (Darmstadt: Wissenschaftliche Buchgesellschaft, 1980), pp. 65 ff.

19. John Stuart Mill, *On Liberty*, ed. John Gracy and G. W. Smith (London: Routledge, 1991), p. 73.

20. Ibid., p. 108.

21. Schlegel, *Georg Forster*, p. 341.

22. Friedrich Schlegel, *Über Goethes Meister*, in *Kritische Schriften*, p. 471; and Humboldt, "Ideen zu einem Versuch," p. 57.

23. Raz, *The Morality of Freedom*, p. 155. For a critical discussion of the idea of

an authorship of our own lives, see Dieter Thomä, *Erzähle dich selbst: Lebensgeschichte als philosophisches Problem* (Munich: Beck, 1998).

24. Raz, *The Morality of Freedom*, p. 369.

25. MacIntyre, *After Virtue*, p. 213; my emphasis.

26. Ibid., p. 216; the reference is the same for the quotes which follow in this paragraph.

27. Mill, *On Liberty*, p. 56.

28. Ibid., p. 64.

29. Nancy Rosenblum, *Another Liberalism: Romanticism and the Reconstruction of Liberal Thought* (Cambridge, Mass.: Harvard University Press, 1987), pp. 103 ff.

30. Richard Rorty, *Contingency, Irony, and Solidarity* (Cambridge: Cambridge University Press, 1989), p. 91.

31. This is a terminologically different version of the tension between equality and individuality described in Chapters 1 and 2. For "liberal justice" implies equality and "subjective freedom" implies the freedom of the individual in the enactment of his life.

32. Kant, "On the Common Saying," p. 73; my emphasis.

33. John Rawls, "Justice as Fairness: Political Not Metaphysical," in *Collected Papers*, p. 413. On what follows, see the critique of Rawls in Cavell, *Conditions Handsome and Unhandsome: The Constitution of Emersonian Perfectionism* (Chicago: University of Chicago Press, 1990), pp. 101 ff.

34. Rawls, *A Theory of Justice*, p. 221.

35. Ibid., p. 220.

36. Royce, *The Philosophy of Loyalty*, p. 37.

37. Rawls, *A Theory of Justice*, p. 565.

38. Ibid., p. 573.

39. Ibid., p. 252.

40. Ibid., p. 529.

41. Ibid.

42. Ibid.

43. Ibid., p. 561.

44. Ibid., p. 568.

45. See ibid., pp. 251–58.

46. Ibid., p. 571.

47. John Rawls, "Fairness to Goodness," in *Collected Papers*, pp. 267–85, pp. 283–85; on what follows, see "Justice as Fairness," pp. 403–8.

48. Sandel, *Liberalism and the Limits of Justice*, pp. 20, 57, and 179 ff.; see also Michael Sandel, "The Procedural Republic and the Unencumbered Self," in *Political Theory*, vol. 1 (1984), pp. 81–96.

49. See Christoph Menke, "Tragedy and the Free Spirits: Nietzsche's Theory

of Aesthetic Freedom," *Philosophy and Social Criticism* 22 (1996): 1, 1–12.

50. Lionel Trilling, *Sincerity and Authenticity* (London: Oxford University Press, 1974). On this perspective on liberalism, see Rorty, *Contingency, Irony, and Solidarity*, pp. 73–95.

51. Rawls, "The Priority of Right and Ideas of the Good," p. 462. See Isaiah Berlin, *Two Concepts of Liberty: An Inaugural Lecture Delivered Before the University of Oxford on 31 October 1958* (Oxford: Clarendon Press, 1958).

CHAPTER 5: THE PERMANENCE OF REVOLUTION

1. Edmund Burke, *Reflections on the Revolution in France*, ed. J. G. A. Pocock (Indianapolis, Ind.: Hackett, 1987), p. 9.

2. Ibid., p. 29.

3. Ibid., p. 22.

4. Ibid., p. 31.

5. Ibid., p. 19.

6. Ibid., p. 9.

7. Ibid.

8. Ibid., p. 153.

9. On the opposition between "metaphysical" and "political," see ibid., p. 160; see also my Preface, "Equality—Political, Not Metaphysical."

10. Burke, *Reflections on the Revolution in France*, p. 53.

11. Ibid., p. 52.

12. The complete title reads: *Reflections on the Revolution in France and on the Proceedings in Certain Societies in London Relative to That Event in a Letter Intended to Have Been Sent to a Gentleman in Paris, 1790.* On what follows, see J. G. A. Pocock's instructive introduction to his edition of Burke's treatise on the revolution.

13. Kant, *Critique of Judgment*, trans. Werner S. Pluhar (Indianapolis, Ind.: Hackett, 1987), § 26; see also Immanuel Kant, *Anthropology from a Pragmatic Point of View*, trans. Mary J. Gregor (The Hague: Nijhoff, 1974), BA 190.

14. The paradigm of such monstrosity is the creation of Dr. Frankenstein. This also explains—if I see things correctly—why the monstrous does not yet appear in Burke's *A Philosophical Enquiry into the Origin of Our Ideas of the Sublime and Beautiful* (1757). This understanding of the monstrous, that is, as an effect of the external stipulation of aims, is, at the same time, a (discursive) effect of the French Revolution. I owe this observation to a conversation with Carlos Thiebaut.

15. Burke, *Reflections on the Revolution in France*, p. 153.

16. Ibid., p. 154.

17. This is, for Burke, a necessary, and not an accidental, "defect" of the attempt to implement the "perfect" idea of equal rights. For the materials into which

these rights are to be implemented—whether political representation or property—are "by nature" or in "[their] characteristic essence" determined by inequality. Burke's judgment of the revolutionary attempt to introduce the "abstract" principle of equal rights thus reads as follows: "In all societies consisting of various descriptions of citizens, some description must be uppermost. The levelers, therefore only change and pervert the natural order of things; they load the edifice of society by setting up in the air what the solidity of the structure requires to be on the ground"; ibid., p. 43.

18. Gracchus Babeuf, *The Defense of Gracchus Babeuf Before the High Court of Vendome*, ed. John A. Scott (Amherst: University of Massachussetts Press), p. 94.

19. Ibid.

20. Ibid., p. 92.

21. "In the state of nature, indeed, all men are born equal, but they cannot continue in this equality. Society makes them lose it, and they recover it only by the protection of the laws." Montesquieu, *L'Esprit des lois* (Paris: Flammarion, 1979), p. III.

22. Louis de Jaucourt, "Egalité naturelle," in *Encyclopédie; ou, Dictionnaire raisonné des sciences, des arts et des métiers*, ed. Denis Diderot and Jean d'Alembert (Paris: Hermann, 1976), vol. 5.

23. Voltaire, "Égalité," in *Dictionnaire philosophique* (Paris: Flammarion, 1964), pp. 172 ff. Voltaire reformulates here the strategy of a restriction of equality by means of a distinction between two worlds, a world of equality and a world of inequality. Something similar can be found in Luther: "This is indeed clear, . . . that in the part in which we are called Christians, the person possesses neither inequality nor advantage, but is the one as the other, man, woman, young, old . . . prince and peasant, master and slave. . . . But afterward, when we begin to enter into external nature and our action . . . there it becomes only inequality and concerns the various differences amongst Christians, not as Christians nor according to Christian nature, but instead according to the fruits of the self"; Martin Luther, "Wochenpredigten über Math. 5–7," quoted in Otto Dann, "Gleichheit," in *Geschichtliche Grundbegriffe*, ed. Otto Brunner, Werner Conze, and Reinhart Koselleck, vol. 2 (Stuttgart: Klett-Cotta, 1975), p. 1006.

24. John Locke, "The Second Treatise of Government," in *Two Treatises of Government*, ed. Peter Laslett (Cambridge: Cambridge University Press, 1988), p. 304. The reference is to § 4, p. 269, in which we read that "the State all Men are naturally in" is not only "a *State of perfect Freedom*," but "[a] *State* also *of Equality*, wherein all the Power and Jurisdiction is reciprocal, no one having more than another." On the argument for a necessarily restricted legal equality, see Kant, "On the Common Saying 'This May Be True in Theory, but It Does Not Apply in Practice,'" in *Political Writings*, ed. Hans Reiss, trans. H. B. Nisbet (Cambridge: Cambridge University Press, 1970), pp. 74–77.

25. Locke, "The Second Treatise of Government," § 54, p. 304.

26. Kant, *The Metaphysics of Morals*, pp. 55–57.

27. Babeuf, *The Defense of Gracchus Babeuf*, pp. 84 and 91.

28. Ibid., p. 82.

29. Ibid., pp. 91 and 82.

30. Ibid., p. 82.

31. Ibid., p. 92.

32. Amartya Sen, *Inequality Reexamined* (Cambridge, Mass.: Harvard University Press, 1995), pp. ix ff. and 1 ff.

33. Babeuf, *The Defense of Gracchus Babeuf*.

34. Montesquieu, *L'Esprit des lois*, p. 75. On the appeal to antiquity in Louis David's revolutionary celebrations, see Jean Starobinski, *1789: The Emblems of Reason* (Charlottesville: University Press of Virginia, 1982), pp. 99–124.

35. Montesquieu, *L'Esprit des lois*, p. 44.

36. Ibid., p. 45.

37. Ibid., p. 41.

38. On the basis of his observations of the first months of the French Revolution, Burke receives the impression that the state-form it is striving for is that of a "pure democracy," according to the model of the "ancients"; Burke, *Reflections on the Revolution in France*, pp. 109 ff.

39. Montesquieu, *L'Esprit des lois*, bk. 5, chap. 3, p. 168.

40. Babeuf, *The Defense of Gracchus Babeuf*, p. 94.

41. "But historians, and even common sense, may inform us, that, however specious these ideas of *perfect* equality may seem, they are really, at bottom, *impracticable*; and were they not so, would be extremely pernicious to human society. . . . [For:] The most rigorous inquisition too is requisite to watch every inequality on its first appearance; and the most severe jurisdiction, to punish and redress it. But besides, that so much authority must soon degenerate into tyranny, and be exerted with great partialities; who can possibly be possessed by it, in such a situation that is here supposed?"; David Hume, *An Enquiry Concerning the Principles of Morals*, ed. L. A. Selby-Bigge (Oxford: Clarendon Press, 1975), § 3, pt. 2, p. 194.

42. Karl Marx, "A Contribution to the Critique of Hegel's Philosophy of Right: Introduction," trans. Gregor Benton, in *Early Writings* (New York: Vintage, 1975), pp. 243–57, p. 251.

43. See Albrecht Wellmer, *Revolution und Interpretation: Demokratie ohne Letztbegründung* (Assen: Van Gorcum, 1998).

44. See Judith N. Shklar, *The Faces of Injustice* (New Haven, Conn.: Yale University Press, 1990), pp. 15–50.

45. As Marx makes clear, above all, the revolutionary demand is not exhausted by the demand for equality. Along with the asymmetry between the individual experience of injury and the revolutionary demand, this constitutes a second asymmetry which I cannot discuss here further: the asymmetry between the objection to oppression and the demand for (more) equality. For there are clearly forms of

oppression—Marx calls them "alienation," Lukács "reification," Horkheimer and Adorno the "administered world," and Habermas the "colonization of the life-world"—which are not forms of inequality; they affect everybody in an equal manner. In a political philosophy which normatively restricts itself to justice as equality, these forms can no longer be considered.

46. In this way, Marx's categorical imperative of revolution resembles the "de-sire for no-rule," which Miguel Vatter, in his interpretation of Machiavelli, has identified as the basis of a republican determination of the political. Miguel E. Vatter, *Between Form and Event: Machiavelli's Theory of Political Freedom* (Dordre-cht: Kluwer, 2000). Despite their opposing contentful determination (in the first case, an objection to determinate suffering, in the second, a desire for indetermin-able freedom), the two coincide in understanding the impetus of revolution as something which can be fulfilled by no order.

47. See Rawls, "The Priority of Right and Ideas of the Good," in *Collected Papers*, ed. Samuel Freeman (Cambridge, Mass.: Harvard University Press, 1999), pp. 461–65. For more detail, see Christoph Menke, *Tragödie im Sittlichen: Gerechtig-keit und Freiheit nach Hegel* (Frankfurt am Main: Suhrkamp, 1996), pp. 295 ff. See above, Chapter 4, "Liberalism in Conflict: Between Justice and Freedom."

48. "Revolutionary politics" can mean two things: a politics that makes a rev-olution or a politics that *continues* a revolution. The first politics is revolutionary in its external form, the second is revolutionary in its content and impetus. Con-temporary politics, under the conditions of legal-democratic constitutions, can be revolutionary only in the second sense. This is also true of a politics which ap-peals, under these conditions, to Marx's categorical imperative. To this extent, it *resembles* the politics proposed by political or social liberalism; like this politics, it does not demand permanent revolutionary upheaval. *Unlike* this liberal politics, however, it demands a permanent and practically effective *questioning* of existing political, social, and cultural relationships—a questioning which certainly does without Marx's formulation of a revolutionary objection to all relationships of in-dividual injury. I thank Gerhard Gamm and Tom Mitchell for their remarks on this problem.

CHAPTER 6: MERCY AND LAW

1. Carl Schmitt, *Der Begriff des Politischen: Text von 1932 mit einem Vorwort und drei Corollarien* (Berlin: Duncker und Humblot, 1991), pp. 79–95.

2. Carl Schmitt, *Die Diktatur* (Berlin: Duncker und Humblot, 1994), p. xviii. Quotes from Schmitt are translated by the translators of the present volume.

3. Carl Schmitt, *Gesetz und Urteil: Eine Untersuchung zum Problem der Rechts-praxis* (Munich: Beck, 1969), p. 2. For a more detailed discussion of this text, see Friedrich Balke, *Der Staat nach seinem Ende: Die Versuchung Carl Schmitts* (Mu-

nich: Fink, 1996), pp. 383 ff. The quote is from Carl Schmitt, *Politische Theologie: Vier Kapitel zur Lehre von der Souveranität* (Berlin: Duncker und Humblot, 1979), p. 31.

4. Carl Schmitt, *Die geistesgeschichtliche Lage des heutigen Parlamentarismus* (Berlin: Duncker und Humblot, 1991), p. 79.

5. Schmitt, *Politische Theologie,* p. 18.

6. Schmitt, *Die geistesgeschichtliche Lage des heutigen Parlamentarismus,* p. 55.

7. Carl Schmitt, *Legalität und Legitimität* (Berlin: Duncker und Humblot, 1993), p. 18.

8. Schmitt, *Politische Theologie,* p. 41.

9. Ibid.

10. Schmitt, *Legalität und Legitimität,* p. 53.

11. Schmitt, *Politische Theologie,* p. 41.

12. See Ronald Dworkin, "How Law Is Like Literature," in *A Matter of Principle,* by Ronald Dworkin (Cambridge, Mass.: Harvard University Press, 1985), pp. 146 ff.

13. Schmitt, *Die geistesgeschichtliche Lage des heutigen Parlamentarismus,* p. 54.

14. Schmitt, *Politische Theologie,* p. 12.

15. Sovereignty is not the "greatest power," for "there does not exist in political reality an irresistible and highest, that is, greatest, power which functions with the security of natural law." Above all, however: "power proves nothing about law"; *Politische Theologie,* p. 26. Sovereignty is, then, the "legally highest power"; ibid., p. 27. And this legality or legitimacy of sovereign power ensues from its relationship to the exception.

16. Søren Kierkegaard, *Either/Or,* pt. 2, trans. Howard V. Hong and Edna H. Hong (Princeton, N.J.: Princeton University Press, 1987), pp. 163 ff.

17. Schmitt, *Politische Theologie,* p. 19.

18. Ibid.

19. Ibid.

20. See Klaus Günther, *Der Sinn für Angemessenheit* (Frankfurt am Main: Suhrkamp, 1985).

21. Schmitt, *Politische Theologie,* p. 12.

22. Schmitt, *Legalität und Legitimität,* p. 29.

23. See Carl Schmitt, *Über die drei Arten des rechtswissenschaftlichen Denkens* (Hamburg: Hanseatische Verlagsanstalt, 1934); and Christian Graf von Krockow, *Die Entscheidung: Eine Untersuchung über Ernst Jünger, Carl Schmitt, Martin Heidegger* (Frankfurt am Main: Campus, 1990), pp. 94 ff.

24. See Carl Schmitt, *Politische Romantik* (Berlin: Duncker und Humblot, 1968), pp. 77 ff.

25. Schmitt, *Der Begriff des Politischen,* p. 27.

26. On the friend-enemy criterion of the political and its existential dimen-

sion, see Heinrich Meier, *Die Lehre Carl Schmitts* (Stuttgart: Metzler, 1994), pp. 44 ff. In contrast to Meier (ibid., pp. 85 ff.), I see it as an advantage that in the determination of political unity the friend-enemy criterion proceeds only negatively, and does not succeed in a positive determination of political friendship. On Schmitt's concept of political homogeneity, see the contributions in Andreas Göbel, Dirk van Laak, and Ingeborg Villinger, eds., *Metamorphosen des Politischen: Grundfragen politischer Einheitsbildung seit den 20er Jahren* (Berlin: Akademie, 1995).

27. Schmitt, *Die geistesgeschichtliche Lage des heutigen Parlamentarismus*, p. 14.

28. Schmitt, *Der Begriff des Politischen*, p. 88.

29. Ibid., p. 89.

30. Ibid., p. 46.

31. Schmitt, *Politische Theologie*, p. 19. The reference is the same for the quotes which follow in this paragraph.

32. Schmitt, *Die Diktatur*, p. xviii; see also p. 143, note; *Politische Theologie*, p. 51. The wider context of these references to mercy is Schmitt's remembrance of the tradition of a right of emergency and resistance, in contrast to the modern claim of an unconditional duty of obedience with respect to legal norms; see also ibid., pp. 32 and 62; and *Legalität und Legitimität*, p. 21. See below, Section E.

33. Seneca, *De clementia*, bk. 5, ed. Manfred Rosenbach (Darmstadt: Wissenschaftliche Buchgesellschaft, 1995), para. 3, pp. xvii ff. See also Gustav Radbruch, *Rechtsphilosophie* (Stuttgart: Koehler, 1950), p. 342.

34. The waiving of punishment can follow a judgment which has been made or it can come in anticipation of a judgment which is expected. The first case presupposes the conclusion of a legal procedure, the second signifies its abolition. On the gradation of the "objects of pardon," see Horst Butz, *Gnadengewalt und Gnadensachen in der Enstehungsphase des modernen Verwaltungsrechts* (Cologne: Hanstein, 1975), pp. 22 ff; and Renate Just, *Recht und Gnade in Heinrich von Kleists Schauspiel "Prinz Friedrich von Homburg"* (Göttingen: Wallstein, 1993), pp. 69 ff.

35. Otto Kirchheimer, "Gnade in der politischen Strafverfolgung," in *Funktionen des Staats und der Verfassung*, by Otto Kirchheimer (Frankfurt am Main: Suhrkamp, 1972), p. 203. On the connection between the revision of judgment and the waiving of punishment, see Martha C. Nussbaum, "Equity and Mercy," *Philosophy and Public Affairs* 22, no. 2 (Spring 1993): 83 ff. Nussbaum only calls the waiving of punishment mercy; by contrast, she calls the revision of judgment "equity." I elucidate my objections to this talk of equity below, in Section E.

36. Radbruch, *Rechtsphilosophie*, p. 278; and Kirchheimer, "Gnade in der politischen Strafverfolgung," p. 190.

37. Friedrich Nietzsche, *On the Genealogy of Morals*, trans. Walter Kaufmann (New York: Random House, 1967), pp. 65–66.

38. Ibid., p. 63.

39. Ibid., p. 75.

40. Ibid., p. 86.

41. Ibid., pp. 72–73.

42. Ibid., p. 87.

43. In the text of Schmitt which most clearly demonstrates his proximity to Nietzsche's concept of the political "creation of form," we can find an indirect reference to this definition of mercy: because "the opposition between power and goodness is dissolved without remainder" in God, the possibility of "an appeal directed against the justice of God" becomes conceivable—an appeal which "dialectically takes justice to the extreme"; Carl Schmitt, *Römischer Katholizismus und politische Form* (Stuttgart: Klett-Cotta, 1984), pp. 54 ff. See also the comment on the "incalculability and immeasurability" of mercy, in Schmitt, *Über die drei Arten des rechtswissenschaftlichen Denkens*, pp. 26 ff.

44. Immanuel Kant, *The Metaphysics of Morals*, trans. Mary Gregor (Cambridge: Cambridge University Press, 1991), p. 145. On the Enlightenment critique of mercy, see Heinz Dieter Kittsteiner, "Von der Gnade zur Tugend: Über eine Veränderung in der Darstellung des Gleichnisses vom verlorenen Sohn im 18. und frühen 19. Jahrhundert," in *Spiegel und Gleichnis: Festschrift für Jacob Taubes*, ed. Norbert W. Bolz and Wolfgang Hübener (Würzburg: Königshausen und Neumann, 1983), pp. 135 ff.

45. Hegel criticizes here a concept of "effective mercy" which claims that "mercy discovers nothing immanent to man." Mercy is, for Hegel—in the consideration of the monarch's right to exercise it—an "ungrounded decision," because it cannot be made into law. At the same time, however, it rests upon reasons of "clemency." G. W. F. Hegel, *Elements of the Philosophy of Right*, trans. H. B. Nisbet (Cambridge: Cambridge University Press, 1991), § 140A.

46. Wilhelm Georg Grewe, *Gnade und Recht* (Hamburg: Hanseatische Verlagsanstalt, 1936), p. 104. On the discussion of *justa causa aggratiandi*, see Just, *Recht und Gnade*, pp. 74 ff. and 122 ff. On the confessional aspects of this discussion, see ibid., pp. 65 ff. Translations from Grewe are by the translators of the present volume.

47. Grewe, *Gnade und Recht*, p. 38.

48. Ibid., p. 104. See also Detlef Merten, *Rechtsstaatlichkeit und Gnade* (Berlin: Duncker und Humblot, 1978).

49. Arthur Kaufmann, *Recht und Gnade in der Literatur* (Stuttgart: Boorberg, 1991), p. 16.

50. Grewe, *Gnade und Recht*, p. 19.

51. Jacques Derrida, "Force of Law: The 'Mystical Foundation of Authority,'" in *Deconstruction and the Possibility of Justice*, ed. Drucilla Cornell, Michel Rosenfeld, and David Gray Carlson (New York: Routledge, 1992), p. 17. On the details and problems of this argument of Derrida, see above, Chapter 2. Derrida's con-

sideration of Schmitt refers to the concepts of hostility and friendship; see Jacques Derrida, *Politics of Friendship*, trans. George Collins (London, Verso: 1997), pp. 112–37.

52. Derrida, "Force of Law," p. 17.

53. Plato, *The Statesman*, trans. Harold N. Fowler (Cambridge, Mass.: Harvard University Press, 1925), 196b.

54. Aristotle, *Nicomachean Ethics*, trans. H. Rackham (Cambridge, Mass.: Harvard University Press, 1934), 5.10.4.

55. Ibid., 5.10.6.

56. For a more detailed discussion, see Chapters 3 and 4.

57. Ivan Nagel, *Autonomie und Gnade: Über Mozarts Opern* (Munich: Deutscher Taschenbuch, 1998), p. 136.

58. Schmitt, *Legalität und Legitimität*, p. 21.

Index of Names

Cultural Memory | *in the Present*

Jacques Derrida and Elisabeth Roudinesco, *For What Tomorrow . . . : A Dialogue*

Elisabeth Weber, *Questioning Judaism: Interviews by Elisabeth Weber*

Jacques Derrida and Catherine Malabou, *Counterpath: Traveling with Jacques Derrida*

Martin Seel, *Aesthetics of Appearing*

Nanette Salomon, *Shifting Priorities: Gender and Genre in Seventeenth-Century Dutch Painting*

Jacob Taubes, *The Political Theology of Paul*

Jean-Luc Marion, *The Crossing of the Visible*

Eric Michaud, *The Cult of Art in Nazi Germany*

Anne Freadman, *The Machinery of Talk: Charles Peirce and the Sign Hypothesis*

Stanley Cavell, *Emerson's Transcendental Etudes*

Stuart McLean, *The Event and its Terrors: Ireland, Famine, Modernity*

Beate Rössler, ed., *Privacies: Philosophical Evaluations*

Bernard Faure, *Double Exposure: Cutting Across Buddhist and Western Discourses*

Alessia Ricciardi, *The Ends Of Mourning: Psychoanalysis, Literature, Film*

Alain Badiou, *Saint Paul: The Foundation of Universalism*

Gil Anidjar, *The Jew, the Arab: A History of the Enemy*

Jonathan Culler and Kevin Lamb, eds., *Just Being Difficult? Academic Writing in the Public Arena*

Jean-Luc Nancy, *A Finite Thinking*, edited by Simon Sparks

Theodor W. Adorno, *Can One Live after Auschwitz? A Philosophical Reader*, edited by Rolf Tiedemann

Patricia Pisters, *The Matrix of Visual Culture: Working with Deleuze in Film Theory*

Andreas Huyssen, *Present Pasts: Urban Palimpsests and the Politics of Memory*

Talal Asad, *Formations of the Secular: Christianity, Islam, Modernity*

Dorothea von Mücke, *The Rise of the Fantastic Tale*

Marc Redfield, *The Politics of Aesthetics: Nationalism, Gender, Romanticism*

Emmanuel Levinas, *On Escape*

Dan Zahavi, *Husserl's Phenomenology*

Rodolphe Gasché, *The Idea of Form: Rethinking Kant's Aesthetics*

Michael Naas, *Taking on the Tradition: Jacques Derrida and the Legacies of Deconstruction*

Herlinde Pauer-Studer, ed., *Constructions of Practical Reason: Interviews on Moral and Political Philosophy*

Jean-Luc Marion, *Being Given That: Toward a Phenomenology of Givenness*

Theodor W. Adorno and Max Horkheimer, *Dialectic of Enlightenment*

Ian Balfour, *The Rhetoric of Romantic Prophecy*

Martin Stokhof, *World and Life as One: Ethics and Ontology in Wittgenstein's Early Thought*

Gianni Vattimo, *Nietzsche: An Introduction*

Jacques Derrida, *Negotiations: Interventions and Interviews, 1971-1998*, edited by Elizabeth Rottenberg

Brett Levinson, *The Ends of Literature: The Latin American "Boom" in the Neoliberal Marketplace*

Timothy J. Reiss, *Against Autonomy: Cultural Instruments, Mutualities, and the Fictive Imagination*

Hent de Vries and Samuel Weber, editors, *Religion and Media*

Niklas Luhmann, *Theories of Distinction: Re-Describing the Descriptions of Modernity*, edited and Introduction by William Rasch

Johannes Fabian, *Anthropology with an Attitude: Critical Essays*

Michel Henry, *I am the Truth: Toward a Philosophy of Christianity*

Gil Anidjar, *"Our Place in Al-Andalus": Kabbalah, Philosophy, Literature in Arab-Jewish Letters*

Hélène Cixous and Jacques Derrida, *Veils*

F. R. Ankersmit, *Historical Representation*

F. R. Ankersmit, *Political Representation*

Elissa Marder, *Dead Time: Temporal Disorders in the Wake of Modernity (Baudelaire and Flaubert)*

Reinhart Koselleck, *The Practice of Conceptual History: Timing History, Spacing Concepts*

Niklas Luhmann, *The Reality of the Mass Media*

Hubert Damisch, *A Childhood Memory by Piero della Francesca*

Hubert Damisch, *A Theory of /Cloud/: Toward a History of Painting*

Jean-Luc Nancy, *The Speculative Remark: (One of Hegel's bon mots)*

Jean-François Lyotard, *Soundproof Room: Malraux's Anti-Aesthetics*

Jan Patočka, *Plato and Europe*

Hubert Damisch, *Skyline: The Narcissistic City*

Isabel Hoving, *In Praise of New Travelers: Reading Caribbean Migrant Women Writers*

Richard Rand, ed., *Futures: Of Jacques Derrida*